REIHE SIEGEN
Beiträge zur Literatur- und Sprachwissenschaft
Band 51

Eine Schriftenreihe der Universität - Gesamthochschule - Siegen

Herausgegeben von
Wolfgang Drost, Helmut Kreuzer
Wolfgang Raible, Karl Riha
und Christian W. Thomsen

GERMANISTISCHE ABTEILUNG

Verantwortlicher Herausgeber dieses Bandes: *Helmut Kreuzer*

ROBERT A. JONES

Art and Entertainment: German Literature and the Circus 1890–1933

HEIDELBERG 1985
CARL WINTER · UNIVERSITÄTSVERLAG

Gedruckt mit Unterstützung der
Alexander von Humboldt-Stiftung

CIP-Kurztitelaufnahme der Deutschen Bibliothek

Jones, Robert A.:

Art and entertainment: German literature and the circus 1890–1933 / Robert A. Jones. – Heidelberg: Winter, 1985.

(Reihe Siegen; Bd. 50)

ISBN 3-533-03507-7 kart.
ISBN 3-533-03508-5 Gewebe

NE: GT

ISBN 3-533-03507-7 kart.
ISBN 3-533-03508-5 Ln.

Imprimé en Allemagne. Printed in Germany
Photosatz und Druck: Carl Winter Universitätsverlag, Abteilung Druckerei, Darmstadt

for

Mary

and

Katie, Andy and Brant

TABLE OF CONTENTS

Preface

The present status of the circus, for decades an entertainment form designated "the greatest show on earth," is tenuous to say the least. In America, the circus has been reduced to an annual event for those with small children, sponsored by civic and/or fraternal organizations and performed in the sterility of metropolitan auditoriums and arenas. Museums in Wisconsin and Florida preserve the circus as an element of the past and suggest that although it persists it is no longer organic to our mass-media culture. In Europe, it perhaps enjoys slightly more recognition and functions somewhat more in line with distinct aspects of its heritage, but there too it is being pushed to the limits of its adaptability.

Not that long ago, however, the European circus functioned in a different context. By the end of the nineteenth century it had reached a zenith in its development and, despite an inherent outsider status, had become an integral part of the European social fabric. In Germany, what can be called the "Golden Age" of the German circus had begun already in 1857 when the innovations of Ernst Renz attracted a public that was to increase exponentially within the next half century. Renz's ideas were subsequently modified and extended by competitors and successors such as Schumann, Busch, Hagenbeck, Sarassani, and Krone, each of whom contributed uniquely to the format and character of the circus and made the German circus in particular a leader in the field.

As a result of its extreme popularity, the circus exerted a considerable force on the world of art. It was appropriated as thematic material by virtually every art form and in a number of cases influenced the aesthetic principles of individual artists. Its re-presentation in the respective arts attests to the multiple and varied attempts on the part of artists to articulate their own personal enthusiasm for the circus as well as their eagerness to exploit the public's interest in this exotic world of spectacle and illusion. Instances of such an interaction are noticeably numerous within the realm of German literature from the turn of the twentieth century up to the historical caesura that began in 1933. It is the nature of this interaction, and the implications of it as well, that I wish to explicate. In its totality this study is an effort to demonstrate the many and complex ways in which the circus as an entertainment form from the "popular" sphere exerted a force on what we regard as the canonical world of "legitimate" art. In the separate chapters I examine the specific ways in which certain writers, poets, and playwrights exhibited a receptiveness to the circus and the probable context for their individual reactions to it as stimulus. Upon analysis, such reactions and their manifestations within the artists' work have aesthetic implications and bring to light relationships frequently overlooked or relegated to a domain lying outside the realm of traditional literary inquiry.

The chapter entitled "Definitions and Demarcations" is a brief historical introduction intended to set the stage for the explorations which follow. It delineates the evolution (in admittedly cursory fashion) of that split between "popular" and "legitimate" forms and focuses particularly on the instances in which the separation itself, i.e., the disjunction between those respective spheres of artistic activity, led to their reunification and integration by those artists seeking aesthetic innovation. The chapter designated "Motifs, Themes, and Characters," reveals the circus as primary thematic material in the work of Carl and Gerhart Hauptmann and Carl Zuckmayer. In the case of Gerhart Hauptmann a number of his female characters exhibit traits which originate in the poet's adolescent enthusiasm for Ozeana Renz, a high-wire artiste whom he saw in performance in 1877. The same traits are demonstrably present in the women with whom the maturing writer shared his life, the reality of his personal existence reflecting, as it were, the dissonances inherent in the personification of those traits. The culmination of the original experience is Hauptmann's 1927 circus novel *Wanda,* a work that can be read as a final exorcism of a conflict that nettled him into his later years. Hauptmann's lesser known brother Carl includes circus-like characters in a number of his works in a fervent attempt, albeit unsuccessful, to express through that work his own ongoing search for a satisfactory solution to genuine discomfort in the real world. In the final essay in this section I demonstrate how the dramatist Carl Zuckmayer put the theater to work to explicate and affirm those model qualities of the "folk" which he saw embodied in the world of a transient family of circus performers.

Under the next heading "Metaphor and Symbol," I attempt to move beyond such thematic treatments to examine the more complex metaphoric and symbolic expressions of the world of the circus. Here it is possible to see a phenomenon manifesting itself in both contradictory and complementary ways. The cases of Thomas Mann and Franz Kafka are good examples. A proper seriousness characterizes the tone of Mann's ironic, controlled, and somewhat didactic prose. Throughout the better part of his orderly lifetime he worked on his *Felix Krull*, an unfinished "Confession" in an intentionally lighter vein. The novel fuses profoundly with the work that precedes it, and with a hindsight afforded by its lateness, caps an oeuvre which for all its dialectic is almost academic in its consistency. In contrast, the younger Kafka endured a Chaplinesque existence in Bohemia, where he struggled constantly to maintain his sanity in his "legal" life through his writing, and came close to losing it in his efforts to give that writing a legality he felt to be lacking. By virtue of pieces such as *Erstes Leid* and *Auf der Galerie* one suspects that his world was more problematic than Mann's and his dilemma more personal in origin. Unlike the Lübeck citizen, the Prague Jew was considerably more handicapped, not only through the complex liability of his racial heritage, but by a mind prone to run in vicious circles and a body of a less than healthy constitution. Despite such completely different personal contexts and artistic intentions, both Kafka and Thomas Mann held onto their respective situations in such a way as to make the latter the substance of much of their art. Both are recognized for their expression of the artist's contention with the modern world. It is therefore not without significance that the circus allowed both of them to shape their argument uniquely in that regard. In a different vein, Rilke's and Georg Heym's metaphorical treatments of the circus constitute a variant set of essentially complementary perspectives. Theirs are both unmistakably negative assessments of the performer/audience relationship within the framework of the circus, statements ultimately less personal, more analytic, and laden with aesthetic and sociological implications.

In an effort to further expand the study's scope, in the penultimate chapter "Form and Structure" I explore the ramifications of the circus and related popular forms on structural and formal elements within the work of Frank Wedekind, Bertolt Brecht, and Georg Kaiser. All three may be viewed as renegades whose desire to break with tradition allowed them to consider new means, and whose conscious efforts to redirect and channel their respective audience's awareness took them into areas that lay beyond what had come to be aesthetically normative. The work of each of them can be viewed as having stretched the parameters of the traditional genres in which they worked and having manipulated a structural relationship with facets of popular entertainment.

The "Nachwort" is a kind of review as well as a tentative assessment. For the most part I have consciously avoided the temptation to tie tight knots around the package presented here. I do not offer in these pages a history of popular entertainment forms, nor do I propose that the case studies be regarded as a complete compendium of all the instances in which such forms were embodied or reflected in German literature within the specified period. Insofar as I suggest throughout that the penetration of the circus into German literature of this period must be viewed against the larger question of the relationship between popular entertainment and legitimate art, in the "Nachwort" I try to bring into play some of the rather subtle extensions which may be drawn outward from that interface. I am convinced that the multiplicities involved are not to be forced into a reductionist scheme. Here and in a number of places I suggest that the relationship between the circus and literature deserves more than a purely historical or descriptive account. Despite its ups and downs and complex turnings, the history of the circus can be viewed as a sequence intimately linked to the general course of social and cultural developments during this period. I ultimately want to propose that while the circus remained a form of "popular" entertainment, in the latter stages of its evolution it became in increasingly bourgeois institution. If it was by virtue of society's bourgeois nature that it was willing and inclined to accord to the circus the kind of popularity, attention, and support which the latter in fact enjoyed, it was as well the circus' ability to respond to, and capitalize, on the demands, likes, and dislikes of the audience that allowed it to continue in the public's favor. *That* Circus Renz, to cite a specific example, could make such a mark on Berlin life from the mid-nineteenth century until the late 1890s is a phenomenon closely tied to the changes in the population's rural and urban status and to the increase in leisure time on the part of audiences. The latter not only needed diversions from their increasingly technologized and organized lives, but their financial resources were undergoing change as well, both with regard to the sources of income and to the priorities according to which such income was used within contexts that were becoming increasingly diversified. *How* Ernst Renz created and developed such an appealing showplace for nineteenth century audiences is doubtless a function of his acumen in giving them what he knew they wanted: one suspects that the highly organized, well-turned and well-outfitted crews that transformed the arena into a spectacular world of precision and beauty answered the needs of a society that was coming to thrive on such bourgeois qualities as *Pünktlichkeit, Ordentlichkelt,* and *Sauberkeit.*

Until relatively recently, little serious attention has been paid to the relevance of forms of "popular" culture to the general sociological and aesthetic matrix. In the case of the circus, for example, there is a considerable body of literature on the institution itself but it is primarily descriptive or historical in nature and frequently tainted by an overbearing enthusiasm that cancels out any hint of objective scholarship. This lack of analytic attention and the absence of any attempt to put the circus into a larger framework is surely a factor of the former's popular status — as if the topic itself were a curiosity and not a legitimate subject for investigation.[1] As an exception, one must cite the work of Neo-marxist philosopher/critics such as Ernst Bloch, Walter Benjamin, and Theodor Adorno. Each of them found the circus sufficiently "legitimate" to incorporate comments on it into their work on the nature and substance of western mass culture. Their analyses consistently suggest broader dimensions in the assessment of cultural forms generally not considered worthy of critical attention. Their suggestions validate the legitimacy of establishing "mooring lines" between those "popular" forms floating in the waters of nontraditional art and the aesthetic doctrines of our largely bourgeois culture. I have no delusions of having fully exhausted the intriguing sociological and aesthetic questions they raise on this level. I have rather used their cues to posit the open-ended nature of the circus' relevance to the broader cultural and aesthetic framework. As I acknowledged earlier, the collective impact of those instances in which the circus as a form of popular entertainment was exploited by authors working both within and against the field of "legitimate" art raises questions to which there are few definitive answers. Nevertheless, supported by philosophers' insights and intrigued with writers' perceptions, it seems timely and appropriate to explore what begs to be placed in perspective and given credit long overdue.

The impetus for this study lies further back in the past than I would care to admit. During its development I have benefit-

[1] The recent work by Günter Bose and Erich Brinkmann, *Circus: Geschichte und Ästhetik einer niederen Kunst,* Berlin, 1978, is perhaps an indication that a reverse trend is underway. They relate how even now their own best intentions met with the usual prejudice: "Als wir dem Verleger vorschlugen, ein Buch über Zirkus zu machen, fragte er, ob wir vom Metier seien. Wir haben nein gesagt und das Buch trotzdem geschrieben."

ted from the good graces of many individuals, among whom I specifically want to thank the following: Ms. Kathleen Blow and Mr. Charles Dwyer, reference librarians at the University of Texas-Austin library, whose interest and untiring efforts on my behalf helped in laying the groundwork for all my subsequent work; Professor Leroy R. Shaw, whose initial suggestion got me started and whose later encouragement kept me from faltering; Professor Dr. Hans Mayer, Eberhard-Karls Universität, Tübingen, whose perception so often crystallized much that threatened to dissolve and whose enthusiasm for my work served as both real and symbolic support; the Alexander von Humboldt Stiftung, for fellowship monies which gave me time for most of the preliminary writing, and for funds in support of publication costs; the Graduate School, The University of Wisconsin-Milwaukee, for financial assistance in the early stages of my research; the UWM College of Letters and Science administration, particularly Associate Dean G. Micheal Riley; my colleagues in the Department of German at the University of Wisconsin-Milwaukee; Rose Liesenfeld, a departmental secretary who performed over and over again beyond the proverbial demands of duty in typing early drafts of the manuscript; finally, although in truth first of all, my wife and children to whom I have given the dedication page, but for whom that is small payment for having stood by and stood with for such a long time.

Milwaukee, Wisconsin
August, 1983

ONE:

Definitions and Demarcations

1. *Sociological considerations*

Having referred so boldly in my preceding remarks to the circus as a form of "popular" entertainment in contrast to the realm of "legitimate" art, I want here at the beginning to discuss that dichotomy briefly. I do not, however, want to attempt to justify it or to trace its origins in any great detail. To advance the numerous arguments given and positions taken on this issue would serve little and would extend us beyond the purview of this analysis. Nonetheless, a number of basic premises are sufficiently inviolate so as not to cause heated arguments from the historians or sociologists while permitting us, so to speak, to fix our own position.

There can be little doubt that the term "popular" has been applied rather indiscriminately to cultural phenomena of great variety. One theorist concedes that the concept is often "no more than a broad umbrella covering ... an open series." He cites as examples ancient romances (second century AD), religious, hagiographic literature in seventeenth century France, didactic literature in seventeenth century England, peasant art in contemporary Romania, Scottish country dance, horror, pornographic, or scientific fiction in contemporary industrial societies, the cinema, and most forms of entertainment" — on the whole any form of cultural activity and product which is by one criterion or another reckoned to arouse a relatively widespread interest, or achieve a high degree of consumption in a given society."[1] Like others, we are

[1] Zev Barbu, "Popular Culture: A Sociological Approach," *Approaches to Popular Culture,* C. W. E. Bigsby, ed., Bowling Green, Ohio, 1976, p. 40.

almost forced to attempt a refinement of that kind of broad definition.

Another look at the examples confirms that it is indeed difficult to find common ground among them. We can note nonetheless that in every instance in which the divers phenomena cited have been designated as "popular", the speaker has presupposed an intracultural and intrasocial differentiation between spheres which polarize themselves variously as "high" vs "low", "majority" vs "minority", "learned" vs "unlearned", "highbrow" vs "lowbrow" (even "middlebrow"), "mass" vs "elite", "democratic" vs ""aristocratic", "popular" vs "genuine" culture. In whatever terms, one cannot escape the assumption of an accepted dichotomization plus the value judgment inherent in it as well. In other words, the dichotomy itself precedes the designation.

We must also note in the examples that the conception of what constitutes "popular" culture encompasses cultural phenomena not solely of recent origin. In recognition of this fact, the point can be, and is often, made that "popular" culture has existed all along, whether or not the nineteenth century made a cultural polarization seem obvious. It is within this kind of linear perspective which relates the former to the more recent, the old or traditional to the new without tradition, that the question is begged as to the relationship between "folk" and "popular" culture, both historically as well as generically. It has been suggested that the two be distinguished by defining the former as a "communal art rooted in daily experience, a product of *gemeinschaft* in which the distinction between audience and performer is inprecise, and the latter as entertainment, a product of *gesellschaft,* in which that distinction becomes vital."[2] This permits a view of folk culture as "pre-industrial, preliterate popular culture," but necessitates a caveat to the effect that the post-literate, post-industrial phase is not to be understood as a product of the

[2] C. W. E. Bigsby, "The Politics of Popular Culture," *Approaches to Popular Culture,* C. W. E. Bigsby, ed., Bowling Green, Ohio, 1976, p. 18.

nineteenth century. In other words, neither chronologically nor generically can one hope to find clear-cut distinctions among those phenomena which find themselves on one side or the other of this cultural bifurcation.

For our purposes, however, we can concede that modern industrialized society has a highly differentiated and internally divided structure that facilitates and accentuates cultural and aesthetic distinctions. There is little reason to dispute the notion that the focus of urbanization and industrialization, togehger with the concomitant economic changes and the formation of a middle class, have served as prerequisite conditions necessary to the creation of a mass public and a popular culture as we tend to speak of it at present.[3] If we can accept this qualification in the interest of economy of argument, it is possible to accomodate the various historical phases of the dichotomy between "popular" and "legitimate" (or however one may wish to label that "higher" aesthetic and cultural activity) by understanding them as evolving along a continuum that begins before, then moves toward, the nineteenth century watershed as a culminating point in the dichotomization of art and culture, subsequently progressing beyond it into the present. It is from this vantage point that we want to view the circus as a form of popular culture that reached its zenith at the end of the nineteenth century and which was clearly operant within the cultural and aesthetic classification system dominant at the time.

Having accepted the dichotomy as the given framework in the late nineteenth century, we still need to establish the circus as a facet of "popular" culture. Three relationships are important here in considering, from a sociological standpoint, the popular status of the circus and how it functioned within the turn-of-the-century cultural milieu: the circus relative to class and culture, the circus relative to its producers and performers, and the circus relative to the market as an economically organized institution affecting cultural production. A brief discussion of these relationships makes it clear that the

[3] Ibid., p. 18.

circus can be placed within the "popular" sphere with a considerable degree of sociological certainty.

The question of class and culture simply reiterates the split into "popular" and "legitimate", "high" and "low" culture. That dichotomization virtually always has been formulated along class lines, with high culture the domain of the upper classes. There are obvious difficulties in this kind of simplistic duality, but the polarity nicely incorporates the relational substance, that is, between superior and inferior, minority and majority. The simplicity does not undercut the implicit fact that high is superior and elite, and that in that context, popular is inferior, common, and of the many. To be sure, these distinctions have undergone significant modifications as theorists have questioned their validity and pointed out exceptions and variations.[4] Moreover, each culture has its own unique stamp, and the closer the analyst to the contemporary scene, the greater the need to take into consideration the changing nature of present-day society and its institutions, most certainly the concept of "class" per se. For our purposes, however, the simplistic duality is a relevant one, inasmuch as we take up the circus at an historical point that coincides with European society in its most class-conscious phase. As will be shown shortly, the circus stems indeed from common stock. From its earliest origins, throughout its century-old history, and even in its present role, its performers have been and are considered to be of "low" class, from a cultural "fringe" or periphery that presumes a "center", or from cultural "depths" that presume "heights". If ever these distinctions were functional and significant, it was during the nineteenth century as the circus moved toward the culmination of its development.

With regard to the other two relationships, we can propose that all those who entered into production of the circus, whether performers with individual acts or producers/directors with managerial skills and entrepreneurial acumen, did so in full cognizance of the audience for whom they were at

[4] See Barbu, p. 55.

work, so that the circus as institution assumed a mediating role between the two. In the sense that those producers/performers related to the institution as they related to the audience, that relationship determined the substance of what the former did and what they made the circus. Insofar as their efforts in their work since the very beginning had been geared toward satisfying perceived needs and tastes on the part of a general public, they sought to give that public what it demanded and what it responded to. The public came, and had always come, for entertainment pure and simple. It responded primarily to what it saw. The circus producers/performers thus responded to the audience by concerning themselves with the nature of the effect in pursuit of entertaining that public.[5] They made a principle of heightened effects and an increased appeal of their product to as wide an audience as possible. To that end they pursued form over content, the physical over the intellectual. Their intent was thus distinct from that of those "legitimate" and "serious" art forms where intent itself was absent, or at the least, designed for intellectual absorption and enlightenment.

Addressing the audience thusly, the circus performers/producers clearly reveal themselves in the third relationship, i. e. as principals in a market relationship involving reception and consumption of a product. Interestingly enough, however, out of this and the preceding relationship involving the institution and its performers/producers we find something of a sociological twist occuring. At precisely the point in time that the circus was movlng toward its zenith, it appeared to supercede the kind of binary distinction that had previously determined its place in the social and cultural matrix. While the history of the circus bears out the fact that from the mid-nineteenth century the circus rose in popularity to the point that toward the close of the century it was culturally at the very center of attraction, it was functioning at that time as a "popular" form of dispersed and common heritage that had gained acceptance such that it could assume a role previously forbidden it.

[5] Ibid., p. 62.

What had always operated in the domain of the majority was transformed into a kind of specialty of a minority elite producing for a market which was becoming general enough to include not only the "people" but the "elite" of society as well. The circus was thus able to maintain and capitalize on its distinctly popular heritage at the same time it could orient itself for its public as a bourgeois institution in an increasingly bourgeois society. This sociological twist and the relationships that were established with the circus because of it are thus central to our attempt to understand the circus at this point in its history and in the history of German literature.

2. *Historia circensis*

As one of the oldest forms of popular entertainment, the circus traces its history back to Roman times. From those ancient roots it has withstood the flux of time and the whim of spectators so that even today it persists — stubbornly and tenaciously in inhospitable times. The circus' genealogy is sufficiently complex and often too obscure for us to draw tight threads through the course of its heritage, and given the focus of this study, there would be little purpose in attempting a sequential account of past to present. It is, however, possible to point to components of that heritage which mark critical junctures in the development of the modern circus and which give a fairly consistent picture of the circus' derivation and nature.

The Roman beginnings, of course, provide the term "circus" — the circle of the Circus Maximus where a variety of entertainment was set before the Emperor and the public. The dissolution of the Empire set much and many in motion, among them those who during the centuries to follow seemed never to find a secure footing or permanency of any kind, a "fahrendes Volk" who traversed the European mainland up to the eighteenth century. Many of its progeny are interspersed among circus performers of the present, their residence still no more than a mobile home or its equivalent. These peripatetic wanderers from the beginning were classifiable as outsiders, disenfranchised, of little social consequence, the riff-raff with little aspiration to station or status. Bose and Brinkmann point out that already around the tenth century certain types were in evidence which persisted throughout the middle ages. i.e., "Waffenkämpfer, starke Männer und Ringer, Possenreißer und Mimiker, dann Seiltänzer, Puppenspieler, Leute mit abgerichteten Tieren, Bären, Affen, Hunden, Schlangen, allerlei Spielleute, Zauberer, Wahrsager und Quacksalber, Tänzerinnen und Huren."[6] They all come to be lumped together as a common grouping, not only by virtue of their transient nature, but also because of their lack of steady employment — a factor which brought them much disdain. They were most often in evidence at the fairs and "Jahrmärkte" which dominated medieval life and which functioned as meeting places along routes of trade and commerce until long after towns and cities solidified society into a network of distinct places and peoples. These fairs were not only commercial markets but places of pleasure and entertainment as well, a factor which placed a distinct aura on those who performed, in contrast to those who came for commercial and/or amusement purposes. In time, animals assumed a role in this setting as performers moved beyond the exhibition of their own selves in one way or another to routines which incorporated an entertaining "performance" by one sort of animal or another. Initially at least, the animal's role would have been based on its performance capabilities since performers would have had few means of obtaining or purchasing truly exotic specimens. Only later did the exhibition of previously unseen and exotic animals add to the lure which brought the public to the performers. An elephant was shown in Frankfurt for the first time in 1443.[7]

Entertainment was a factor at the court as well as at the marketplace. The former could come to the latter since it

[6] Günter Bose and Erich Brinkmann, *Circus: Geschichte und Ästhetik einer niederen Kunst,* Berlin, 1978, p. 20.

[7] Ibid., p. 26.

could pay the price and could buy the entire show if it so desired. The transplantation of entertainers to the court, where "Hofnarr" was a title, legitimized and sanctioned what otherwise belonged very much still outside the official and proper life of the developing bourgeois existence. It is possible in fact to propose that this contradiction is the essence of the bifurcation that characterizes the split into high and low, popular and legitimate, facets of culture. If the medieval citizen found himself in the midst of two worlds it was the carnival that united them: "Der Karneval vereinigt, vermengt und vermählt das Geheiligte mit dem Profanen, das Weise mit dem Törichten."[8]

The seventeenth century brought a further accentuation of the dichotomy. By this time, as Bose and Brinkmann point out, the court had reached a culminating point in artificiality, pompousness and boredom such that Rousseau's critique of that world of appearances was not only justified but taken up and enforced by the citizens and subjects as well. Bourgeois eyes were opened to see things in a new light. What they confronted was to a certain degree their own corporeality – in most instances best exemplified in those who had all along been exhibiting and training the body. If the performing artist first had had to be taken in by the court in order to receive some degree of legitimation, he was now able to function more in his own realm where both burgher and aristocrat seemed anxious to become his audience. For the aristocrat and his royal cousins, such performances were a diversion and an entertaining escape from ennui. For the bourgeois citizen it had a much stronger attraction. It was nature and natural. It belonged to him. He could observe the performing artist as if he himself were the performer. In that sense, all was possible that was demonstrated to him and he was the focus of attention.[9]

The latter part of the eighteenth century marks the inception of the modern circus in a format roughly identifiable

8 Michail Bachtin, *Literatur und Karneval. Zur Romantheorie und Lachkultur,* Munich, 1969, p. 49.

9 See Bose and Brinkmann, p. 33.

with what we know today. Individuals and/or small troupes offering hardly more than entertaining showmanship and a single highly developed skill were in evidence on the Continent as early as 1767. More often that not a family enterprise, these small troupes provided a kind seasonal, transient entertainment for a largely rural populace. The origin in 1789 of one of the most famous of these groups — the Franconis — dates back to this period when family ties and intermarriages established and nurtured talents that carried circus blood into succeeding generations. The permanent structures built by Phillip Astley in London and Paris in 1778, 1782, and 1794 mark the first attempts to establish a more secure footing for the modern European circus.

By the middle of the nineteenth century a distinctly German circus tradition had emerged. Karl von Holtei's classic work *Die Vagabunden* enthusiastically described the talents of numerous troupes and sundry personalities. Based on von Holtei's knowledge of the lives of circus people, the work capitalized on an aura of confidentiality, providing behind-the-scene glimpses of what by now were considered a distinct breed of performers and entertainers. The book was widely read and, through its consistently positive tone, contributed substantially to the receptive attitude accorded the circus on the part of the German public at large.

In conjunction with other demographic factors during the second half of the century, the circus gravitated toward the urban centers. In Germany, Berlin became the operational base of a number of circuses, several of which enjoyed international prominence. What rather quickly developed in the more cosmopolitan context were circus dynasties whose wealth and appeal displayed little connection with the wandering troupes of the recent past. The first German circus to rise beyond purely local fame was a troupe under the direction of Eduard Wollschläger. His circus was established in permanent quarters in Berlin as early as 1842. In 1851 Ernst Renz initiated a tradition that would carry the German circus to the apex of its development when he brought his performers to Berlin. In competition with a popular French troupe under Lejean, Renz won the favor of the public by incorporating into his productions a level of sophistication previously unknown. Under a standard of strict discipline and excellence, Renz transformed the circus into a visual spectacle through the use of huge pantomimic productions. These served for years to give the Renz circus a unique quality, bringing into the circus arena an impressive combination of music, pantomime, and dance. In obvious competition with the more established forms of theater, ballet, and concert, Renz took over a former Berlin market hall in 1888, outfitted and enlarged it to a seating capacity of 6000, and set before the public a spectacular new production in September of 1859. The circus became a cultural and social event for all of Berlin. Until the death of its founder in 1892, the Renz circus was the home of virtually all the first-class talent in the German circus world.

Significant contributions to the development of the German circus were made by a number of other troupes, among them those bearing the names of Schumann, Busch, Hagenbeck, Sarassani and Krone. Albert Schumann's special talents lay in his renowned ability to train animals, particularly horses. Using highly developed training methods, he offered the public a splendid spectacle of performing animals just as Renz had done with choreographed dancers and performers. Paul Busch, whose talented daughter Paula carried the Busch circus name into the 1960s, chose Hamburg as a permanent home in 1891 and subsequently brought the enterprise into such renown that Circus Busch had permanent buildings in Vienna, Breslau, and Berlin. Busch carried the Renz tradition of the *Schaustück* one step further and perfected an arena whose floor could be raised and lowered hydraulically.[10] This technology enabled him to transform the arena into an enormous pool for the production of aquatic pantomimes. Renz himself had introduced this kind of spectacle in 1891, and

[10] This innovation was also part of the Parisian circus. The Arènes Nautiques was built in 1886 and soon became the stamp of the Cirque Nouveau. Bose and Brinkmann, *Circus,* p. 133.

others tried it as well, but Busch carried it to its most impressive extremes. His acclaimed production "Siberia" featured one hundred and twenty polar bears hurtling down a slide into the water, a sight which must have delighted his audiences. Hagenbeck, Sarassani, and Krone developed a different emphasis and established their circuses primarily on the fascination of the public for wild animals. It was in their arenas and menageries that many a citizen first saw and became conscious of animals native to other parts of the world. Hagenbeck's zoo is still an attraction in Hamburg. Sarasanni brought an American immensity to the German circus with a conscious effort to follow the lead of Barnum and Bailey. For his productions in Dresden he established a permanent home with a seating capacity of 5000, and performances with as many as twenty well-trained elephants became standard fare. If Karl Krone's circus beginnings were inauspicious, he was ultimately able to establish one of the largest undertakings on the Continent. His name came to be associated with trained lions by virtue of an impressive act he developed with his wife and twenty-four magnificent animals. His circus withstood both World Wars, but not before he moved his operation first to Munich, then to Italy, then to Switzerland and finally back to Munich. Krone established the American tradition of the three ring circus within the European circus context, a factor that encouraged his undertaking to grow ever larger — even by contemporary standards: at a relatively early point he could count twenty-seven elephants, over one hundred sundry wild animals, among them fifty tigers, plus some two hundred and fifty horses.[11] Circus Krone is still quartered in Munich and perserveringly survives the multi-media pressures of contemporary society even though its present function is hardly comparable to the role it played in the past.

The German and European circus had in fact already reached its zenith by the time Paul Busch died in 1927. By the early 1930s, what Gautier had once described as the era of the

[11] See Emil Gobbers, *Artisten: Zirkus und Variété in alter und neuer Zeit,* Düsseldorf, 1949, p. 71.

purely visual spectacle had run its course. While the visual aspect of the spectacle was to persist to a degree as the circus was pushed into a lesser role by the emerging medium of the film and, subsequently, by television, the mutation of live spectacle performance into the instrumented, duplicative image inherent in and symbolized by those more technical media was virtually complete. After that, the circus would find it increasingly difficult to perform for a world that could find its thrills elsewhere and which had been weaned from the immediacy of the world of acrobats, animals, and clown.

3. *The circus in context*

All evidence suggests that the heyday which the European circus experienced from roughly 1875 through the first decades of the twentieth century was not an isolated phenomenon. This was a period of rapid and momentous change, an era of technological, economic, and social growth and expansion almost without parallel, a difficult time for many, for those whose status was in ascendancy as well as for those who were sensitive to the fact that they and theirs was in decline. In such transitional times, when conventions are shaken and become inadequate, the pressures are released in digressions and diversions, not infrequently in those which promise either a closer relationship to what can be perceived as reality or which operate at the other extreme in a kind of fantasy world unencumbered by the exigencies of everyday life. Doubtless any attempt to reduce cultural history to a few lines runs the risk of blatant oversimplification. Nonetheless, it is safe to suggest that it was precisely in such a context that the circus and other forms of popular entertainment came to be regarded with great favor during the period in question. Out of a combination of the public's receptivity to being entertained and amused and the entrepreneurial skills of those ready to capitalize on the prevailing mood, forms of "popular" entertainment such as the circus, which enjoyed a lengthy heritage, as well as those such as the *Kabarett*, which seemed to spring from nowhere, rose to new heights of popularity. Within a setting characterized by a remarkable degree of internationalism, of tolerance for borrowing (engendered no doubt by the general mood of innovation and experimentation), of fluidity between forms not yet confirmed and hardened into traditions to be defended or broken, we find numerous connecting links, reciprocal exchanges, and mutually-shared structural elements among those forms — as if to emphasize their common counterdistinction to the "legitimate" forms now seemingly less appealing and less entertaining.

The dichotomous cultural situation outlined earlier, however, was not so set as to prevent at the same time a similar kind of osmotic transference between forms on the "popular" side and those on the "legitimate" side of the coin. In the case of the circus, its sheer popularity caused it to take on a significance far beyond its surface appeal of high-wire thrills and animal smells. The fascination on the part of most artists with what came to be called "the greatest show on earth" was based most often on an insight more penetrating than that of those who simply paid their money and watched the show. Those who were contemporary to the circus' great appeal, if they were not already locked into an aesthetic custom, were anxious to experiment and were receptive to the myriad ideas suggested by the multifaceted world of the circus.

Within the broad spectrum of the graphic arts, for example, the circus as thematic material surfaced as early as 1881 in Seurat's *Le Cirque*. Cézanne's Harlequin paintings (1888–1890) just a few years later represent a borrowing which was certainly not without precedent, but which nonetheless coincided with Harlequin's status within the contemporary circus context. Degas' ballet dancers appear to be unrelated here, but actually follow the line of Cézanne's motif and represent a thematic variation of the same world. Toulouse-Lautrec, living in Montmartre and moving openly in bohemian circles, set the circus squarely in front of that intensely experiential world. The subsequent popularity of his work left the motiv engraved in his oeuvre and in the graphic arts in general.[12] It was ultimately through the impetus from Toulouse-Lautrec that Picasso created his works depicting various aspects of the circus world — creations which brought the world of clowns and acrobats into the sphere of legitimate art — if not initially, then later after reaction became cognizant of genius. Toulouse-Lautrec's depiction of brothel life in his *Elles* series represents a conscious choice of subject matter heretofore inappropriate and not without a certain intrigue and eroticism, despite the artist's serious intent in showing the female subject in the most mundane aspects of her everyday life. Circus-related figures, particularly the Pierrot and Harlequin which were much in evidence in pantomimes popular at the time, became increasingly popular as subject matter. Henri Ibel's characterization gives them a sadness and melancholy that would find expression, again, in Picasso's later treatments of them as symbols of human isolation in an alien world.

Beyond this kind of widespread thematic treatment of circus motifs, the close kinship between the circus and the various forms of the variety stage demonstrates a similarity in cultural function. In its Montmartre origins, the cabaret was literally as well as artistically "just around the corner" from the circus. The French cabaret served as experimental ground for artists and performers who consciously sought to negate most of the elements of legitimate art, although it succeeded in engendering much that later came to be recognized as the best art produced at the time. In Germany, the cabaret took hold largely through the efforts of Otto Julius Bierbaum and, once initiated, became a thriving aspect of the popular entertainment world for the first third of the century. From the beginning, however, Bierbaum mistakenly sought to take the revolutionary, though "lowly," elements indigenous to the ca-

[12] It is interesting to note that Toulouse-Lautrec's efforts to prove his sanity at the Neuilly sanatorium centered around a series of circus pictures entitled *Au Cirque*. They were inspired by his enthusiasm for the Cirque Nouveau which had held Paris' rapt attention since the 1880s. See Grete Wehmeyer, *Erik Satie*, Regensburg, 1974, p. 174.

baret and variety stage and ennobel them so that they could be considered "serious" art. He was never fully successful in transferring those elements onto a "higher" level, and the publication of his *Deutsche Chansons* in 1900, although giving the popular form a certain degree of legitimacy by putting it in print, did not completely institutionalize it so as to prevent further experimentation in this genre. Nor did it cancel out the antagonistic stance which was organic to the cabaret's format and the style of those artists who worked within this context. In however varied a format, the satire, the exoticism of the performers, the eroticism of much of the material, the strongly rhythmic music, and the serial format of one routine followed by another all reveal a heritage common with the circus. What transpired on the cabaret stage frequently was to be seen in the circus arena and vice versa, with modifications as dictated by spatial and acoustical considerations. The cabaret in its unique style came to thrive as a viable meeting ground between high and low art, bringing popular forms almost to the verge of legitimate status, and at the very least, forcing a meeting between the separate spheres.

The relationship between the pantomime and the circus is another case of mutual enhancement. Although pantomimic performance in the context of theater as well as pantomime in general represents a tradition with ancient roots, its great popularity toward the end of the nineteenth century must be viewed as a late development or revival, and its turn-of-the-century evolution into spectacle the unique result of its ties to the circus. Experimenting with the pantomime within the circus setting had been a hallmark of the pioneering Eduard Wollschläger earlier in the century in Germany,[13] but it was in the Parisian circus that it assumed a new destiny. Incorporating pantomimic elements into the circus afforded a unique opportunity for spectacle, and the role of such elements was gradually increased to major proportions. As an art form it developed in Paris with little trouble, insofar as the Parisian

[13] Recall that Wollschläger had been one of the early German circus directors to establish permanent quarters in Berlin (1842).

public more than any other seemed intent on searching for exciting innovations and ready-made escape hatches from the routine of everyday life. Moreover, in Paris the pantomime enjoyed something of a tradition. At least once before the city had responded to that mode of expression when in 1832 Jean Gaspard Deburau had inspired some of Paris' best known artists to attend his performances eagerly and to write pantomimes for him. After seeing him in performance, Théophile Gautier wrote: "Le temps des spectacles purement oculaires est arrivé!"[14] and Thomas de Banville acknowledged in his memoires that Deburau was an incomparable actor who had everything necessary to enchant the masses.[15] As an art form appealing more to the senses than to the mind, the pantomime easily found a favorable reception among members of the public at the turn of the century. As a theatrical medium, moreover, the pantomime was adaptable: in the music hall or café, it developed within the parameters of the traditional stage, and in the circus its potential was extended in proportion to the possibilities offered by the circus' increased spatial dimensions, outfittings, and the number of potential performers. Within the latter framework it relied on the spectacle effect of large numbers of performers, elaborate costumes, and intricate staging, and maintained the traditional and rather banal and overblown tableau format of narrative tale with grouped performers in choreographed routines. Outside the actual circus framework, it found its most innovative outlet on the stages of music halls and cafés in the context of the dance.

Defiant of the traditional ballet and oriented toward pure rhythmic movement, pantomimic dance developed as a hallmark of dance performance of the period. Popular interpreters such as Loie Fuller, Ruth St. Denis, Mary Wigman, Isadora Duncan, the Loheland School, Sent M'ahesa, Niddy Im-

[14] Quoted in Karl Gunther Simon, *Pantomime: Ursprung, Wesen, Möglichkeiten,* Munich, 1960, p. 32.

[15] Quoted in Georges Cain, *Anciens Théâtres de Paris,* Paris, 1906, p. 15.

pehoven, Valeska Gert, et al, consciously rejected the limitations of the ballet and sought to release the human body from the paralysis of classical form and routines. Their experimentation was avidly received by a public eager for a less contrived and more natural depiction of the human form. A contributing impetus was the increasing popularity of the folk dance, a generic form which enjoyed a significant renaissance of its own at the time. It was the folk dance as natural expression that inspired the leading expressive dance artists to adapt it for their individual interpretations — each of them recognizing and capitalizing on the public's enthusiasm for everything that appeared exotic.[16] The naturalness of the costumes, the frequent reduction of the dress to less than had ever clothed a dancer previously, did much to create a favorable context. The dance achieved at this point a sensuality that had long been lost and hidden, and both the exotic and the erotic elements struck a responsive chord at a time when the strictures of a previous age were being rejected.

In contrast to those instances in which individual circus types such as the clown and the acrobat were transferred as subject matter to other artistic forms of the period, it was the kind of stylized "natural" body movements observable in circus animals and well-trained performers that made the latter interesting for the expressive dance.[17] Many of the turn-of-

[16] The same phenomenon is to be observed in the realm of music where, toward the latter part of the nineteenth and in the early decades of the twentieth century, the folk idiom and folk-dance music was used by composers such as Berlioz, Liszt, Smetana, Brahms, and Dvorak to lighten and enliven a heavier musical context grown stale. Written in response to a condescending remark by a "serious" and quite famous composer-conductor (Johann Franz von Herbeck) to the effect that Czechs were no more than "reproductive artists," Bedrich Smetana's *The Bartered Bride* is an entire opera of folk elements and folk melodies with the whole third act revolving around the performance by a circus troupe. It was the epitome of ethnic exoticism and comic gaiety which a number of "national" composers would bring to the world of "serious" music and opera.

[17] In a reciprocal mode, there were instances of the expressive dance programmed for large audiences in the permanent circus build-

the-century innovations in the dance would culminate somewhat later in the work of George Balanchine, a man whose originality and creative genius repeatedly bridged the chronological distance between earlier experimentation and the modern dance of today. In validation of the proposal that the development of modern dance has been repeatedly subject to the force of the circus, we may note that one of Balanchine's most "uncomfortable" works stemming from his early collaboration with the Ballet Russe, his well-known *Prodigal Son,* harks back to a Russian circus setting of clowns and acrobats.[18] The piece, in fact, constitutes a high point in the enigmatic choreography of his early work.

New forms and sounds for the cabaret and variety stage appeared on music's threshold and served to mark its twentieth-century character. Jazz began to sweep from America across Europe. Few were satisfied with anything that looked back toward the old. Wagner, for all his musical dramatics, was by now not considered by everyone to be the direction of the future. The new composers, if they lacked a clear conception of a unique form and style, were sure of their opposition to, and rebellion against, established traditions no longer appropriate to the contemporary scene.

As we might expect, the circus made its mark on this "new" music as well. One of the newcomers during the period in question, Erik Satie (1866–1925), had very definite ideas about what the new music should be. For the most part these were sufficient to exclude him from the official musical lea-

ings of the era. The pantomimes of the dramatist Frank Wedekind are an interesting case wherein both the individual expressive dance (Wedekind designates them by title according to the mood to be expressed, e. g. *Schmerzenstanz, Freudentanz,* etc.) and the more expansive collective pantomimic dramatizations work together in a single presentation suitable for the stage or the circus arena. Wedekind was particularly aware of the animal/human relationship, specifically in the matter of natural movement, and wrote his pantomimes very much in celebration of such relationships.

18 Horst Koegler, *Balanchine und das moderne Ballett,* Hannover, 1964, p. 25.

gues. An impish recluse often frustratingly close to a musical breakthrough, he both longed for a hint of success and abhorred the kind of constraints success would bring.[19] His *Parade* of 1915 is an almost unmatched example of cooperative genius and a case in point of an "extended" impetus originating in the circus. The history of the piece is worth a brief digression: Satie would doubtless have remained in obscurity had he not become part of a remarkable artistic constellation composed of Serge de Diaghilev, Jean Cocteau, Leonide Massine and Pablo Picasso. These were the collaborators on *Parade,* artists each in his own right, each of whom has left his mark on the history of the modern theater, ballet, art, and music. That they all came together in this cooperative effort can likely be ascribed to the magnetism of the eldest of them, the impressario Diaghilev. During his twenty years as one of the leading figures in the world of opera and ballet (1909–1929) in Paris Diaghilev effectively supervised, either by virtue of his genius or his eccentricity, the direction of modern dance until it no longer resembled its traditional precedents.[20] Diaghilev's emphasis was remarkably interdisciplinary, bringing dance, music, and stage setting into a new relationship premised on equality of the various parts. Writing to the *London Times* in 1914, his choreographer Michael Fokine declared that the "new ballet" had no intention of being a slave to music or stage setting. It would make it clear instead that those elements coexisted on equal footing and would promote the freedom of the cooperating artists.[21] While that

[19] Although Roger Shattuck chose him as one of four studies in his analysis of the arts in France up to 1918 (*The Banquet Years,* New York, 1968), Satie's work has only recently received serious attention, and his place in the history of French music is frequently accorded only borderline status.

[20] In 1937 Ninette de Valois wrote: "His work was done at the time he died, and the lull that followed was a valuable relaxation for all concerned. What is happening in the ballet world today may ultimately stand as a memorial to the man who succeeded in saving the ballet from itself." Quoted in John Percival, *The World of Diaghilev,* London, 1971, p. 150.

[21] See Wehmeyer, *Satie,* p. 198.

kind of philosophy proved volatile often enough, it was excitingly productive, and *Parade* is one of the best examples of that artistic approach.

The genesis of the work reveals an inspiration coming from the circus on both the part of Satie and Cocteau, the two collaborators who gave most shape to the piece. From early childhood Satie was a devotee of the circus world. As a child he often went to the circus and was acquainted with many of the artists in a backstage, dressing-room familiarity. In 1887 he lived at the foot of Montmartre close to the Cirque Médrano where he was a frequent visitor. Thus when he met Cocteau in 1915 he had every reason to be receptive to the latter's suggestion that they collaborate with Diaghilev on a work based on a circus motif. Cocteau had been brewing the idea for several years, and the meeting with Satie apparently provided the ingredient that had been lacking at an earlier point. Cocteau's version of the origin of the ballet is delineated in his pamphlet *Coc et Arlequin* in which he recalls that the idea surfaced in 1913 when he saw Stravinsky's *Le Sacre du Printemps* under the direction of Diaghilev. At that time he wanted to collaborate with Stravinsky on a work based on the David motif. The two worked on the idea together in Switzerland in March of 1914, shaping the biblical account into what looked like a circus number, The work remained incomplete, however, and when Cocteau later met Satie he apparently forsook his work with Stravinsky. Cocteau's inclinations to this kind of theme were nonetheless considerable: in an earlier collaboration with Edgard Varèse, he had worked an another circus piece — a circus version of *A Midsummer Night's Dream* in which Oberon was supposed to make his entrance into the ring of the Cirque Médrano while the orchestra played *Tipperary*.[22] It was doubtless the similar inclination on the part of Satie that enabled Cocteau finally to give shape to his circus fascination. In his best anti-traditional stance, Cocteau later referred to Satie as one of his masters — an artist whose "direction" went against the cur-

[22] Shattuck, *Banquet Years*, p. 152.

rent of musical impressionism and whose reductionist compositions baffled the dilettantes.[23]

The credits for the 1917 performance of *Parade* read like a lineup of this century's early avant-garde: Ballet réaliste / sur un thème de Jean Cocteau / avec la collaboration de / Picasso / pour les décors et costumes et de / Erik Satie / pour la musique / Représenté au Théâtre du Châtelet / en 1917 par la / Compagnie des Ballets Russes de / Serge de Diaghilew / Choréographie de / Leonide Massine / d'après les indications plastiques / de l'auteur.[24] Despite the cooperation of such complex personalities, the plot was a simple one. The scene shows the outside of a circus booth. The performers appear one after the other and attempt to lure the audience inside. First a Chinese conjurer performing tricks with an egg, then a figure representing a little American girl mimicking the riding of a bronco, bicycling, and dancing ragtime. This followed by two acrobats in blue and white tights performing a lyrical adagio. In the midst of all are two managers wearing cubist costumes, plus a comically constructed horse. The action, aside from the comedy per se, involves nothing more than the repeated attempts to get the audience passing in front of the booth to move inside. The spectators seem not to understand and are convinced that what they are seeing is all that is to be seen. The performers become increasingly frustrated. The artists despair over this tragic misunderstanding, the manager collapses, the American girl imploringly spreads her arms wide, the acrobats tremble from exhaustion, the magician appears to be reconciled in true oriental fashion, and the horse falls exhausted in a heap. Not exactly a happy ending, nor an overtly profound scenario.

The plot is so obviously thin that Apollinaire in his program notes devoted his attention to the choreography and the sets. One can sympathize with his dilemma: there is very little in the end that warrants analysis. One wants to be suspicious of the negative ending. The performers are unable to convince

23 Wehmeyer, *Satie,* p. 178.
24 Ibid., p. 174.

the spectators that what they see is not the real thing, that beneath the surface, i. e., inside the tent, there is more. Cocteau's point would thus be directed to both the obstinate audience as well as to the frustrated performers, yet it is not at all clear who is on the wrong track. The piece simply ends, and one is forced to believe it is ultimately less the point and more the entire mise-en-scène that is the essence of the work. It appears to be purely and simply an opportunity to confront the real audience with images, music, and choreography heretofore unknown. A kind of nonsense and somewhat heretical context was appropriately provided by the circus, and it made the scandal the collaborators had hoped for. For Satie, it was the closest he ever got to success.

Satie's music for the circus piece clearly indicates the direction of the new. He openly rejected anything barely resembling Wagnerian enormity, complexity, and density, or the French fluidity and vagueness of Debussy. His style was acutely clean, clear, and small in scale, his musical ideas sometimes extending no further than a few measures. He incorporated a music-hall style and gave the French audience its first concert treatment of jazz. In its musical aspects, the piece has been described as "a serious-humorous exploitation of popular elements in art, a turning to jazz and musical hall and to all the paraphernalia of modern life, not in a spirit of realism, but with a sense of exhilaration in the absurd."[25] To state that the spirit of the piece was not one of realism, however, is not to suggest that it was removed from the reality of the day. The jazz which Satie saw fit to incorporate into *Parade* was very much the rage and had made its way into the life of the populace via — once again — the circus. The Cakewalk had made a hit in 1904 in the Nouveau Cirque. Scott Joplin's rag opera *A Guest of Honor* had come to Europe already in 1903, and for years his rags expressed the syncopation that dominated real life. Cocteau saw in jazz a return to the human and a victory over a mechanistic age. He referred to it as a kind of "tamed catastrophy," and stated unequivo-

[25] Shattuck, *Banquet Years,* p. 154–155.

cally that it was the "form of the day."[26] Satie must have sensed in jazz's rhythms, melodies, and timbres a rich counterforce to the whole European tradition of "absolute" music. It was a case of musical style growing out of one social reality and transposed for use into another. Jazz was to become the basis for much of twentieth century music and, as a form of musical expression of humbler origin and therefore closer in touch with reality, it provided the desired opposition to the staleness and politeness of Straußian/Offenbachian melodies and the complexities and strictures of the classical tradition still limping along. It was also an alternative to those serious composers such as Prokofiev and Stravinsky who in their own ways were remolding "high" music to fit the times.[27]

It is thus no overstatement to assert that the cultural matrix of the era in question was shaped by the circus and those related forms such as the pantomime, the music hall, varieté, cabaret, and revue that borrowed from, as well as contributed to, its form and content. The kind of popularity these forms of entertainment enjoyed, their essentially non-traditional format and innovative substance, is perhaps best exemplified in what emerged as a characteristic art form of the period — the poster. In France. where it originated and where it flourished most pronouncedly, the poster's ubiquity was manifestly a factor of that conjunction referred to earlier, that is, the public's hunger for entertainment and its receptivity to the new, including the burgeoning world of commercial ventures and manufactured products. Under the auspices of the World's Fair of 1889 and the centenary of the French Revolution, Paris blossomed as a kind of mecca, a world stage and bustling metropolis whose bourgeois and elite populace was wealthy and demanding in its preferences and which insisted on being wined, dined, and amused on every possible front. "Die Straße war zur *Galerie en plein air* geworden, die Werbegraphik zur *Art democratisé,* die sich an alle Bevölkerungs-

[26] Wehmeyer, *Satie,* p. 184.
[27] See Henry Raynor, *Music and Society since 1815,* London, 1976, p. 157.

schichten wandte und von der man außer der Werbewirkung auch einen Einfluß auf die Geschmacksbildung der Massen erwartete."[28] In its format, the poster took much from the style of Toulouse-Lautrec in terms of graphic simplification, a disregard for spatial exactitude in favor of spatial illusion, the simultaneous use of intense color contrasts together with sharp delineation of shapes and contours. What originated as an artistic reaction against the impressionism that had dominated previously led directly to the later *art nouveau/Jugendstil* with its strong feeling for the linear, a similar inclination toward stylization, simplification, concentration of color, and ornamental decoration and elaboration. Taking precisely the elements of simplification, bright color, and strong lines, the poster addressed the public, advertising the circus, ice rinks, theaters, dance halls, bicycles, soap, etc., in what was generally an aesthetically creative use of the medium's potential. The subjects shown boldly on the French posters provide a unique key to the life of that period around the turn of the century, and as the quoted passage suggests, most of them communicate considerably more than a simple advertising message. The poster functioned to put life on view for the public's receptive eyes by successfully transforming facets of popular culture into art for a commercial purpose traditionally shunned by the world of legitimate artistic endeavor.

In the end, the evolution of these popular forms clearly signals the split from the realm of legitimate and high art that in many ways reflected the reality of the social milieu of the time. That split as we have seen was no simple breach, but itself, in a kind of perverse complexity, the product of a long tradition. If it is impossible to fit the puzzle together exactly (the contours of this essay allow only the suggestion of the number of pieces) it is fairly obvious that the circus and its cultural brethren take their place within that lineage extending back over centuries and including such diverse elements as jugglers, acrobats, animal trainers, the Commedia dell'arte,

[28] Christiana Thon, *Französische Plakate des 19. Jahrhunderts,* Berlin, 1968, p. 6.

wandering troupes of magicians, prestidigitators, actors, court fools, fairground performers, and gypsy wagons. My efforts in the following pages to analyze how the circus impinged on authors and their work is thus forced into that broader framework. But before we examine the individual cases, we need to expand that framework further by looking briefly at some of the aesthetic issues involved.

4. *Aesthetic considerations*

Although in the essays on individual German novelists, dramatists, and poets that follow and which constitute the body of this study there will be few instances in which I can point with certainty to a direct or causal relationship to the circus in explanation of an author's artistic formulation of circus-related ideas, I will attempt in this section to analyze what it was in the popular world of the circus that generated sufficient interest to force an aesthetic imprint onto a single work or the entire oeuvre of any of these authors — authors whose purpose was primarily directed toward the realm of serious and legitimate art.

On a kind of superficial level, we can suppose that the receptivity of authors to the circus likely involved their recognition of the fact that principles and attitudes were fostered in the circus that were elsewhere excluded and denied. For the writer chafing under the puritanical restrictions of a turn-of-the-century moral code, for example, the circus provided a singular opportunity to view the physical human form in relatively unrestricted fashion — in dress and costume that was more revealing, and in movement more unfettered, than under any other conditions. In a number of cases to be examined, we find that the initial enchantment of the male author with the circus rested purely on ardent admiration for one of the female performers. The admiration is usually romantic, rarely physical, and invariably matures at a later point into more complex associations. Infatuation is superseded by recognition of the aesthetic principles behind the poised movements exhibiting the body in advantageous and complimentary positions. The human form is seen to take on a kind of animal grace missing in its social and culturally restricted movements. In rather dialectical fashion, these tightly trained and practiced poses acquire an elemental and therefore "natural" quality which contrasts to the awkwardness in the "nature" of the normally untrained body. The similarity between the animal and human form assumes significance. The methods used to train animals and the obvious results in terms of physical grace and discipline are impressive at a time when rigid educational codes and inhumane pedagogical practices seemed to result only in frustration for teacher and pupil alike. The intelligence of animals both domestic (the horse) and exotic (lions, tigers, elephants, etc.) displayed in the circus setting with finesse appears to put the human counterpart to shame. The circus stimulates questions as to whether the methods used in the arena to bring animals to such demonstrable achievement might not be of value if transferred to the human context. The work of Frank Wedekind will be illustrative of these points, although the Hauptmann brothers' and Thomas Mann's initial impressions of the circus will also indicate that such were the auspices under which their circus-related work was generated as well.

Somewhat more subtly, these authors perceived that the circus world is premised to a considerable degree on an illusion and that that illusion reflects some of the fallacies within the reality of the audience itself. The leagues of clowns play an exemplary role in this respect. In an ageless tradition, these eternal favorites of the public have done their tricks and played their jokes before audiences which rarely realize that they are laughing at themselves. The clown routine invariably encompasses a basic philosophical attitude and not infrequently a fairly complex one: it comprises a subtle invitation to the spectator to reflect upon his own awkwardness and inadequacies and is therefore a natural vehicle for social criticism. In a process in which the artist looks behind the spectacle to understand the reality of that shining world of the circus, the attending, reading, or viewing audience is challenged to perceive the reflection and reversed images of its own ills. Even if the acumen of the respective audience frequently falls short of the artistic expectations and the point is lost, the intention is almost always a reflective one. From Tom Belling, "der dumme August," to Chocolat, to Grock, and all the others famous and not so famous, the clown's routine tirelessly represents man's eternal struggle to overcome obstacles, those put in his way by others as well as those inherent in his own nature. The chapters on Wedekind, Thomas Mann, Kaiser, and Brecht will show them as having been conscious of this kind of relationship to the extent that they built innovative and experimental structures on their perception of this aspect of the circus context.

In his *Prinzip Hoffnung* the philosopher Ernst Bloch reflected on another facet of the circus' illusionary nature and posited within his comprehensive view of things an essentially positive tendency on society's part to find in, and to respond to, certain aspects of cultural life as reflections of its own need and desire for a benign aura, for what he refers to as *bessere Luftschlösser,* for *das Wahre am Schein.* He saw the circus as the most "open" of forms, the original "round," equally visible from all angles and, because of such exposure, preclusive of dishonesty. He considered it an honest "Wunschwelt aus Exzentrik und präziser Leichtigkeit," "eine Art bürgerliche Rechtschaffenheit in der Kunst und das Vorbild dafür," an "arabische Fantasia in der aufgeheitersten römischen Arena."[29] In a related way, he proposed that dance can be seen as an expression of man's almost constant desire to be "other" or "elsewhere." The folk dance, specifically, "sei ... Zeuge und Maß jenes unverdorbenen, gruppenhaft gelingenden Ausdrucks von Trieb- und Wunschbildern. Ob deutscher Ländler, spanischer Bolero, polnische Krakowiak oder russischer Hopak: Die Form ist genau und verständlich der bedeutete Inhalt, ist Freude jenseits des Lasttags."[30] The

[29] Ernst Bloch, *Ästhetik des Vorscheins I,* Gerd Ueding, ed., Frankfurt/Main, 1974., p. 85.

[30] Ibid., p. 119. The broader ramifications of the dance are worked out in Fritz Strich's chapter "Tanz als Lebenssymbol im Drama

technique of performers like Sent M'ahesa, he suggests, is "völkerkundlich und kunstgewerblich-mythisch dekoriert" — totally false, but entirely appropriate to the audience's longing for aesthetic "transportation" to other realms. The break with the traditional forms so obviously articulated by dancers such as Loie Fuller, Isadora Duncan, and the Loheland School he saw as an expression of the desire to depict and reveal "ein schöneres Menschenbild im Fleische." These reflections on both the circus and the dance suggest the interplay between art and reality, between a social context grown weary and colorless and the need and desire to find an escape to more satisfying regions. They underline the function of popular forms such as the circus — and here the folk and exotic dance — on both a cultural and aesthetic level. Most importantly, however, the mention of the dance and the circus in the context of wish-fulfillment and/or fantasy denied brings into better focus a phenomenon that prevailed in many sectors of art around the turn of the century, namely the overwhelming doubt about the capacity of language to articulate the products of artistic inspiration and the consequent turn to other forms in response to this doubt. In myriad manifestions this "Sprachkrise" determined form and content and, in many instances, became itself the topic of artistic endeavor. Hofmannsthal's Chandos letter of 1901 formulated the substance of the problem. His 1895 summary statement to the effect that "audiences are sick of words and have developed a liking to those art forms that are performed without them, for example, music, dance, and the various feats of acrobats and jugglers,"[31] had already put the issue on the line and fur-

um 1900," in his *Zur deutschen Literatur seit der Jahrhundertwende,* Stuttgart, 1967.

31 "Die Leute sind es nämlich müde, reden zu hören. Sie haben einen tiefen Ekel vor den Worten: Denn die Worte haben sich vor die Dinge gestellt. ... Wir sind im Besitz eines entsetzlichen Verfahrens, das Denken völlig unter den Begriffen zu ersticken. ... So ist eine verzweifelte Liebe zu allen Künsten erwacht, die schweigend ausgeübt werden: die Musik, das Tanzen und alle Künste der Akrobaten und Gaukler." Hugo von Hofmannsthal, *Prosa I,*

nished a classic instance in which the circus and the dance were linked together as representative of those nonverbal forms to which many artists felt drawn and in which many felt inclined to experiment. In their efforts to enhance whatever they were anxious to articulate through the use of forms and structures which did not rely on words, they would — consciously or not — capitalize on the circus' and the dance's inherent capacity to remove the spectator from the realm of frustrated fantasy and the dictates of normative bourgeois culture. Wedekind's experimentation with the pantomime will be seen as one of the strongest cases of this shift away from the word, and the integration of the pantomime, the dance, and circus elements within his oeuvre shows the extent to which the inherent relationships among these forms come to bear on a dramatist concerned with putting life back into the theater with the help of non-literary and non-verbal elements.

Similar to the drive to find more suitable formal structures was the need to break with those structures and the themes that had become canon. We can discern, for example, that in the case of Frank Wedekind, Carl Hauptmann, and Carl Zuckmayer it was primarily on an act of intellectual reactionism against prevailing aesthetic standards that their relationship to the circus is based. The circus provided them with an opportunity to break with what was normative, a chance to put something unusual and unexplored into the stream of art, an occasion to set themselves against the aesthetic current. In this regard, the reality of the circus' extraliterary status cannot be overemphasized. No matter what degree of popularity at any given time, no matter that circus performers were frequently acquaintances or favorites of princes, kings, and queens, the circus on any or all of its performance levels — whether musical, acrobatic, theatrical, or balletic — has al-

Frankfurt/Main, 1956, p. 228. Fritz Strich's chapter, "Tanz als Lebenssymbol im Drama um 1900" delineates this point extensively, and his "Aspekte der deutschen Literatur um 1900" provides a broad perspective on this and other factors at work during this period. See Strich, *op. cit.,* pp. 1–48.

ways been considered something less than art. Whatever specific aspects of the circus the individual artist found on which to concentrate and focus attention, the subject itself invited reaction from the defenders of "serious" literature. If it was fashion to go to the circus. if the public and the audience in a kind of non-thinking way found it enjoyable and much to their liking, it was something less than acceptable to write about it: the subject matter was apt to be considered unworthy of the *Wohlstandsgemeinschaft* to which the legitimate art world catered and which had long viewed itself as protector of the arts.

In connection with the rebellious stance in which many turned to the circus it is interesting to theorize why in most instances this artistic rebelliousness cast itself predominantly in a thematic mode, while those whose relationship to the circus rested on other foundations articulated that relationship in essentially metaphorical form. It strikes one that in the cases of Carl and Gerhart Hauptmann, Zuckmayer, and Wedekind, for example, the rebellion represents a liberation and enjoys a positive orientation despite all that it is against. The thematic — and for that matter the formal — integration of the circus is relatively straightforward and to a large degree prescriptive. In the cases, say, of Kafka, Thomas Mann, Heym, Rilke, and Kaiser, the metaphors will be seen to articulate a more sceptical view, and bespeak a largely negative or at least ambiguous relationship between the writers and the circus. The integration here may be viewed as less straightforward, more poetic, though in both cases remarkably akin to the aesthetic stance of the individual author. There is a recognizably enormous difference between Wedekind's *Zirkusdirektor* in the Prologue to *Erdgeist* and Kafka's *Zirkusdirektor* in *Auf der Galerie,* both in function and form — to oppose just one such pair. Rilke's troupe in the Fifth Elegy is certainly viewed through different eyes than G. Hauptmann's gypsy tribe in *Wanda* or his brother's characterization of the group that leads Einhart der Lächler off into the wild blue yonder. There is admittedly little possibility of being definitive on this issue, however. Insofar as these differences need to be recognized, they speak to the variety and the profundity of the circus "experience" for the respective figures under scrutiny here as well as to the ambiguity of the phenomenon in general. The separate analyses will attempt to make clear the complexity of each individual case.

In their efforts to move out of the confines of an elitist legitimacy and to intensify and broaden their appeal, these authors were fully aware that writing about or for the circus potentially brought their work into the purview of a wider public. If the legitimate forms drew their audiences from among those citizens who could afford such delights and who considered the theater, concert, ballet, and opera their social and cultural due, the circus was much more democratic in its appeal, and could count among its guests and fans those from virtually every level of society. Although Wedekind is the only one of the writers who, as will be shown, envisioned an actual circus context for some of his work, authors such as Zuckmayer, Brecht, and Kaiser will be seen as consciously striving to establish a link with the broader kind of audience. Even if in practice the connection to the popular sphere was for these writers associative and confined to a thematic, characterizational, or formal principle in their work, they demonstrate an acute awareness that the world of the arena was one attuned to the sensitivities of the times and, by virtue of experimentation and innovation, one that enjoyed a certain vogue and popularity. Both on the basis of its popularity with an attending public as well as its cult status with the reading or viewing public, then, the circus as forum or as subject matter promised a potentially less restricted and more vital field of reception.

The nature and significance of the circus in a socially instrumental role which goes beyond the individual artist's perception of it as a more "democratic" kind of audience is found in some of the musings of Walter Benjamin. In his analysis of mass culture, he suggests that the circus might be thought of as "ein soziologischer Naturschutzpark" in which the various animal types are both thrown together and differentiated from each other. He proposes that (at an earlier point) the world of the circus embodied the elements of democratization and differentiation to be found in mass culture, that the circus audience represented the gamut of social castes and classes, drew them together insofar as it was open to all yet kept all separated as if by general admission and reserved seating. The same idea is at work in what actually developed as a circus tradition: the visit to the menagerie during the intermission. At the time of the circus' zenith, such an interlude was not much different than attendance at a public *salon:* one rubbed shoulders with the best and the worst and yet was never allowed to be forgetful of one's place. It was at once a perfect expression of the social setting as well as a potentially negative statement of the status quo. Benjamin implies that while the interlude allowed such interaction to take place, it served to stabilize the situation into a potentially tensionless system in the same way that a nature preserve fosters an order that frequently has little relationship to the tension-filled configuration of nature's free structure.[32]

With few exceptions and as previously indicated, it will become almost conspicuous that the infusion of popular elements into the codified realms of traditional and legitimate art represented for a number of authors a potential means of restoring relevance and vitality to the respective forms. If by contemporary standards it is less obvious that widely variant artistic activities are segregated into distinctly separate aesthetic spheres, we are nonetheless frequently impressed with an artist's ability to creatively juxtapose elements that seem to belong to otherwise incongruous realms. The trick was not so overworked then as perhaps now, nor, one can propose, is the practice ever as conscious on the part of the artist as in the mind of the aesthetician. There is nonetheless ample evidence to suggest that most of the authors to be treated in the following pages recognized the distinction between a "lower" and a "higher" artistic realm and thought of themselves as working creatively as they brought the one to bear upon the other. We

[32] Walter Benjamin, *Gesammelte Schriften,* Frankfurt/Main, 1972, III, 71.

may assume, then, that the popularity of the circus and other associated forms of popular and "lesser" art developed in conjunction with, as as a factor of, a dichotomous aesthetic within western European, late nineteenth century, bourgeois society. The exploitation of such forms by German authors working out of the "legitimate" realms, moreover, must be understood to have been in large part a function of the general aesthetic revolution reshaping the world of art in most pronounced fashion immediately preceding and following the turn of the century. Virtually every case to be examined can be related to this broader aesthetic crisis developing, reaching its culminating point, and finally by the late 1930s, slackening off. Even though none of the authors belonged in any obvious way to any one of the better known modernist groups of futurists, constructivists, or surrealists, it will become clear that each worked within the general desire to somehow effect a connection in the split between life and art and to be an agent of the modernist mission to reincorporate art back into the praxis of life. At the time, the extradition of the circus from its milieu on the boundaries of art but in the midst of life with the intent of reification in the other realm was as bold a stroke as most of them could manage.

In a well known treatise on the theory of the avant-garde[33] wherein he argues that the concept of the avant-garde is a post-Romantic phenomenon, Renato Poggioli proposes that "a cultural sociology for our time can only be construed from the now certain hypothesis that a plurality of diverse and contradictory intellectual strata exists." This diversity, to be sure, has increased since the turn of the present century, but Poggioli's point is distinctly applicable to the situation confronting the authors examined here. The complexity of social structures, the relative freedom of movement across class boundaries, and the confusion derived from the flux and change have for some time now forced the artist and the intellectual to form their own group and to assume a stance of dis-

[33] Renato Poggioli, *The Theory of the Avant-Garde,* Gerald Fitzgerald, trans., Cambridge, Mass., 1968.

tance or detachment from the traditional culture of the society. "This reduction of the link between art and society to a purely negative function, which from the artist's point of view is alienation, is a new historical fact of incalculable importance and profound meaning." The avant-garde he thus views "not only as the direct expression of a negative cultural relation, but ... also the expression of the human and social condition that created this schism in the cultural order."[34] Poggioli treats the avant-garde as a sociological as well as an aesthetic fact and claims that its ideology is a "social phenomenon precisely because of the social and antisocial character of the cultural and artistic manifestations that it sustains and expresses."[35]

The negative and negating stance of the avant-garde had been argued a few years earlier by Herbert Marcuse who suggested that the struggle of the avant-garde was to "create ... estrangement" in the process of making the artistic "truth" once again communicable.[36] In his view of things, it is again our complex, multi-level though one-dimensional society that operates a "flattening out" process — "repressive desublimation" — for the purpose of making the contradiction between art and life more tolerable and less threatening.

In a more recent book on the theory of the avant-garde,[37] Peter Bürger explains the separation between art and life as a logical consequence to the development of bourgeois society, arguing that the emergence of the concept *l'art pour l'art* was a factor of the division of labor that began to shape society as soon as forces such as industrialization, technostructures, and capitalism evolved as determinants of modern western culture. The evolving division between the two resulted in the aestheticism that dominated toward the end of the nineteenth century in which art became a kind of stronghold of the nonproductive in opposition to the rest of society. Bürger proposes that the development of the avant-garde is to be under-

[34] Ibid., p. 118.
[35] Ibid., p. 4.
[36] Herbert Marcuse, *One-Dimensional Man,* Boston, 1964, p. 68.
[37] Peter Bürger, *Theorie der Avantgarde,* Frankfurt/Main, 1974.

stood as occurring within that context and posits that the avant-garde reached its full potential and zenith when art became self-critical to the extent that it developed a consciousness of what he terms "Institution Art." The avant-garde found its justification and cause in the destruction of that bourgeois instrument, its rebellious and subversive character molded by its desire to reintegrate art into life and, in turn, to put life back into art. In slightly different terms this situation would evolve to the point that Marcuse could argue that as "artistic alienation succumbs, together with other modes of negation, to the process of technological rationality," the avant-garde moves to prevent the threat of integration and to "communicate the break with communication."[38]

These theories of the avant-garde are cited to provide credence to my argument that the reification of the circus by the authors under examination here can be understood, at least partially, as a function of the aesthetic and sociological phenomenon of the avant-garde within the cultural framework of the turn of the century. Most of the qualities which Poggioli specifies as characteristic of the avant-garde, such as its emphasis on youth and vigor, the idea of evasion, i. e. flight toward a world "where things are not horribly fixed in unalterable correctness,"[39] an experimentalism that "tends not so much to form the artist as to transform the public, that is, to educate it,"[40] its activism, its antagonism derived from a basic nonconformism, its tendencies toward eccentricity, exhibitionism, defiance, provocation, scandal — all these and more are discernible in any attempt to ascribe rhyme and reason to what brought these authors to the circus.[41]

[38] Marcuse, *One-Dimensional Man,* pp. 65, 68.

[39] Poggioli, *Theory of the Avant-Garde,* p. 36.

[40] Ibid., p. 135.

[41] I am forced to resort here to a rather broad perspective. I am aware that finer distinctions are possible. In the particular case of Poggioli, for example, Jochen Schulte-Sasse (Theory of Modernism vs Theory of the Avant-Garde, unpublished) argues that Poggioli's theory is more accurately one of modernism rather than of the avant-garde, speaking as it does more to modernism's general

In time, it would become increasingly more difficult to understand the separation by virtue of any clear-cut demarcations and therefore increasingly difficult to justify a creative and fruitful interface. If the circus had held sway for a few years as the impetus and inspiration of much that was put before the public, that public audience, on the basis of its bourgeois origins, would seek entertainment elsewhere in response to what was evolving as Adorno's twentieth century "culture industry." In his 1971 essay "Kulturindustrie: Aufklärung als Massenbetrug," he analyzes the almost insidious manipulative effects of that "industry" on society, the creation of that contemporary aesthetic state in which virtually nothing escapes a kind of rationalized unity of purpose. The compulsion of that industry toward unification of previously opposite poles, e.g., Naiveté and Intellectualism, Entertainment and Art, works to defuse the clash but to the detriment of both elements. He suggests both the historical significance of the circus as well as its present import when he cites it as a preserving medium for aspects of our culture which are otherwise denied and repressed by that culture industry within the industrial/technological complex: "Die Spur des Besseren bewahrt Kulturindustrie in den Zügen, die sie dem Zirkus annähern, in der eigensinnig-sinnverlassenen Könnerschaft von Reitern, Akrobaten und Clowns, der 'Verteidigung und Rechtfertigung körperlicher Kunst gegenüber geistiger Kunst.' Aber die Schlupfwinkel der seelenlosen Artistik, die gegen den gesellschaftlichen Mechanismus das Menschliche vertritt, werden unerbittlich von einer planenden Vernunft aufgestöbert, die alles nach Bedeutung und Wirkung sich auszuweisen zwingt. Sie läßt das Sinnlose drunten so radikal verschwinden wie oben den Sinn der Kunstwerke."[42] The

attack on language and a rebellion against a traditional stance of art, and less to the avant-garde's intent on changing the link between art and commerce. The point is well taken. For the purpose of the argument here, however, Poggioli's description of the social and aesthetic schism has its own efficacy.

42 "Kulturindustrie: Aufklärung als Massenbetrug," *Dialektik der Aufklärung*, Frankfurt/Main, 1971, p. 128.

words of the internal quote belong to Wedekind, and Adorno thereby effectively underscores what the dramatist had sensed even before the circus had so noticeably been reduced to museum status. Adorno's comments on the function of the present-day circus as haven for that which society needs to keep at a safe distance speaks to the point that the circus still exists. Its status is still a factor of a societal arrangement with a *drunten* and an *oben,* but its role has been superseded by other elements which found the audiences' favor and became fashion. Thus within a relatively brief period of time, the circus flourished on the basis of its distinctive origins, assumed a function which caused its own transformation from an element of popular culture into a facet of mass culture while instrumentalizing the evolution of the bourgeois audience into a more homogeneous proletarian one, and finally gave way to other forms whose origins lay in technology's advance into the present. Still in tenuous ways a facet of our present-day society, the circus as institution — both in its essence and its evolution — impinged on the authors under scrutiny in the variety of ways examined in the pages that follow. The authors' testimonies are as varied as that to which they responded and attest to the riches offered by the circus world and its related spheres to those intent on looking beneath the surface in search of that something only inadequately described as "der Zauber der Manege."

TWO:

Motifs, Themes, and Characters

1. *Carl Hauptmann*

Gerhart Hauptmann describes his and his brother Carl's encounter with the circus as "eine Ballung von Glanz, Leben, Natur, todesverachtender Kühnheit, berückender und betörender Schönheit und Kunst, die alles in ihren Wirbel zog und in Rausch versetzte."[1] He then remarks somewhat cryptically: "Natürlich, daß auch Carl und ich, und mehr als andere, dieses Rausches teilhaftig zu werden suchten." Carl was four years Gerhart's senior and apparently had managed to procure tickets so that the two of them could go to several performances. Gerhard is careful to acknowledge Carl's fraternal beneficence in making the circus visits possible, but he does not clarify why specifically their attendance should be of special significance. The account seems indeed to be more than the ordinary enthusiasm of a small child (the brothers are fifteen and nineteen respectively at the time) but no further explanation is furnished for the puzzled reader. Gerhart's subsequent confession that both he and his brother needed the kind of catharsis brought on by the festive atmosphere indicates nonetheless that at the time both brothers were extremely receptive spectators at these (and possibly other) performances of the Renz troupe, and that they in particular were ripe for the impressions the circus was making on them. Their receptivity to the circus as an institution and to the kind of life it represented is reaffirmed three years later in Gerhart's account of the funeral of Karl von Holtei, the author

[1] See Gerhart Hauptmann, "Das Abenteuer meiner Jugend." in *Das Gesammelte Werk,* XIV, Berlin, 1943, pp. 303–306.

whose four volume circus romance *Die Vagabunden* (1852) had quickly attained the status of a classic:

> In corpore wohnten wir eines Tages dem Begräbnis Karl von Holteis bei. Ich hatte die schöne auffällige Greisenerscheinung mit dem weißen, bis auf die Schultern hängenden, wohlgepflegten Haar einmal auf der Straße gesehen. Ein unauslöschlicher Eindruck, daß die ganze Stadt mit ihm zu Grabe zog. Aber tausende Menschen, unter die wir hineingerieten, gaben ihm das letzte Geleit. ... Ich war gerührt, als ich einen Jungen, der auf einem Lattenzaune saß, immer wieder sagen hörte: Das ist der größte Dichter gewesen! Das ist der größte deutsche Dichter gewesen! wiederholte er, unter eigener Rührung lehrhaft unherblickend.[2]

Both reports are admittedly recollections with hindsight by the mature Hauptmann, and as such beg the question whether the memory might not indicate more than an old man's fondness for childhood adventure. As we shall see, there is ample evidence that for both Hauptmann brothers the circus experience of their youth proved to be a matter of lasting significance. The manner in which it was incorporated into their respective work, however, is remarkably different, so that both cases warrant our attention. The separate responses to a common experience reveal much about the vast differences between the brothers themselves.

Within about a decade after the visit to the Renz circus in Breslau, Carl Hauptmann's fate of being relegated to the shadows of his younger brother's fame was already sealed. His reputation to this day, despite the efforts of some who would have rescued him from obscurity, remains minimal. His place in the history of German letters has no doubt been accorded as much attention as his rather sophomoric work warrants, although his limited following stemmed initially quite simply from the fact that he was an individualist to the core. At a time when there were ample *causes célèbres* with enticing programms that promised more than could ever be delivered, Carl Hauptmann was resolute in listening to the sounds of his own distant drums. His literary position, as

[2] Ibid., p. 431.

Walter Goldstein put it in 1931, was absolutely unique. At the turn of the century, when much seemed to hang precariously in limbo between the old and the new, when the German spirit reached intoxicating peaks with discoveries in the natural sciences, the voice of Carl Hauptmann called out a warning as he read the faults of the moment and sensed the dangers of the future. What made him unique to his time was the fact that he seemed to know what he was doing. While his contemporaries were struggling with the problems of the emerging modern age, Carl Hauptmann seemed quietly sure of his philosophic and aesthetic goals.[3] One of his diary entries describes what he felt to be his business: "Ich fahnde allenthalben nach Seele. Seele ist immer gut, wie Licht immer leuchtend. Alles um mich, alle Wesen, Felsen, Bäume, Tier und Mensch, alles ist ein Grab des Lichts, wie ein Grab der Seele."[4]

The elder Hauptmann came to such a credo via a rather devious route, and despite the risks of digression, we need to establish this framework of belief before we examine his interest in the circus. Under the influence of Ernst Haeckel and Richard Avenarius (both of them his teachers, the one a natural scientist, the other a philosopher), Hauptmann began a career which proved misdirected. During his student years in Jena and Zurich (1880–1888) he worked diligently on two scientific-philosophical discourses, the one involving the relevance of embryonic cell theory to the concept of hereditary personality traits, the other on metaphysics in contemporary physiology. He had difficulty completing both works as they kept him more and more from a totally different philosophy that was emerging. While the task of convincing himself that he was indeed on the wrong track must have been unpleasant, the gradual switch from scientific metaphysics to human ide-

[3] Walter Goldstein, *Carl Hauptmann: Eine Werkdeutung,* (Vol. 65 of *Germanistische Abhandlungen,* Walter Steller, ed.), Breslau, 1931, p. 214f.

[4] Quoted in Hubert Razinger, *Carl Hauptmann: Gestalt und Werk,* Krummhübel i. R., 1928, p. 53.

ology allowed the dichotomy he sensed in the world to crystallize before he set forth his solutions to it and began proselytizing for converts to his cause.

Reverberating within Hauptman's philosophical world are echoes of the uncertainty of turn-of-the-century life. Materialism and its associated concepts had been accruing interest during the preceding years, and the account had begun to weigh heavily on some minds. A counter movement toward a less materialistic orientation began to assert itself, evidencing a religious-supernatural longing, a craving for a spiritual essence. With his *Zarathustra,* Nietzsche in 1883–85 outlined for the seemingly unshakable bourgeois world a catalog of its faults. Blatant dichotomies came to the surface, dilemmas circled unanswered around basic conflicts such as Life vs the Contemplation of Life, Instinct vs Intellect, Body vs Soul, the Material vs the Spiritual. The overwhelming and often stifling penchant toward intellectualism gave rise to a free-wheeling, "gay-nineties," less restrictive, pleasure-seeking sensualism intended to counteract that intellectualism and its moral consequences.

In his own search for "soul" Hauptmann quite soon became a renegade with a declared allegiance only to himself. While many of the young authors at the time — including his own brother — were involved in popular literary trends of the day to the extent that they could then, and can now, be identified with them, such is not the case with Hauptmann. If within his literary and dramatic work one can detect elements of the earlier Romanticism, of the contemporary Naturalism, of Neo-Romanticism, and in some instances even the Expressionism that surfaced somewhat later, none of these labels is by itself validly descriptive of his work. One ultimately has to resort to describing Hauptmann in terms of what he opposed in order to ascertain the nature of his advocacy.

Once he had terminated his scientific-metaphysical treatises, Hauptmann's life in service to the soul began to take shape. It appears that he was in favor of some aspects of the popular Naturalist movement developing at the time — the movement that was to catapult his brother to fame in 1889 —

but he also found much in it to criticize. Man suppressed by the social facets of life was a pitiable creature whose salvation could only be found in other realms. All the determinism encountered in the platforms of Naturalism — the tracings backward, the projections forward, the causes and results, the social orientation — decreased the freedom of the individual and the individual's opportunity for development. Hauptmann advocated the "natural" which the Naturalists seemed ready to forego. The ultimate, most "natural" reality was in his opinion the individual, earthbound, life-oriented, personality. Walter Meckauer labels him the prophetic herald of the individual personality and points to the similarity here with the "personality cult" of some of the later Expressionists.[5] Even much later, when European society had succeeded in toppling the insecure world by the events of 1914, Hauptmann was sure of his convictions and relentless in his campaign for them. The answer then, as before, revolved around the central concept of *Seele* — that unseen and intangible source of all life-values.

Hauptmann likewise had little sympathy with many of the trends associated with the so-called Neo-Romantic movement — although here again some of the features associated with it seem tailormade to much of his work. While he disapproved of art for art's sake, of fancy form and "artiness," of visual and aural pattern, decoration and ornamentation per se, he could still reverently proclaim that art was a celebration to be preserved and protected from anything "common." When he called for the abandonment of all social purpose and societal restrictions in favor of the freedom of the soul's infinite potential, he viewed it as a distinctly individual and private "happening": "Heute wollen wir wieder heraus aus der Welt, wo der Mensch starr als eingeschnürter, rein dürr und intellektuell gedeuteter Mensch lebt. Wollen wir hinein in eine Welt, wo er nicht Mensch, wo er nur Wesen ist."[6]

[5] Walter Meckauer, "Carl Hauptmanns dichterische Hinterlassenschaft," *Monatshefte,* 42 (1950), p. 226.

[6] Quoted in Razinger, *Carl Hauptmann,* p. 81. Hauptmann's rejection of the superficial world and his asocial penchant are, howev-

There were thus few aspects of contemporary life to which Hauptmann did not in some degree take exception. He found little in modern existence to be proud of and even less to be pleased about — with the exception of the joys he found asserting his own kind of existence. In the same remarkable way that he could work on his early scientific theses while shouting mutiny to all that they represented, he seems constantly to have suffered at the hands of life all the while he was asserting the possibilities of existence. Razinger views Hauptmann's heroes as saints, and proposes that through all his tribulations Hauptmann smiles the smile of his hero Einhart — the surprised smile of an eternal youth.[7] It is ultimately behind that smile that Hauptmann's circus experiences lie, and in that connection that the influence of the circus on his life and philosophy can be interpreted.

Besides the early Breslau encounter with the circus, there is nothing to attest to any subsequent circus associations on the part of Hauptmann. Only on the basis of his circus drama *Tobias Buntschuh* and the fact that a number of his other pieces incorporate a circus-type character can we assume that the interest he showed in his youth was kept alive throughout his career. The one additional bit of information on Hauptmann and the circus is possibly more confusing than it is helpful: In his 1917 essay *Luise und Radiana,* the dramatist Frank Wedekind recounts that while he and Hauptmann were friends in Zurich during the 1880s, both of them fell under the spell of the tightrope artiste Ella Belling. In their enthusiasm both men tried to attract public attention to her. Wedekind claims to have praised her charms in a newspaper article (he was then a reporter for the *Neue Zürcher Zeitung);* Hauptmann

er, not to be interpreted in Nietzschean terms. Razinger points out that despite all similarities — the call to life, the rejection of social factors, the cult of the personality, the "super" attitude, the projection of the Dionysian/ecstatic/artistic as antithesis to the scientific/theoretical, the instinctual as antithesis to the rational/intellectual — Hauptmann had little sympathy with what he interpreted as the overbearing, potentially revolutionary Nietzschean stance.

7 Razinger, *Carl Hauptmann, p. 39.*

supposedly took issue with the article and published a rebuttal in the *Zürcher Post,* only to have Wedekind capitalize on the situation and write a second article. In the latter article Wedekind purportedly worked in a love poem to Miss Belling (doubtless one of the two poems to her contained in his *Gesammelte Werke* – see below, p. 144) and was successful in winning some recognition for himself from Miss Belling. None of the articles has been found, however, and the whole affair, as Wedekind's biographer Artur Kutscher suggests, seems to be of questionable authenticity. The issue is further complicated by the fact that Kutscher proposes that Hauptmann's *Tobias Buntschuh* is based on his attraction for Miss Belling.[8] There is, of course, no way of proving or disproving this, and whether Kutscher had facts on which to base such a claim is not stated. Razinger suggests that the play is based on an experience Hauptmann had with the circus in Berlin "around 1911/12"[9] — but again the matter is not further clarified. Thus it is difficult, if not impossible, to be definitive about the issue of influence. The fact that *Tobias Buntschuh* is part of Hauptmann's mature work, however, suggests at the very least that Hauptmann's earlier circus experiences culminated in an attempt to depict the circus world as a complex reflecting his more mature ideology.

Throughout Hauptmann's work the gypsy — or a character with similar characteristics — occurs so often that one is inclined to see in that figure Hauptmann's chief protagonist. The author's intense preoccupation with this figure culminated in his *Einhart der Lächler,* a work which can be aptly described as "genuine" Carl Hauptmann. The characteristic elements which Hauptmann sets forth in Einhart, however, are perceptible from the very beginning of Hauptmann's literary career. In his very early (1890) collection *Sonnenwanderer* the story "Fahrendes Volk" establishes the theme of escape into freedom. The intent is blatantly to communicate a kind of universal relevance despite autobiographical traces of the

[8] See Artur Kutscher, *Frank Wedekind: Sein Leben und seine Werke,* Munich, 1922, I, 148.

[9] Razinger, *Carl Hauptmann,* p. 131.

author's infatuation with a Polish woman, Josepha Kodis-Krzyzanowska. The 1894 play *Marianne* depicts the courage of a nineteen-year-old wife who deserts her despotic pastor-husband and flees into the unknown with a young painter. It clearly expresses the same desire for escape and demonstrates Hauptmann's fascination with the prospects of turning his back on it all and setting off for the life of the vagabond.

Ephraims Breite (1889) is an early play focusing on the schism between "soul" and "reality," a theme that emerges to run throughout Hauptmann's work. The story of a young farm girl in conflict with the external world that Joseph, a gypsy youth, injects into her rural serenity, the play articulates the anguish of that dialectic and allows Hauptmann, if somewhat ambivalently, to express his preferences in favor of the gypsy. There is a figure similar to Joseph in Hauptmann's 1904 story *Der Landstreicher,* this time in the role suggested by the title. The account tells of a stranger who interrupts a Sunday church service of self-centered and self-satisfied villagers. He enters the lives of these people as an obvious Christ figure, for after be leaves there is a noticeable change for the better in their attitude. His appearance in the door of the church is heralded by a shaft of sunlight and his exit is similarly marked. There is little difficulty in associating such a figure with an antibourgeois, free, unfettered, gypsy ideal. If there exists any doubt, Hauptmann takes pains to have the reader fit the figure into the paradigm he is constructing. Black hair strands fall into the pale face of the vagabond, the same hair strands that mark Joseph in *Ephraims Breite* and the same black hair that is the most striking and oft-repeated physical feature of Hauptmann's chief gypsy figure, Einhard.

[10] Razinger makes the distinction between Hauptmann's *Zigeunererlebnis* and his *Landstreichererlebnis,* but there are virtually no differences between the two. The latter stems from Hauptmann's personal acquaintance with a "noble" vagrant whom he met somewhere in or around Berlin. Hauptmann named him Graf di Santa Rocca and uses him as prototype for the vagabond in *Musik,* the third drama in the much later trilogy, *Die Goldenen Straßen.*

This vagabond figure is spread over a wide span of Hauptmann's creative period, and like the gypsy is rather heavy-handedly representative of a life style that Hauptmann felt to be more genuine — so much so that he became its advocate.

In the story of Einhard (1907) Hauptmann states everything he had already said over again — and then some. The work is his contribution to that tradition of souls divided in two — the progeny of bourgeois father and gypsy mother — whose problems seemed to hold special fascination for writers during this period. Einhard is the son of an honorable civil servant. He runs away from school, joins up with a band of gypsies, is brought back into society's fold but leaves again for the freedom "out there." Einhart's search for himself and an existence more meaningful than that to be found in his native (one-half native!) bourgeois sphere is Hauptmann's gypsy developed to the fullest extent. It is both the author's and the hero's longing for adventure that would allow an escape from the accepted, sober, dilettantish, everyday world of the bourgeois into the unusual, unexpected, twilight-like, less defined, less determined, less restricted, less socially ordered world disdained by the bourgeois.

Two instances in the story of Einhart attest to the fact that Hauptmann's gypsy/vagabond is never far removed from a circus orientation. The ease with which Hauptmann's associations glide from a gypsy context to a circus context is illustrated in this passage describing the hero: "Wer ihn so sah in seinem braunen Röckel und dem dunklen Rundhut, wußte nicht, ob er einen dürftigen Photographen oder einen von einer fliegenden Theatertruppe vor sich hatte. Man konnte auch an einen Gaukler denken, der auf dem Seile tanzen, oder mit goldenen Kugeln vor den Augen seiner Zuschauer spielen, und sie in die Luft werfen könnte, daß dann gleich, wie im Märchen die schöne Quellfrau es tat, die goldenen Bälle wieder mit Donner und Blitz herniederführen unter die strömende Menge."[11] Somewhat later in the novel, as biblical

[11] Carl Hauptmann, *Einhard der Lächler,* Berlin, 1907, p. 101.

connotations enter the picture with Einhart reading the Bible and professing a philosophy based on the Christian ideal, he makes a diary entry in which he transforms Christ's entry into Jerusalem and His mixing with the crowd into the equivalent of a circus parade:

> Wie Christus sich entschloß, auf den Markt in die Großstadt zu ziehen, mußte er sicherlich noch einmal tüchtig lachen erst. Er wußte sehr genau, daß jetzt das Theater begann. Wie er sich Palmen wedeln ließ, wie er großartig unter Jauchzen und Geschrei des Volkes auf einer Eslin in Jerusalems Tore eintritt, da war das Theater fertig. Noch heute reiten die Kunstreiter auf Pferden mit ihren großen Trommeln auf die Straßen und Märkte und locken das Volk zusammen. Da mußte dieser ganz Innerliche, der sein Herz vom Himmelreich der Güte und Menschenliebe überall auf den Markt unter den Pöbel trug, heimlich blutig lachen.[12]

Hauptmann's Einhart could thus just as easily be a circus performer as a gypsy vagabond or the unorthodox (according to his family's standards) individualist in search of an essence in life that he himself was. The one was for all intents and purposes the equivalent of the other. When Hauptmann has Einhart utter the dictum: "Das Leben ist gar keine Idealität. Es ist immer nur das einfache Leben," followed by the narrator's (Hauptmann's) assertion that "er wußte es nicht, daß er damit den tiefsten Lebenssinn gegen all die großen Worte in Wissenschaft und Religion verteidigte,"[13] the reader cannot but be convinced of Hauptmann's earnestness in the matter.

The circus-related ideal comes to its clearest expression in Hauptmann's most most mature work, the trilogy *Die Goldenen Straßen.* The three plays were not written as connected parts of a tripartite structure but rather were lumped together by Hauptmann after it became obvious to him that he had composed three pieces which were indeed consonant. In a letter to Armin Wegner of March 14, 1916, he claims that he had composed one of the plays, *Tobias Buntschuh,* three years previously, i.e., between 1912 and 1913 — a fact that would seem

[12] Ibid., p. 195.
[13] Ibid., II, p. 66.

to support Razinger's thesis that the play is based on a circus experience from 1912–13 rather than on Hauptmann's enthusiasm for Ella Belling as Artur Kutscher asserts — and only in September of 1917, according to a letter to his friend Zeiß, did he discover that he had written a trilogy: "Ich habe nämlich eine Trilogie gemacht. Jetzt wo der 3. Teil vor mir liegt, sehe ich den großen Zusammenhang, in dem die letzten drei Jahre meine Arbeit verlaufen ist. Das Erlebnis ist das seltsamste und offenbarendste meines bisherigen Schaffens."[14]

As the first play in the trilogy and also the one most clearly infused with circus elements, *Tobias Buntschuh* is of primary interest here. Buntschuh — whose very name carries connotations of clown or jester — is a renowned inventor who has the world at his fingertips but who feels maligned by life. Happiness eludes him. His initial appearance in the beginning of the second act puts him immediately in the category of the comic, and his physical characteristics suggest the cause of his problem. He steps out of the doorway blinking and shielding his eyes from the light, a small hunchbacked man in his 30s with a longish nose, thin legs in white silk drawers and undershirt, an old purple silk robe thrown around him, his bare feet in worn-out slippers. The weakness expressed in the physical appearance of Buntschuh has nonetheless not kept him from genuine intellectual achievements, and in this realm he enjoys a superior position. He is recognized as an ingenious mathematician, physicist, and chemist; he has used his knowledge and ability philanthropically, has reaped his due monetarily, and enjoys the fruits of his labor. But, as his goldsmith-friend and companion Wendelborn explains, his mental accomplishments have left his other senses atrophied.

Together with Wendelborn, the two seem to be a formulation of the type of situation found in Wedekind's *Marquis von Keith*. Tobias, longing for love, seeks his fulfillment in Radiana, but can never be successful in his quest, i.e., he wants

[14] Carl Hauptmann, *Leben mit Freunden: Gesammelte Briefe,* Will-Erich Peuckert, ed., Berlin-Grunewald, 1928, p. 277.

what he can never have and has what he does not particularly want, i.e., Luisa, a girl whose affections can be bought. In an inverted parallel, Wendelborn has to be satisfied with only a vicariously enjoyed exercise of his own intellectual fervor through Tobias, but finds Radiana longing to throw herself at his feet. He too wants something he cannot achieve and gets what he does not especially want. Through all of this shines the rather shopworn motif of the conflict between the Spirit and Nature, between Science and Art, between the Senses and the Intellect — another depiction of the man overloaded with knowledge who wanders too far astray from the golden path of Nature.

As the first of three heroes, Buntschuh ends in a stance of resignation and disappointment in his quest for the "golden way." His intellectual genius, overdeveloped to the point of atrophy of his other capacities, is ultimately forced to forego the complement it seeks in Radiana. The fulfillment sought by Tobias is once again circus-oriented, for the object of his affection, Radiana, happens to be what Hauptmann innocently calls a "circus maiden." To look on Radiana as Hauptmann's ideal, however, is to ignore the complications he seems to put in the way of that kind of interpretation. In addition to this sweet young contortionist there are two other figures in the drama: Luisa, bareback rider and trapeze artiste and the clown Oderbrecht. Taken all together they allow a more mature Hauptmann to present somewhat ambigous feelings with regard to the circus world. The desirability of seeing the circus as his ideal is unmistakably brought into question.

The first act takes place entirely in the circus setting of Luisa's dressing room. In a conversation between her and her clown-suitor Oderbrecht we get a negative picture of Luisa the circus star: cold, temperamental, haughty. She is portrayed as nothing short of cruel as she tries to get rid of Oderbrecht. Her fury rages unabated as she throws glasses at him. She accuses him of hypocrisy because he goes to church every Sunday, listens to the parrot in the pulpit, and prays that God bless his leap over the horses' backs for loud applause and large receipts. In contrast to the sad figure he represents, she reminds him that she is something better than the rest of them: "Ich bin eine Kunstreiterin ... eine Athletin ... eine Tochter der Anmut und der Kraft ..." To Oderbrecht's meek reply that she is just like all the rest she retorts: "Ich habe nun einmal Zigeunerblut ... ich bin von einem englishen Vater aus Liebe erzeugt ... und vereinige die Kälte mit der Glut ... ich hasse alle Männer, die nichts sind als Clowns und Seiltänzer und Lustigmacher ... es ist ein Schandegewerbe ..." What she wants is a man who can offer her the bourgeois ideal, a measure of security, someone who can set her up behind "silvered oak doors" where she can order her morning cocoa on a silver tray.

Now within this rather bitter dialog the author reveals himself on several counts with regard to the circus. Despite Hauptmann's rather affirmative connection between the gypsy and the circus performer, one cannot overlook the implications behind Luisa's desire to get free of the circus, to lead a different kind of life. Hauptmann was apparently objective enough to be able to perceive the cracks in that world's structures; he can be scornful of her bourgeois desire at the same time he is impressed by her innate pride in herself and her circus art. Oderbrecht's admiration of her and the terms he uses to express it are in this instance temptingly supportive of Kutscher's assertion that Ella Belling inspired Hauptmann, or at least figured in his writing this play. Oderbrecht's references to her as goddess with a quality both predatorily sure and sweet, with eyes that long for the moon and stars are convincingly close to Wedekind's terms of praise. When Luisa characterizes herself as "a child of grace and strength" it is impossible not to associate this kind of heady admiration with that articulated by Wedekind back in 1888 when he, along with the Hauptmann brothers, was in Zurich and caught up in his admiration for Ella Belling (see below, p. 144). In the composite, however, Luisa is a figure full of contradictions, a woman who can inspire and disgust, who combines innocence with cunning. If in Hauptmann's mind she represents the epitome of the circus star, a combination of grace, beauty, and athletic prowess, she is ambiguous as an ideal and is ultimately scorned by Tobias.

The second female in this circus cast, Radiana, is depicted as ambiguously as the first, for just like Luisa she is only dubiously a part of the circus world. She describes herself as follows: "Ich heiße nämlich gar nicht Radiana ... das ist nur so ein roter Klecks auf der Stirn ... ich heiße eigentlich ganz gewöhnlich Lotte Grassmück ... nur als Schlangenmädchen heiße ich Radiana ... nur für die Kunststücke im Zirkus heiße ich Radiana ... weil ich noch so junge und gewandte Glieder habe ... sonst bin ich ein ganz gewöhnliches Mädel." [15] Her "just an ordinary girl" notwithstanding, she embodies the kind of girl Tobias is looking for. Here Hauptmann proposes a different kind of circus girl, the antithesis (as we might expect) to Luisa. She demurely reveals her "self" throughout Act V. Her job, she clains, has no relationship to her character. She is remarkably, coyly innocent; she has admirable qualities, specifically fidelity in love. She maintains her integrity and is not taken in by all the gold that glitters; and if one could still ask for more, she is a "natural" creature, untamed and untainted by civilization and the modern world.

This "circus maiden" Radiana, then, is certainly Tobias' ideal, and in light of so many of Hauptmann's other characters, can be understood as the author's as well. A variation on the tune Hauptmann had been whistling for so long, Radiana's naturalness, her untamed, unspoiled nature, her purity, her beauty, her grace and charm represent just about all that could be rolled into one little girl from the circus. Yet she proves elusive to Tobias — as one would expect, given the contrasts as they exist in the play. Radiana's "circus maiden" characteristics are the other side of the coin relative to Luisa's "circus star" characteristics. If Oderbrecht is blind to Luisa's true self, Tobias can see in Radiana what he wants to see. Neither realizes the attractiveness and seductiveness of the ladies' ambiguity. As for Hauptmann, it was as if even now he were letting them perform on the trapeze in his mind before

[15] Carl Hauptmann, *Tobias Buntschuh* in *Die Goldenen Straßen,* Leipzig, [n.d.], p. 43.

deciding to let Luisa (who ironically belonged up there) fall from his grace to the net below. If Luisa is based on Hauptmann's enthusiasm for Ella Belling as Kutscher and Wedekind suggest, then Radiana was created by Hauptmann as her counterpart and antipode within the circus world.

The hero's lack of success in his attempts to find *the* way – in the case of Tobias with the help of a companion from the circus who supposedly is a repository of those qualities that will enable him to do so – is reformulated in the other two plays of the trilogy, *Gaukler, Tod und Juwelier,* and *Musik.* The latter are so obviously variations on the main theme that we need not examine them as closely as *Tobias Buntschuh.* In the second play we meet the imposter Lionel Mander whose life is described as having been a constant balance act on life's high-wire. Circus imagery is liberally dispensed in this play as Hauptmann reverses the sides of the coin and the direction of the search to the opposite of what it was with Tobias. Throughout his life Mander has been frantically seeking the "Rosa mystica" and up until now had sought it in association with the demimonde. Suddenly he finds it, or so he believes, manifested in his own daughter Lisiska. Beautiful, radiant, innocent, untouched, fresh from the convent, she is at the opposite end of the spectrum in comparison to Radiana. In this play she is contrasted to Ottilie Kopriva, an actress whom Mander rejects in favor of his sweet young daughter. Not surprisingly, all is not as positive and glorious as it might appear to Mander. Despite the fact that he has convinced himself that he has found the possibility of a new life, there is no mercy in heaven. The clubfooted jeweler of the title seems unmistakably to be a devil/death figure and is unrelenting in giving Mander the final bill for the jewelry and for his life. Mander's misdirected solution at the end of Act IV as he exits with Lisiska, "wie mit einer Braut,“ is a symbolic juggling act about to collapse. At the end of Act V his juggling is over. Even at Mander's death, the jeweler gets the last word: "heute gaukelt er sich wirklich die reinste Erlösung vor ...“

Now if these two heroes were less than successful in finding the/ir way, the cathedral organist Josua in the third play

Musik seems to be more fortunate. Here all the previous imagery of Hauptmann comes together — to wit, a gypsy woman prophesying the truth, a vagrant who refers to himself as a "staubgrauer Heiland" (he had "gray" qualities also in *Der Landstreicher* back in 1904) and who has chosen to live outside human society. And finally, Josua's wife Georginel, who by virtue of the gypsy appearing to her in a vision as "Botschaft der Wahrheit," is made to wake up to her destiny with Josua. In all her purity she must be considered the white cat of the prophet in the piece's original title.[16] Through a selflessness on her part that facilitates his artistry, Josua appears to have attained the goal that eludes his two predecessors. If they had been looking in the wrong places, to Josua — in an almost mystical transcendency into the realm of music and art and accompanied by the unreal Georginel (according to Razinger, the "purest dream-figure in Hauptmann's drama")[17] — is granted the privilege of walking down the "golden road." Hauptmann could describe this third play in terms of music, because here at last it was ringing for Josua and for the author, not as a faintly perceivable echo, but loudly and clearly.

With the hindsight afforded at this point, the circus world and all the ideals that Hauptmann associated with it — or tried to impart to it — were in the end not the answer after all. Josua, as Hauptmann's character who finally achieves the long-sought goal, has no connection whatsoever with that world, and Georginel, as the agent of his success, is only tangentially associated with a circus-related figure. We are forced to acknowledge that the golden road proved to be a dead-end street if it went by way of the circus. Like all of Hauptmann's attempted solutions, the circus proved not up to the challenge. But understandably so, given Hauptmann and what he was after. The harmonious music he was looking

[16] In the letter to Zeiß referred to previously, Hauptmann had proposed that the third play (Musik) bear the title "Die weiße Katze des Propheten." See Hauptmann, *Briefe,* p. 277.

[17] Razinger, *Carl Hauptmann,* p. 134.

for could not be found anywhere but in the individual soul: not of this world, but reverberating in its transcendancy toward the divine.

2. *Gerhart Hauptmann*

In addition to those comments relevant to both brothers' experience at the Renz circus performances, the younger Gerhart's account contains a number of associated remarks that are most revealing. The pertinent passages give some indication of the importance the writer attributed to the experience and provide a backdrop to our discussion of the role the circus played in the life of the famous Hauptmann brother.

"Es handelt sich hier um ein Phänomen, das mit allem Ernste zu würdigen ist: eine traditionelle, eine fast erbliche Form der Kunst, und zwar fast die einzige noch wahrhaft volkstümliche.“ That is a straightforward statement of Hauptmann's opinion that the circus functioned as a traditional form of art in its own right, neither to be underestimated nor undervalued. He takes pains to put the circus on an equal footing with the more legitimate drama and acknowledges that for him the circus at times even took precedence over that other theater: "Eine Zeitlang wurden durch die Erlebnisse in der Manege des Zirkus Renz die Erinnerungen an die Meininger Truppe und ihr Theater zurückgedrängt. Sie vermochten sich auch bei Vergleichen, die ich anstellte, nicht durchzusetzen. Ihr Scheinwesen löste sich gleichsam auf vor dieser kompakten Wirklichkeit.“ Despite the fact that in this comparison the make-believe of the theater pales before the gripping reality of the circus arena, the relationship between the theater and the circus in the dramatist's mind underscores the interpenetration and kinship of the two areas. For the dramatist moreover, the experience was a long-lived one: "Wie oft in meinem langen Leben habe ich mit innerer Dankbarkeit und Heiterkeit, wenn sie zu erlöschen drohte, die Kerze der schönen Illusion, die Fackel des Ehrgeizes an dieser Erinnerung neu belebt und lodern gemacht!“

In somewhat less philosophical terms Hauptmann ends his account of the circus' visit to Breslau with human interest, confidential-type gossip. As innocent as it might at first appear, it is nonetheless information that is revealing. He claims, for example, that the atmosphere of the circus world was an important one and instructive for the local adolescents. Rumors were rampant concerning the love affairs that supposedly developed between the cavalry officers in the Breslau garrison and the ladies of the circus. With tongue in cheek, he suggests that if the interest in horses, horse training, and horsemanship was natural enough for those imposing horsemen with clanging swords and spurs, their interest in the beautiful haute école riders and other ladies was certainly not unnatural. In a situation similar to the one Thomas Mann's Felix Krull enjoys with the Circus Stoudebecker's Andromache, the entire corps of officers falls head over heels in love with Ozeana, the sylph of the air. Each tries to outdo the other in winning her favor. The competition of these men — usually described as tall, handsome, and wealthy members of old and established aristocratic families — causes her husband considerable anguish. Hauptmann makes a class-conscious comment relative to the frustrated spouse who in his profession as circus rider was not even *satisfaktionsfähig,* and seems to find the husband's defense of his honor particularly impressive.

It is clear from the entire passage that over and above the general excitement that marked the circus visits, most of the author's lasting impressions are rooted in one way or another in his own personal and vicarious relationship with the star of the show, Ozeana Renz:

> Fast ein jeder dieser Artisten von unvergleichlichem Können regte meinen Ehrgeiz an ähnlichen Leistungen auf. Noch staunenerregender, noch unnachahmlicher, noch gefährlicher wollten sie womöglich sein. Die knabenhaften Träumereien ... wurden durch eine kaum geahnte Wirklichkeit zu neuem Aufflammen gebracht. Auf diesem zornig blickenden, schwarzen arabischen Hengst sah ich mich, um die Schloßherrin zu gewinnen, den Mauerkranz des Kynast umreiten. Kunigunde war Ozeana Renz. Die wahrhaft aphrodisische Frau in ihrer

> wunderbaren Anmut strömte, wenn sie als Sylphide der Luft auf dem Drahtseil stand, den Schönheitsglanz einer Göttin aus. Dem berückenden Reiz dieses Anblicks vermochte sich niemand zu entziehen. Ich habe in meinem späteren Leben ihresgleichen nicht wieder gesehen.[18]

Interestingly enough, Ozeana Renz was an Amerlcan born in 1856 in Dubuque, Iowa. She was married to the son of Ernst Renz, founder of the Renz Circus, worked primarily as a high-wire artiste, and in that capacity appeared to Hauptmann as the graceful "Sylphide der Luft." Hauptmann first associates her with Kunigunde and the Kynast, and envisions himself as suitor to her, bravely riding on an imaginary black stallion. It is obvious enough that the object of the young Hauptmann's admiration is a lovely young lady, that she has a certain erotic charm in combination with physical grace, and that she has impressed the author as much as, if not more than, any of the other spectators watching her performance. It is questionable whether any of the rest of them thought of her as Kunigunde, much less of themselves as a knight trying to win her favor. Hauptmann would have come upon this fantasy innocently enought — the Kynast is a wellknown (certainly to anyone from Silesia) medieval fortress, and the legend connected with it and its lady Kunigunde would have been the mental property of any youngster in Breslau — but it is the range of associations generated by the legend that certifies the significance for Hauptmann: under close scrutiny, the Kynast leads us to character configurations that function centrally throughout the author's work.

Hauptmann's *Nachlaß* contains dramatic fragments from the two decades between 1897 and 1918 that revolve around the Kynast. The fact that these Kynast-Kunigunde associations do not appear until some twenty years after the original experience in the circus is not pure chance. It was during the first part of 1897 that Hauptmann made the journey to Italy with Margarete Marschalk (whom he had met already in

[18] Gerhart Hauptmann, "Das Abenteuer meiner Jugend," *Das Gesammelte Werk,* Berlin, 1943, XIV. The cited passages are found on pp. 303–306.

1889), and it was from August of that year that we have the first dated mention of the Kynast saga. Hauptmann's marriage with Marie Thienemann was virtually finished, and it was as if his new relationshp with Margarete had brought former figures into play again. This was to happen more than once in the poet's life — the personal experience repeatedly finding expression in an aesthetic formulation — and this particular liaison crystallized only one of many poetic representations. What is interesting is that a number of these literary manipulations are formulated in Ozeanean terms, so that several of his personal relationships with women in the course of his life seem prefigured here in the Circus Renz experience. Thus the original experience can in fact be accorded as much importance as Hauptmann himself is obviously willing to give it. It culminates in his 1927 circus novel *Wanda*, a work that functions as a final exorcism of a conflict that had nettled him over an extended period. As for the record itself, the question whether the experience was actually as described, or whether later events shaped Hauptmann's recollections in such a way that the episodes of his youth simply reflect a configuration rather than prefigure it, is a valid one. Unfortunately, no answer is available. The psychology is nonetheless interesting in either instance and, for our purposes, equally significant.

The Kynast fragments show the original knight/Hauptmann-Kunigunde/Ozeana relationship gradually taking shape as a play involving a ride on the circular wall of the castle.[19] Cast in terms of a medieval contest of knight-suitors competing for the lady Kunigunde, the scenario calls for the hero's death as the demonstrably negative result of his hapless attraction for the lady. The idea for the play then retreats into the shadows of Hauptmann's dramatic interests until about 1900. It is revived in 1912 by a visit of some friends who remind Hauptmann of the Kynast legend in terms of its incorporating a natural/unspoiled vs cultivated/spoiled di-

[19] Gerhart Hauptmann, *Sämtliche Werke,* Hans-Egon Hass, ed., Berlin, 1969, IX. The Kynast fragments are found on pp. 191–221.

chotomy within a Minnesang context. Subsequently, we find Hauptmann putting the question to himself whether the Kynast saga might not also be viewed as just another variant of the Odyssey. He is thinking here about Penelope, not in the context of her faithfulness to Odysseus, but of her attractiveness to the suitors seeking her hand. All three situations depict the suitor hopelessly ensnared in adoration of an unattainable ideal — an archetypal configuration that was to become a real facet of Hauptmann's personal and aesthetic life.

It was subsequently in 1905 that Hauptmann met the young actress Ida Orloff in Berlin where she had made a name for herself in the role of Hannele in Hauptmann's play *Hanneles Himmelfahrt* at the Lessing Theater. Just as the original Kynast-Kunigunde configuration seems to have been brought forth by the poet's relationship with Margarete Marschalk, here again his enthusiasm for Miss Orloff set him off on a creative course that lasted many years after the personal affair was over. In the most complete account of the poet's relationship with the actress, F. W. J. Heuser asserts that the acquaintance functioned as a basis for what Hauptmann was ultimately to create in the *Wanda* novel. If however, we consider this liaison with Ida Orloff as another, more mature experience of a nature similar to the earlier Ozeana infatuation, the affair comes to stand more accurately at midpoint and links the more seasoned expression of the conflict in the 1927 novel to the original circus experience of the author's youth.

In his immediate enthusiasm Hauptmann modeled his Pippa in *Und Pippa tanzt* after Miss Orloff. That role subsequently established her fame and brought the poet and the actress into a warm but precarious relationship which lasted about a year. Hauptmann was forty-three, Ida only sixteen, and the difference in ages only increased the severity of the spell the young girl cast on the by then distinguished author. Regardless of the fact that much of the correspondence between Hauptmann and Ida Orloff was apparently based on a paternalistic attitude on the part of Hauptmann, there is evident a sense of physical excitement which Hauptmann is unable to suppress. That Hauptmann should try to suppress it in the first place can doubtless be attributed to the obvious age differential, though this did not prevent him from wooing and marrying Margarete Marschalk in spite of a thirteen-year difference in their ages. Heuser asserts that this fascination with younger women was characteristic of Hauptmann, and the large number of characters in his works who are portrayed in this kind of relationship would seem to bear this out. The poet must have sensed, as Heuser proposes, "that these adolescents were more genuine, less self-conscious, more natural, and yet also more of a riddle to themselves and to others than the older women he had met."[20]

The various characters for which Ida ultimately served as model are numerous indeed. Starting with Pippa, Hauptmann molded her into Gersuind in *Kaiser Karls Geisel,* Ludowike in *Die Jungfrau vom Bischofsberg,* Ingigerd in *Atlantis,* Melitta in *Phantom,* Wanda in the circus novel, Hamida in *Hamlet in Wittenberg,* Irene Bell in *Im Wirbel der Berufung,* Minka in the rejected manuscript portion of *Das Buch der Leidenschaft,* as well as the heroine in at least two projected novels. While the female characters are all sufficiently varied to give them character of their own, Heuser points out that they all bear "an unmistakable family resemblance and in certain details there is almost complete identity with their prototype. All are about sixteen years of age, or at least appear so. All have Ida's delicate frame, her mass of flowing hair, her entrancing beauty, her gracefulness, her seeming childlike innocence and Madonna-like purity, her irresistible personal charm, her lack of inhibitions, her stubborn determination, her demonic power over men." Heuser makes the case that Hauptmann had dealt with the issue of love vs sex in practically all of his works up to *Kaiser Karls Geisel* (1908) but that only after Ida Orloff "did he essay the portrayal of polyerotic young women who give themselves to several men with whom for a time

[20] Frederick W. J. Heuser, "The Life of Ida Orloff and her relations to Gerhart Hauptmann," *PMLA,* LXXII (September 1957), p. 753.

they are in love." The heroines therefore "are not just women in whom sex is raised to the nth degree, but rather women of much more complicated makeup. They do not simply inspire lust in the individual man. On the contrary, they are themselves capable at times of sincere devotion and selfless affection, and can arouse genuine love in men. There is a magic compulsion about it all which may lead to the highest and purest ecstacies, but never to peace and bliss for any length of time."[21]

As soon as one attempts to establish the qualities common to these post-Orloff character portraits, it becomes clear that those qualities are also in evidence in many of Hauptmann's heroines that precede the writer's acquaintance with her. It is, in fact, possible to go back to the Renz circus experience and see that when Hauptmann refers to Ozeana as "Sylphide der Luft" with aphrodisiacal qualities, he marks her as one of the *Elementargeister* and thereby establishes her as the first of an extended series that had had its inception long before the writer met Ida Orloff. Already in *Die versunkene Glocke* (1896), for example, we meet such a "spirit" with magnetic attraction for the protagonist, and who by virtue of the separation of their two worlds is almost as much enticed to his as he to hers. In the 1906 play *Und Pippa tanzt* Hauptmann draws Pippa as something young, happy, and lively, and underscores one of her entrances with an introit-like "incipit vita nova."[22]

By the time Hauptmann broke off his relationship with Ida at the beginning of 1907 he had added yet another element to his conception of this female type. In *Kaiser Karls Geisel,* for example, we find a distinctly negative aspect polarized with the attraction that the figure wields. The personal connection is difficult to avoid. Heuser points out that Kaiser Karl (with Gersuind) and Hauptmann (with Ida) vacillate between idealization of an adolescent and derogation of her. In the 1912 novel *Atlantis* the character type that was first described as

[21] Ibid., p. 758.
[22] *Und Pippa tanzt,* Act III, *Das Gesammelte Werk,* IV, 427.

"Sylphide der Luft" is given more earthy qualities — as Heuser puts it, she "comes pretty close to being an ordinary hussy."[23] As a varieté dancer (from the same side of the tracks as a circus performer!) with a special dance number called "Mara or the Spider," Ingigerd is a liberated woman intent on living according to her own rules and desires. She functions as a spider for the male lead even though the latter is aware of her powers of attraction as well as her potential for destruction.

These several qualities, then, the heroine's youth and beauty, her elusiveness, her magnetism, her deadliness, are almost blatantly the fruit of personal experience and are consistently the mark of female characters throughout Hauptmann's oeuvre. In no single work, however, do they come together as forcefully as in his novel *Wanda*. Subtitled *der Dämon,* the novel's heroine Wanda acts precisely in that capacity with regard to Paul Haake, a young Breslau sculptor. In this rather obvious autobiographical analog to Hauptmann's own early career as sculptor (1880–84), Paul Haake "rescues" Wanda from her circus existence, and she serves for a time as his model, inspiring him to create as never before. The relationship progresses along rather bourgeois lines until Wanda tires of the cage she feels shutting her in and flees. Haake's search for her then becomes the story of his life. He is capable of risking all under the auspices of a rationale that suggests that her kind of life is superior to a bourgeois existence, but in the next breath plunges into the depths of despair to curse his enslavement to Wanda: "Mache mich frei! Mach mich rein ! Rotte sie aus meinem Herzen!"[24] When she returns to him they marry, and the battle between the two poles of the dichotomy seems momentarily quelled. The peace, however, is short lived and the division becomes more and more noticeable. Haake is possessed by jealousy and assumes a role similar to that of Ozeana's husband as recorded in the *Abenteuer*

[23] Heuser, "Life of Ida Orloff," p. 762.

[24] *Wanda, Das Gesammelte Werk,* XI, 180. Subsequent quotes will be referenced with page numbers in parentheses after the quote.

meiner Jugend account. In a moment of desperation he tells her:

> Meine Liebe zu dir ist jetzt, wo ich dich täglich und stündlich und ganz besitze, beinahe noch schmerzhafter, quälender, sinnlos unmäßiger als in der Zeiten, da ich dich suchen ging. Ich weiß ja, du bist zu nichts anderem da. Alle müssen ja auf dich fliegen und in dich hineinstürzen. Du bist ja die reinste männermordende Gottesanbeterin: das aber macht mich ja eben zu deinem Hörigen! Und trotzdem, wenn ich dir je wieder etwas nachweise, Wanda, bist du nicht mehr! Du bist von der Straße, du bist eine, die dorthin gehört! Eine Allerweltshure bist du! Den Kerl möchte ich morden, der nicht für eine Nacht mit dir seine Seele verkaufen würde. Aber wehe! wehe! wehe!, wenn auch nur der kleinste Gedanke an Untreue in dir ist! (197)

Once again she leaves him — to follow the circus that comes to town. And here we cannot help but sense a mirror effect, for the circus that appears in the novel is not just any circus, but the Renz troupe with Ozeana, described in terms that are unmistakably familiar: the circus encounter which functions so dramatically in the lives of Haake and Wanda is an almost verbatim recounting of the childhood experience of the young Hauptmann. Regardless whether one argues here that in the *Abenteuer* account Hauptmann is remembering the terms of his childhood visit or only remembering his childhood visit in terms he later acquired, the validity of the parallel between Haake and Hauptmann is not in the least diminished.[25] Here he cites the curiosity of the eager townspeople, calls Ozeana the "schönste Frau der Welt," and mentions her again as "Sylphide der Luft." The same phenomenon whereby the legitimate theater is made to take a back seat is there too: "Das große Stadttheater, Oper und Schauspiel sowie das Lobetheater blieben leer und verloren ihre Leuchtkraft wie Licht-

[25] Hauptmann had completed *Wanda* in 1927. It appeared in serial form in the *Vossische Zeitung* under the title *Der Dämon,* and was subsequently published, virtually unchanged, in book form. See Hans Daibler, *Gerhart Hauptmann,* Vienna, 1971, p. 213. The *Abenteuer meiner Jugend,* in which he records the circus experience, was written mostly after 1929, completed prior to 1935, and subsequently published in 1937.

stumpfe, wenn die Sonne über den Horizont gestiegen ist." (199) Young and old alike are captivated by Ozeana, and as if she were not enough, the second part of the evening is a spectacular steeplechase. Since we are dealing here with the same circus visit as before, it is not difficult to view this spectacle in *Wanda* as analogous to the ride on the wall in the Kunigunde-Kynast fragments originating from Hauptmann's earlier years and subsequently figuring in his storehouse of dramatic ideas. The recounting of the same circus episode, moreover, interweaves the novel theme with the childhood experience and with Hauptmann's relationship with Miss Orloff. As for Hauptmann, as for Franz, so for Paul Haake in the later novel these things signal evil: "Das ganze Ereignis stieg eher wie eine Wolke denn als eine Sonne über dem Horizont herauf. Solchen Veranstaltungen im Grunde leidenschaftlich geneigt [Hauptmann?], stand er ihnen aus Gründen, die in seinen Erlebnissen lagen [Hauptmann?], jetzt mit Zurückhaltung gegenüber. Es war ihm, als sollte er lieber nicht hinblicken, wo etwas dergelichen in Erscheinung trat." (199) Wanda, on the other hand, is described as being "außer Rand und Band", and when Paul finally relents and accompanies her to a performance, the effect it has on her demonstrates the tug-of-war going on in both of them and is symbolic of the chasm separating them. Before the evening is over she has left him again.

Haake is ultimately driven to drink and almost total dissipation. He begins on the road to recovery when he moves to a friend's house where his momentary salvation appears in the forester's daughter, a girl of simple and peaceful nature who functions as a haven from the storms of Wanda. Modelled supposedly after Hauptmann's friend in youth, Anna Grundmann, this Marie Ronke is in obvious contrast to the type portrayed in Wanda, and while she seems momentarily to offer the peace Haake is seeking, he is unable to free himself from Wanda — literally and figuratively. A settlement by means of divorce is unsuccessful in that he cannot prove her guilt, and he sets out again in search of his circus daemon. Finding her and the circus she has returned to, his fall from his profession and his society is virtually complete; there is little resistance from his "legitimate" self once he has come again under her spell. By bourgeois standards, Wanda's behavior is representative of the negative extreme to which she has led Haake. While still carrying on under a pretext with Paul, she has become the mistress of the circus director Flunkert, a man of her own kind who exercises a tenacious hold on her. Paul is himself so completely taken in by the possibilities of his bohemian circus existence that his rationale evolves into hate for the bourgeois world. He wallows in what Hauptmann calls his social *Pariatum*. Wanda ultimately has a child by Flunkert and convinces Paul that it is his son, but the apparent placidity of this arrangement is again short lived. The discovery of the truth causes the final break in Paul; he attacks Flunkert and beats him to within an inch of his life. This ends what Hauptmann refers to as Haake's *Lebenskampf* — ends with Haake himself the victim of his uncontrollable passion and what must be interpreted as a cerebral hemorrhage.

By this point the pattern is clear. This kind of girl and her power over men had been manifested in an embryonic state in Hauptmann's and the garrison soldiers' enthusiasm for Ozeana Renz, and had been at the base of the dramatist's unfinished portrayal of Kunigunde and her suitor Franz. The same configuration recurs subsequently in countless variations in his works as well as in his life, so that it is possible to see the roots of the later, more thorough, expressions of the phenomenon extending all the way back to the original experience of the Renz performances. The circus novel *Wanda,* while by no means one of Hauptmann's better works, gains thereby some significance inasmuch as it is the single work that actually delineates the issue in terms matching the original formative experience. Having met Ida Orloff, it was "as if Hauptmann had asked himself the question: What would become of the young woman with different antecedents, under different circumstances, and in other environments?"[26] It is

[26] Heuser, "Life of Ida Orloff," p. 758.

clear by now that two decades after his romance with Ida Orloff, Hauptmann did not simply fashion the circus context out of the blue, so to speak, but rather turned to an earlier experience to develop the fullest and most revealing version of the situation he was trying to portray. What Heuser terms Hauptmann's "literary reaction to his acquaintance with Ida Orloff" might indeed have been just that, but Ida herself was the affirmation of a phenomenon he had sensed and encountered much earlier. When he chose to shape his literary heroine as a circus girl, it was to bring to fruition a seed that had been planted during his youth. His aesthetic manipulation of the circus motif, moreover, is not only valid for its uniqueness in expressing his own conception of the nature of such women, but is likewise a perfect depiction of the force that the circus world and its performers exercised on the society of the time. Wanda — the circus girl — is at once the ideal to be adored and the agent of possible damnation. As the heroine entices and leads the hero astray, so is the "regular" world (society) drawn to the exotic reality of the circus — to wit, the young men from the "best" society flocking around Ozeana Renz, plus the tone of rebuke, plus the concept of a "lesson to be learned" as they are disappointed in their desires. In that kind of a context Hauptmann's variations on the theme culminate at a point at which he speaks not only of a personal problem but of a more universal one — where the symbols are relating to the issue of Eros and its attraction and danger for the bourgeois artist/individual/society.

Wanda was not the last of the guises in which Hauptmann tried to clothe the issue, but none states the dichotomy so strongly and straightforwardly. Heuser cites other character portrayals in which the influence of Ida and/or the other women in Hauptmann's personal life is in evidence, and how they seem to "line up" at the opposing poles. But Heuser's interpretation, at least as far as the Ida-Wanda pole is concerned, is somewhat misleading. The point he makes central to *Wanda* is that it emphasizes Hauptmann's conviction "of how little man is master of his fate, how large a role chance plays in his life, how little he can lay claim to the good found in him, how ineluctable under given conditions is the power of human passion,"[27] an interpretation that seems to ignore the trees in looking for the forest. His more general comments on all of the characters revolve around Hauptmann's coming to see "tragedy inherent in human nature itself," part of which takes shape as "the most revolting and brutal of ... instincts" to oppose man's other "most glorious and idealistic impulses." In Heuser's total scheme of things, women like Ida and Wanda are "simply the revelation of an irrational and irresistable force" to which the hero by chance falls victim. Hauptmann, he claims, does not condemn these women and the effect they have, but sets up a scale of values "placing pluralistic manifestations of love on a lower plane than the lasting affection of a woman for one man only. ... Only the monogamously conditioned woman can help a man toward an enlargement of his life and a sense of transcendence."[28] This kind of interpretation is the result of Heuser's trying to schematize the women, all of them, into a spectrum to include the ones opposite to Ida-Wanda, such as Ottogebe, Griselda, Agata, etc., and imposes on Hauptmann a scale of values which the poet himself did not envision. One cannot ever say definitely that Hauptmann opted for the one type over the other; what the one could do for the man, the other could not. To appreciate that is precisely the truth in Hauptmann's myriad portrayals of his female characters, and it is therein that that uniqueness of epitomizing the issue in terms of the circus lies. Hauptmann used the circus in the real terms of a personal experience in his youth to symbolize and embody the age-old dilemma involving the forces of salvation and damnation inherent in Eros. It was a case of having sensed its force in his youth, of having manipulated it for all it was worth during his career as poet, playwright, and novelist, and of being able to view his own life as its best exemplification.

[27] Ibid., p. 766.
[28] See Heuser, p. 772ff.

3. *Carl Zuckmayer*

Carl Zuckmayer's play *Katharina Knie* stands as the only complete dramatic treatment of circus life in the German theatrical repertoire — a fact indicative of the unique relationship to the circus which Zuckmayer alone enjoyed. The origins of the playwright's association with the Swiss "national" Circus Knie are related in his memoires *Als wär's ein Stück von mir.*[30] There he states that he had no designs on *the* Knie circus when he wrote the play. Like every other child growing up in Nackenheim am Rhein, Zuckmayer had reacted with nothing less than total enthusiasm for the small troupe of artistes who came every year to perform in the market place. The troupe's appearance each year brought forth excited and rumorous cries of "Der Knie kimmt!" "Knie" had come so often, Zuckmayer claims, that the name had lost any direct association with an individual performer or with a particular group of artistes and had simply become synonymous with any and all tightrope walkers and aerial acrobats. Zuckmayer asserts further that even if as a child he had indeed seen "old man Knie," his 1928 drama was written with no particular individual in mind. The playwright was thus surprised and not a little upset, when in December of that year, a few days before the premiere of *Katharina Knie,* a telegram arrived from the attorney for the Knie Circus in Zurich, issuing an injunction against performing the play — at least with the Knie name as its title. How could he have known, Zuckmayer explains, "daß ... der Urvater der 'Dynastie', ein Friedrich Knie ... in die Schweiz übersiedelt und Bürger von Burgdorf geworden war ... daß seine Söhne schon vor längerer Zeit den 'Schweizer Nationalzirkus' gegründet hatten, eines der bedeutendsten europäischen Zirkusunternehmen, und reiche Leute geworden waren, jeder mit seiner eigenen Villa in Rapperswyl am Zürichsee — das alles war mir unbekannt." (433) Faced with this dilemma, Zuckmayer

[30] Carl Zuckmayer, *Als wär's ein Stück von mir,* Vienna, 1966. Page numbers for subsequent quotes from this work will be given in parentheses within the text.

claimed total ignorance of the Knie circus enterprise and argued against changing the title. A possible solution was tendered by the Knies' press secretary who had enclosed a note, suggesting they could possibly be persuaded. It was worth a try, and Zuckmayer dutifully wrote a letter inviting them to come to Berlin and see for themselves, counting on a performance to avoid any difficulties a mere script-reading might induce. Within days they were on the scene, as Zuckmayer recalls them, a formidable quartet of "Goliaths" to be reckoned with: "Da war der mächtige Frédéric, die Haare tief in die breite Stirn gescheitelt — er trug als einziger noch die kleinen Goldblättchen der alten Zunft in den Ohrläppchen und arbeitete im Zirkus mit Tigern und Eisbären –, da waren seine gleichfalls spektakulären Brüder Charles (Elefanten), Rudolf (Pferde und artistisches Programm) Eugène (Geschäftliches). Sie hatten in ihrer Jugend, alle noch unter freiem Himmel, im bunten Trikot, auf dem Turm- und Sprungseil, als Akrobaten, Trapezkünstler, Trampolinspringer und Menschenpyramide gearbeitet, jetzt trugen sie die Finger voller Ringe und hatten schwere, goldene Uhrketten mit kostbaren Berlocken über die wohlausgefüllten Westen gespannt." (434) By virtue of the fact that the renowned Albert Bassermann was scheduled for the lead,[31] the four agreed to attend a rehearsal. Immediately thereafter the Knies gave their enthusiastic sanction, asking only that the program acknowledge their contemporary situation as an established "national" enterprise enjoying international stature. Zuckmayer and the Knie brothers became fast friends, and on a Viennese New Year's Eve 1929/30, a night on which doubtless much of the world was torn between elation and depression, the poet was taken close to midnight into

[31] As it happened, the "Papa Knie" whose act (cooking pancakes on the high-wire and wheeling his grandmother across in a wheelbarrow) was embedded so vividly in Zuckmayer's memory, was the identical artiste seen by Bassermann as a child in his native Schwetzingen. Because of his own fond memories, Bassermann enthusiastically accepted the role in the Zuckmayer drama when the occasion presented itself in 1928, so that both the script and the acting were grounded uniquely in vivid childhood memories of the circus.

the elephant tent by Charles Knie and allowed to pluck an elephant hair from the tail of Rosa — a good luck charm which Zuckmayer claims to have kept with him throughout his life. Six years later during the Jubilee celebration of the Circus Knie in Zürich, *Katharina Knie* was performed again before an enthusiastic circus audience, and during the intermission Zuckmayer was presented to the audience for recognition — this time standing in the curve of Rosa's trunk. As Zuckmayer records it, "Ich glaube nicht, daß je ein anderer Dramatiker auf einem Elefantenrüssel vorm Publikum erschienen ist." (437)

That evening must have been in many ways a dream for Carl Zuckmayer. His interest in the circus was of long standing, and in all probability not as much "out of the blue" as his account of the play's origin would imply. In another section of *Als wär's* Zuckmayer in fact recalls a visit to the circus as a child, and that recollection is sufficiently rich in implications to convince one that Zuckmayer's *Katharina Knie* is and was something more than an accidental choice of subject matter. In this particular passage he remembers his father's dictum "O selig, selig, ein Kind noch zu sein!" but questions whether any father ever really forgets the context of intrigue, fraud, connivance, hypocrisy, and resulting guilt that pervades the supposedly innocent state of childhood bliss. At issue is a case of hypocrisy and fraud from his own childhood: an intercepted *Strafzettel* from school, fished out of the mailbox before it could reach the father for the necessary signature. Should it be destroyed — in which case it could be claimed that it never arrived? Or will the postman remember delivering it? Should it have been left in the box — in which case the agony would be done with? To make matters worse, the circus is in town — Cordy-Althoff with an impressive menagerie of wild animals. The ominous slip of paper is stuffed into a pocket in hopes that it will be forgotten in the excitement of the gala performance with its bright lights, lively music, and the press of the mob in attendance. All hopes of forgetting are futile, however, and his conscience acts up more than ever. Transfixed by the total atmosphere of the circus, taking it all in with a fervor "almost erotic in nature," the guilty one savours the possibility of running away with the circus: "Mit dem Zirkus als Stallbursche davon? Man könnte sich ein, zwei Jahre älter machen, einen falschen Namen angeben, seine Sprache verstellen. Dann wäre man alles los. Man würde, aus Buenos Aires, eine Karte nach Haus schreiben: Sorgt euch nicht, mir geht es gut, aber ich komme erst wieder, wenn ich ein großer Dompteur geworden bin ... Indessen lacht der Vater über die Affen und weiß von nichts. Harmlose Geschichten. Doch enthalten sie den Keim der Tragödie." (146/47) Humorously, and with the perspective of maturity, Zuckmayer plays with overwrought resignation and the tantalizing tragicomic nature of the predicament with the words "Après le Cirque — le déluge." In such a mood, nonetheless, the configurations were such that the child experienced "the power of sin" — an occurrence that was to be repeated often enough. Who, Zuckmayer asks in this context, is "so höllisch ausgestoßen und sündig selbstverloren, so inbrünstig-tödlich hingegeben an Wollust und Verdammnis wie ein Knabe bei jenem zwangshaften, rauschhaften, opferbetäubten Laster, vor dem man ihn mit dunklen Andeutungen gewarnt hat wie vor einer folgenschweren Krankheit und das ihm doch nichts Ärgeres einträgt als einen narkotischen Schlaf und eine kleine Mattigkeit am Morgen? Es geschieht, wie man ein Opfer darbringt: der großen Mutter, der großen Hure, der Aphrodite, der Hekate, der Nachbarstochter, der Bardame vom 'Malkasten', allen Göttinnen, allen Frauen, allen Brüsten, allen Schößen, Brüsten und Nabeln der Welt." (147) Before drawing the episode to a close, Zuckmayer briefly returns to the "O selig, o selig" of his father and admonishes the reader to give some thought to this — as he (Zuckmayer) seems to suggest — "mutual" experience.

Now this is a remarkable passage for the context in which it places the circus, whether it be Cordy-Althoff, Knie, or any other. Hidden in the middle of the episode is the reference to Eros, and by the end of the passage the erotic associations are all but underlined and in italics. As if to accomplish just this, Zuckmayer begins in the next paragraph to discuss, with no transition whatsoever, what he calls "sex education in Mainz before WWI." What he has actually managed to do here is to describe the circus experience in association with a taboo and empower it with the attractiveness that accompanies all forbidden fruit. If, like the young Frank Wedekind, Zuckmayer could ascribe to the circus the quality of "Wollust," he understood that such was an integral aspect of its attraction, naturally and powerfully part of its pull, the unmistaken and deeply significant "Keim der Tragödie." Choosing the circus as theme for a play, then, was no mere accident. There was more at stake than that: Zuckmayer wanted to clarify and hold up for exhibition those aspects of the circus existence which for him were significant and which he wanted to have recognized as such. His making theater out of the circus ring thus involves both the delineation of basic and natural forces as well as the exploitation of the aura of prohibition that surrounds such elemental forces. The playwright at once dares to legitimize the illegitimate while counting in a positive way on the accompanying prejudice. There is somehow more in his statement that as a result of the success of Katharina Knie he was the "first dramatist to be presented to the audience on the trunk of an elephant": his 1936 presentation of the Knie circus play before an audience in a circus tent together with himself as author in the role of circus performer can be seen as the culmination of his attempt to unite two separate entities — the folk ideal as incorporated in the "illegitimate" circus and the "legitimate" drama as literature. The prospects were exciting in the same way prohibited activities promise delights. The actual realization furnishes insight into the significance of *Katharina Knie* both for Zuckmayer's own work and for this account of the circus in German literature.

Almost as innocent and uncomplicated as the life it depicts, the play focuses on a brief period in the life of Katharina Knie, at her introduction the twenty-four year old daughter of a circus family. Her birth having caused the death of her mother, she has become the dutiful daughter, helpmate, and leading force in the travelling circus troupe of her father, old Vater Knie, now in his sixties. Times have gotten worse: the troupe finds it difficult to earn a living, and life has become a pitiful battle for mere existence. Conditions force Katharina to steal fodder for her pet donkey from a wealthy landowner, Rothacker. The theft is discovered and investigated, the authorities come to question the troupe — they are, after all, the most logical thieves in the vicinity — and the stage action begins at this point. Rothacker withdraws his complaint and leaves them alone, apparently smitten with the young performer Katharina. The integrity of the troupe, and particularly Vater Knie, has been brought into question, however, and Katharina's behavior leaves the old man dumbfounded and confused. Rothacker later returns, he and Katharina find themselves in a timid and delicately intriguing relationship in which wholesome naiveté exhibits strong powers of attraction for the landowner. Vater Knie, through the actions of Katharina, becomes more and more aware of the precarious existence led by himself and the members of his troupe. Discussions bring to the surface the changing nature of the times and the loss of the circus' popularity. Knie's laments encourage Rothacker to propose that Katharina be given a job in his home under assurances to old Knie that she would gain thereby some security in face of increasingly hostile exigencies. Old Knie struggles to preserve the group: he cannot accept the idea of giving up his daughter to Rothacker's kind of bourgeois life, and it is equally painful to let his ideals be sacrificed to the realities of the times. He leaves the decision up to Katharina. She suffers the same qualms but finally agrees. She leaves the troupe and goes with Rothacker to meet her new life.

Life does change, and Katharina is happy in her new life on the farm. She and Rothacker grow fond of each other and make plans to marry. Her predicament, of course, is the conflict between her love for her father and her love for Rothacker. Before the play comes to its end, she confronts the realization that everything in the family's heritage will cease if she leaves the troupe, that the tradition her father carried on so valiantly — the troupe itself and the bonds it represents — will cease to be. She forsakes Rothacker for the circus. The troupe rejoices in her decision and with convincing resolve shouts: "Es geht weiter!" as the final curtain falls.

Such an apparently simple tale has unfortunately engendered some over-simplified and shortsighted interpretations. Setting up the two antitheses of *Volkstum* and *volkstümlich*, the well-known drama critic Alfred Kerr distinguished between what supposedly was genuinely representative of the *Volk* — a depiction of *Volkstum* — and what was only of strong appeal to the *Volk* — a depiction of things or qualities describable as *volkstümlich*. The latter to his way of thinking was of questionable value. Kerr considered Zuckmayer's plays *Der fröhliche Weinberg* and *Schinderhannes* worthy of the first category, but relegated *Katharina Knie* to the second. Arnold Bauer, in his monograph on Zuckmayer, concurs in that judgment and writes sarcastically:

> Die menschlichen Charaktere und ihre Konflikte erscheinen allzu romantisiert. Was der Dichter in einem hübschen, bunten Zirkusbilderbogen vorführt, ist eigentlich noch mit dem naiv verklärenden Blick des Knaben auf die Welt des fahrenden Volkes gesehen. Zuckmayer versucht, seinem Publikum glaubhaft zu machen, der Flitterstaat eines armseligen Wanderzirkusses könne einen Menschen so stark in seinen Bann ziehen, daß er professioneller Passion sein persönliches Glück opfert. ... Katharinas optimistischer Charme und ihre unbeirrbare Zuversicht triumphieren, die anderen mit sich fortreißend. Der Gerichtsvollzieher wird mit dem goldenen Verlobungsring abgefunden, und: "Anspannen!" heißt ihr Befehl zum guten Ende. Das Artistenblut hat noch einmal gesiegt.[32]

He is willing to admit that the milieu and the social background of those inflationary times are genuine, but he maintains that what Zuckmayer makes out of the comedy and tragedy of his circus folk is an almost childishly simplistic swan song. He reports that the Berlin critics, including Herbert Ihering (who was otherwise favorably disposed to Zuckmayer) almost unanimously rejected the play. He writes the piece off as an insignificant work in the German theatrical repertoire.[33]

[32] Arnold Bauer, *Carl Zuckmayer,* Berlin, 1970, p. 47f.
[33] Ibid., p. 48.

Despite such summary critiques, the play can be seen as having a much more intricate framework of values supporting it and represented in it. Within the context of Zuckmayer's own work, it is hardly necessary to argue that *Katharina Knie* is altogether in keeping with his previous and later work. It represents nothing new or radical, but rather fits precisely in a pattern that has become Zuckmayer's trademark. In its fashion it is an encomium to a natural, free kind of existence, to an unsophisticated unity with nature, to a state of being purer and less tainted than possible in traffic with the modern world. Vater Knie's tranquility at the end of Act III expresses a mystical experience accorded only to those whose ways are exhibited as exemplary. The play's characters, except for the antagonists, are all representative of that folk humanity and wholeness with which Zuckmayer identified and which he repeatedly articulated in his works. Despite their rootlessness as members of a *Wanderzirkus* constantly on the move, the extended Knie family embodies that quality of self-assurance and integrity that preserves it against societal forces threatening to destroy it. In contrast to their homelessness, that family represents some of the most "at home" individuals to be seen on the stage. Papa Knie's monolog on the occasion of the reunion leaves little doubt of this:

> Siehste — jetz biste wieder daheim — un bleibst daheim — un wenn wir morge weiterziehn un übermorge noch weiter, un rollen um de ganze Welt erum, ohne fest einzustelle — da biste als noch daheim! ... Die Hauptsach is, daß einer weiß, wo er hingehört, mit Herz, Lung, Leber und Nier, un auch mit sein Kopp und mit seine Händ, un mit all seine Blutstroppe und mit Müh und Plag un Last und Freud, mit der ganze Lebsucht. ... Un da sin mir halt beim Wage besser dran wie viele Leut auf der Welt, weil's doch e Kunscht is, wo mir treibe, un kein leere Wahn, un weil ma's schon mit auf de Welt bringt un nit erst lang zu suche braucht, nur lerne muß ma's noch emal un dann wird's immer besser un geht nie nit zurück.[34]

[34] Carl Zuckmayer, *Gesammelte Werke,* Frankfurt/Main, 1960, III, 284f.

In sum, the joyous affirmation of life that pervades almost all of Zuckmayer's writings finds no better expression than in *Katharina Knie.* In the sense that the play forms a link in a fairly uniform chain, it cannot be cited as a unique delineation of the dramatist's ideas. Nonetheless, the fact that it was precisely in terms of the circus that such "typical" Zuckmayer ideas were given such unqualified expression is not to be overlooked. That Zuckmayer should have seen in the circus ideal the vehicle most suitable for his dramatic and philosophic purposes gives *Katharina Knie* a significance that few have been willing to consider and which has generally not been recognized.

As stated earlier, Zuckmayer's choice of the circus setting cannot very plausibly be considered sheer accident. In addition to his statements referring to the background of the play in *Als wär's ein Stück von mir,* other references to his relationship to the circus world — references which chronologically indicate an ongoing and fruitful relationship — attest to the seriousness with which Zuckmayer approached that world and its people, and consequently, the earnestness with which he undertook to write about it and them. In an article entitled "Von Seiltänzern und Himmelreichsmännern" that appeared two years later in *Gartenlaube,*[35] he describes how closely he mixed with the Knie circus world, traveling with the troupe, sleeping in their wagons, eating at their canteen, helping put up the tent, and sharing countless stories and tales from their past. In a 1967–68 introduction to a volume on the Circus Knie, Zuckmayer acknowledges the earlier, rather humorous recollection of the Knie brothers in *Als wär's.* Here, however, what he writes is intended as a serious testimonial of his admiration and estimation of the Knie family. Instead of "Goliaths" he now praises the brothers as "monuments of a heroic past, monuments of hard work ... courage ... and enterprise."[36] In an unpublished letter of 1972, Zuckmayer viewed

[35] *Gartenlaube,* 1930 (36), pp. 747–48.

[36] Alfred A. Häsler, *Knie: die Geschichte einer Circus-Dynastie,* mit einem Geleitwort von Carl Zuckmayer, Bern, 1968, p. 9.

the then contemporary situation of the circus, specifically the Circus Knie, as the culmination of an historical series of events and forces emerging out of the nineteenth century, developing as a parallel with the natural sciences, particularly zoology and animal psychology, and transformed from simple popular entertainment into a highly cultivated forum of international artistic endeavor. In its ability to mesh myriad levels of work and performance into a single productive effort, the circus comes close to being a model social state. Zuckmayer thus places the realities of circus life in a larger, more complex framework. Such an expanded relevance makes it entirely plausible to look back to 1928 and see that Zuckmayer had more in mind than a romanticized picture of gypsy life when he set forth the story of Katharina Knie. What the audience was getting as dramatic fare was not only a depiction of the struggles of a small wandering circus, but more significantly, a statement on the status of a cultural and historical phenomenon along with a subtle, almost unconscious, sermon on cultural values.

On whatever level one reads the play, it is easy enough to see Katherina's dilemma in terms of her having to choose between two worlds — that represented by her father and that represented by Rothacker, the man she loves and almost marries. Her argument with Rothacker in Act III, her pleading for time to explain her choice to her father, her statement to Rothacker: "Du un er, das sin zwei, da gibt's kei Brück dazwischen"[37] are poignant confirmations of that fact. If we look beyond her personal fate, however, and examine the significance of the opposition of those two worlds we can seen that the Katharina Knie–Martin Rothacker dichotomy is but the smallest ring in a series of increasingly larger circles.

In addition to her own life, Katharina's choice involves the life of the troupe, and we can assume, as almost seems to be happening in the play, that had she stayed with the Rothackers the fate of the troupe would have been sealed upon the death of old Knie. The play moves to the brink of what one of

[37] *Gesammelte Werke,* III, 281.

the characters calls the demise of "die ganze große Seiltänzerei." In an integral way, Katharina's initial attraction and longing for Rothacker and his world, her stint on the farm, and her almost passing into that world were all tied as much to the fate of the troupe as was Knie's death. Times being what they were — and those times are acknowledged as genuinely and accurately portrayed — the kind of circus operation represented by the Knie troupe was threatened as much by the attraction which the more stable bourgeois existence exercised on it as by the passing of those whose leadership was necessary to maintain the tradition. We are given to believe that the historical time was all-important, the economic circumstances and competition having created the kind of context in which, and only in which, Papa Knie could consider giving Katharina over to Rothacker, and in which she in her own way could reject the harshness of the vagabond life. Reneging on her engagement with Rothacker at the last moment, however, she assesses the situation after the death of her father and decides to lead the troupe on a new tour, very possibly to a more successful existence under her leadership than would have been possible under her father's old-fashioned notions. As Bauer stated somewhat sarcastically, "Das Artistenblut hat nochmal gesiegt."

That fact for Zuckmayer was historically significant. In the 1967 introduction he praises the Knies for having the foresight to change with the times, to adapt to circumstances, to expand a small operation into an enterprise of international stature as demanded by contemporary society. Zuckmayer credits them with the ability to contend with society on the latter's terms while still preserving the old traditions. *Katharina Knie* and the heroine's decision and triumph, therefore, are to be viewed as the playwright's statement on the historical status of the circus and its relationship to the rest of society. As such, Katharina Knie and the troupe of artistes she takes charge of — both in their acknowledged past role and in the potential future one — represent a model which, despite the odds at work against it, remains intact, undiminished by those forces, adaptable, constant, and altogether worthy of admiration — unmistakably so in contrast to a time whose values and standards, much of reality in fact, appeared to be disintegrating. If the inflationary era had taken its toll of much of life and its values, here was an exemplary case of a faithful adherence to principles, making possible both a personal as well as a societal victory over forces all blatantly negative in nature.

Beyond that interpretation of an ideal in a less-than-ideal world, Zuckmayer is working further with an intricate structure of relationships. If we indeed consider Katharina's relationship with Rothacker as the essence of something larger, as the smallest of several circles, that configuration then encompasses the circus world's relationship between this particular kind of *Volkstück* and the serious drama — the "legitimate" theater — and possibly even further, the kind of psychological phenomenon which surrounds taboos and proscriptions in the world of accepted and official values and standards. Given the fact that the circus and its people have traditionally been ostracized from society, given that no matter how many and what kind of accoutrements of social normalcy they put to themselves they always remain on the fringes as outsiders shut off from the mainstream of bourgeois life, it cannot be denied that such exclusion is an essential aspect of the game and a sizable portion of their attraction. In the case of *Katharina Knie,* one has the feeling that no matter how close Katharina comes to entering the bourgeois world of Rothacker, the Rothackers are all too relieved at the solution as it comes about. Martin does not even show up at the funeral of Papa Knie, and Mother Rothacker puts the finishing touch to the relationship under a rather supercilious cover. The relationships between Katharina and Rothacker and between the circus and society are thus intended as parallels which enable Zuckmayer to make a statement about the latter. Furthermore, in light of the history of Zuckmayer's earlier work and the difficulties of his reception and success as a dramatist (until *Der fröhliche Weinberg* in 1925), we can venture that the playwright is also addressing the relationship between "his" kind of play and "other" depictions of life within the parameters of the serious theater. Certainly the circus life can be viewed as an ideal rooted fast within his person and his art. But when he placed on the stage such a eulogy to circus society he could well have expected that it would encounter difficulty similar to, or exceeding, that of his previous work. If in writing *Der fröhliche Weinberg* Zuckmayer had opted for comedy material which he felt had little chance of success, he later might have been encouraged by the ultimate popularity which that play had won. In the meantime, however, his *Schinderhannes* had reminded him of what he himself could recognize as the inherent limitations to his dramatic bent. He well knew that with his tendency toward "a popular tone" he was going down a dramatic path that, as Bauer put it, guaranteed him a wide public, but which was also "dangerous" insofar as it brought him into the territory which had been usurped by the more or less provincial guardians of tradition on the ultraconservative right.[38] To a great degree his hesitancy was justified, and the history of *Katharina Knie* as a play has in large part borne out his analysis of the dangers. It was obviously a decision the playwright made for non-dramatic reasons, and in that sense, one that compels a certain amount of admiration for the dramatist willing to buck tradition and tread boldly. In the end, the play and Zuckmayer's decision to write it illustrates how strong a hold old Vater Knie had on those who had watched his daring act and found it wonderful, how symbolically the latter's little circus troupe could articulate the dramatic and social forces playing against each other as the 1920s drew to a close.

[38] See Bauer, *Carl Zuckmayer,* p. 43.

THREE:

Metaphor and Symbol

1. *Franz Kafka*

The one-page narrative *Auf der Galerie,* written during the winter 1916/17 and published as one of the pieces of *Ein Landarzt*[1] in 1919, numbers among Kafka's better-known works and as such has generated its fair share of critical analyses within the enormous body of Kafka criticism produced since his death and particularly after 1945. Most interpretations are perceptive enough in their own right although few adequately examine the piece for what Kafka reveals, and what of Kafka is revealed, through the circus imagery that dominates the brief account.[2]

It should be noted from the onset that it is not the only work of Kafka to utilize a circus motif. Another piece from the same collection, *Ein Bericht für eine Akademie* (written May/June 1917), is related by virtue of the connecting link between the circus and the variety stage to which the reporter belongs. In this well-turned vignette Kafka presents his reader with an ape become human addressing an "academy" on his development from captured ape to varieté artiste. The question posed in the piece is whether such a conversion is to be understood in positive terms, whether or not the change in status represents anything gained. The piece is most frequently seen as a parabolic expression of a predicament in which Kafka could imagine and see himself, and the resolution — if there is one — is not to be regarded as positive. The

[1] Munich, 1919.

[2] Naomi Ritter's article "On the Circus-Motif in Modern German Literature," *German Life and Letters,* XXVII (July 1974), No. 4, pp. 273–285, is exceptionally lucid.

narrator's apeness was the initial cause of his predicament once captured, and to escape his torments he decides to "stop being an ape." He remains externally an ape, however, and the internal change is viewed only as a matter of expediency. There is much in the piece that touches on the predicament of a number of Kafka's fellow countrymen and contemporaries who sought to exchange their Jewishness for the legitimacy that came with conversion but who could not alter their heritage or their person by virtue of an official transaction. Like them, the ape's present "position" as a varieté performer makes him no less an outsider to the academy than a Prague Jew in the company of Czech Christians or an ape in the company of men, or for that matter, a circus performer in the circle of onlookers. The varieté artiste is brother to the circus artiste, and the two can be seen as Kafkaesque symbols of the outsider — variations, both of them, on the pariah theme.

Two other pieces carry the idea further, both from the collection of stories entitled *Ein Hungerkünstler* which appeared shortly after Kafka's death in 1924: *Erstes Leid* (written 1921/22) and the title story *Ein Hungerkünstler* (written Spring 1922). The first leaves little doubt as to the peculiarities and singularity of the trapeze artiste who in this case may be interpreted as the artist in general. As enigmatic as the characters in any number of Kafka's other pieces, this one seems bent on self-castigation though not without a touch of humor. Whatever the interpretative possibilities, however, it is important for us to note that it is explicitly in terms of a circus performer that Kafka describes the artist and his predicament: "Bekanntlich ist diese hoch in den Kuppeln der großen Varietébühnen ausgeübte Kunst eine der schwierigsten unter allen Menschen erreichbaren." From all appearances the uniqueness of such a figure held a considerable attraction for him. The title story, likewise one of Kafka's best known and most frequently interpreted, pushes the outsider theme to the ultimate extreme and puts the hunger-artist's downfall in unmistakably negative terms. In his transformation into something even less interesting than a caged animal the hunger artist's descent into ignominy is marked by his relegation to the animal cages on view for the circus/carnival crowds — and even these come to find him uninteresting. His being replaced by a captive animal is the ultimate degradation and even more condemnatory than Gregor Samsa's sister taking a new lease on life after her brother's death in Kafka's popular story *Die Verwandlung*.

These three pieces show Kafka using the circus context as an essentially negative framework for the dilemma which plagues the artist and with which he himself so strongly identified. The fact that the circus did indeed have particular connotations for Kafka strikes one as not at all remarkable for a writer of his ilk. His entire work, while in many ways a personal testimony and almost provincial in scope, is decidedly non-elitist. Kafka's world was never removed from the ordinary and everyday plane no matter how much his personal plight made him special or his poetic insight removed him from the mundane. Within such a framework, the circus may be viewed as a common facet of his rather ordinary personal milieu. Other references nonetheless would seem to show him more than ordinarily inclined to bring the circus into play, using it to pin down or release meaningful associations or connotations. Shortly after the publication of *Die Verwandlung* he wrote to Felice Bauer of his confusion caused by contradictory reviews. In slight desperation he asks: "Bin ich ein Circusreiter auf zwei Pferden?" Answering his own question, he replies: "Leider bin ich kein Reiter, sondern liege am Boden."[3] In a 1915 diary entry he rails against time-consuming hack work at the office and expresses his frustration with the exasperated exclamation: "Nun stehen vor mir vier oder fünf Geschichten aufgerichtet, wie die Pferde vor dem Zirkusdirektor Schumann bei Beginn der Produktion."[4] In a relatively late fragment, "Es ist ein Mandat" (1920), the circus imagery carries the entire message:

[3] Letter of October 7, 1916. *Briefe an Felice,* Erich Heller and Jürgen Born, eds., in Franz Kafka, *Gesammelte Werke,* Max Brod, ed., Frankfurt/Main, 1967.

[4] Franz Kafka, *Tagebücher:* 1910–1923: New York, 1948 and 1949, p. 456.

> Ich kann meiner Natur nach nur ein Mandat übernehmen, das niemand mir gegeben hat. In diesem Widerspruch, immer nur in einem Widerspruch kann ich leben. Aber wohl jeder, denn lebend stirbt man, sterbend lebt man. So wie zum Beispiel der Zirkus von einer Leinwand umspannt ist, also niemand, der nicht innerhalb dieser Leinwand ist, etwas sehen kann. Nun findet aber jemand ein kleines Loch in der Leinwand und kann doch von außen zusehn. Allerdings muß er dort geduldet werden. Wir alle werden einen Augenblick lang so geduldet. Allerdings — zweites allerdings — meist sieht man durch ein solches Loch nur den Rücken der Stehplatzbesucher. Allerdings — drittes allerdings — die Musik hört man jedenfalls, auch das Brüllen der Tiere. Bis man endlich ohnmächtig vor Schrecken in die Arme des Polizisten zurückfällt, der von Berufs wegen den Zirkus umgeht und nur leise mit der Hand dir auf die Schulter geklopft hat, um dich auf das Ungehörige eines solchen gespannten Zusehens, für das du nichts gezahlt hast, aufmerksam zu machen.[5]

Now in general these latter three references to the circus are somewhat less consistently negative than the first three which showed the circus in actual thematic usage, and the change in tone brings to the surface a kind of basic equivocalness on Kafka's part. Leaving aside comparisons between the two sets of circus references, this second triad is interesting in that it shows Kafka envisioning himself in three distinct circus-related roles: in the first as performing artiste, in the second as circus director, and in the last as spectator — albeit outside the tent. One can ascribe this kind of role-playing variously to changeability, insecurity, slipperiness, or adaptability, but the resulting ambiguity becomes a kind of Kafkaesque symptom that seems to be always present. Inasmuch as this very ambiguity as well as the identical composite of roles may be found in the extremely compact piece *Auf der Galerie* — one of Kafka's stylistic gems — the interpreter is legitimately tempted to view that story as both a representative sample of Kafka's work and a kind of synthesis of what the circus connoted to him. Kafka's own allusion to the piece as an "unanfechtbares

[5] *Gesammelte Werke,* Max Brod, ed., VI, Frankfurt/Main, 1953, p. 302.

Ganze" uniting disparate elements[6] makes it extremely interesting to examine *Auf der Galerie* in detail.

The piece may have been written under the influence of Robert Walser's *Lustspielabend,* a short sketch describing a spectator's reactions to a theatrical event. According to Hartmut Binder,[7] Kafka was in possession of the Walser text as early as October 1913, so that the impetus for the 1916/17 *Galerie* is entirely possible. Yet the differences between the two are pronounced, a fact pointed out by Henry M. Rosenwald.[8] In actuality the sole similarity seems to lie only in the fact that both situations are described from the perspective of a member of the audience. The Walser account precludes the possibility of placing the emphasis on the circus performer and totally lacks the parabolic structure of the Kafka piece. Regardless of whether Kafka got the idea from Walser — tracing sources in Kafka is never very satisfying — the miniature *Auf der Galerie* bears the unique stamp of being genuinely puzzling. It is a perfect example, moreover, of Kafka superimposing a profound idea on a less than profound reality.

The narrative occupies only a page in some editions and consists only of two lengthy sentences. The first is expressed in the subjunctive "if/then" form and proposes that if some sickly, consumptive circus equestrienne were to appear before a voracious audience on a shabby and unsure horse, driven by a merciless trainer for months on end around in her arena circle, throwing kisses and bowing to the spectators, and if this spectacle were to continue thusly under the unrelenting noise of the orchestra and ventilator on into a seemingly endless infinity, accompanied by the recurrent diminishing and increasing applause of the multitude of hands — really noth-

[6] In his piece "Elf Söhne." See Jürgen Kobs, *Kafka,* Bad Homburg, 1970, p. 80–81.

[7] Hartmut Binder, *Motiv und Gestaltung bei Franz Kafka,* Bonn, 1966, p. 149.

[8] See *Jahrhundertwende,* Henry M. Rosenwald, ed., New York, 1968, p. 69.

ing but a concert of steam hammers — perhaps then a young man from the audience would run down from the seats into the arena and call out through all the fanfare of the orchestra: "Stop!" The second sentence states that such, of course, is never the case: "da es aber nicht so ist." Instead, a beautiful lady dressed in red and white flits out from the curtains at the arena entrance; the director devotedly tries to catch her eye, stands ready for her every wish, lifts her onto her dapple-gray steed as if she were his beloved grandchild going on a treacherous journey, hesitates to give the whip signal to begin, but finally forces himself to do so: he follows every movement of the horse, stands in awe of her skill, tries to admonish her with commands in English, makes the grooms stand at attention, hushes the orchestra before her spectacular somersault, and finally lifts his little one down from the horse, kisses her on both cheeks, and considers no amount of applause from the audience sufficient. She meanwhile, supported by him, stands on her tiptoes in a cloud of (saw)dust with arms outstretched and head held back and shares her happiness with the whole circus. And since this is the way it is, the young man leans his face on the railing and, as if sinking into a deep dream during the grande finale, cries without being conscious of his tears.

Not a little enigmatic, this miniature sketch begs interpretation. The first sentence-paragraph in the subjunctive overtly expresses an unreal situation, one that is proposed as an impossibility in the world on view at the circus. Has it ever occurred that a spectator has had to rush into the ring to rescue a performer in distress? The questions raised are clearly rhetorical. The second sentence-paragraph presents a more accurate account of reality, the way it really "is" in the circus, down to the fine details. The spectator crying with his chin on the railing, however, is an odd reaction and sufficiently peculiar to cause the reader to reconsider and view the whole thing in reverse. Thus the first and unreal situation would describe what must be imagined as the "true" world under the grease paint and an "ever-accomodating orchestra": the circle orbed by the horse and performer in the arena is a truly vicious one which only the drastic action of a decisive onlooker with enough sense to appreciate the horror of the situation can break. The second half, despite the indicative mood, also becomes reversed and is seen thus as pure *Schein*. If the first half is *really* the case, the second half is only an act. The first spectator's cry to stop the music — while potentially possible only in the subjunctive — is suggested as an appropriate factor of the "reality," and the reaction of the second onlooker is relegated to emotional weeping in observance of the beautiful perfection of the "illusion."

Interpretations of the piece rest more often than not on the role and reaction of the spectator: earlier analyses stress the sorrowful resignation of the second spectator as the core of Kafka's lament:[9] others go beyond this and relativize the two spectators' reactions to give the reader the benefit of both in play with realistic and illusionary facets of a dually described world. With emphasis on the spectator, the "point" comes to turn on the choice and chance of action to correct the reversals which frequently cloud and distort reality as perceived or deceiving. The spectator role and the responsibility incumbent in it relative to what is transpiring in the center of the ring is here as much fraught with problems as the "Es ist ein Mandat" fragment cited earlier. There the dilemma belongs to a spectator so outside the legitimate circle of onlookers that he cannot even "see" the goings-on, much less "act" on them, but who despite his kind of inactive blind viewing, is "discovered" and made out as guilty for non-payment participation. Here in *Auf der Galerie* the Kafkaesqueness of that situation is condensed into the confrontation of two different reactions centering on the vital issue of *action*.

Beyond the question of the spectator's reaction to the discrepancies between the genuine and the sham, however,

[9] The *Forschungsbericht* by Peter Beicken *(Franz Kafka: Eine kritische Einführung in die Forschung,* Frankfurt/Main, 1974) cites such as the "herrschende Meinung" proposed in the interpretations of Binder, Emrich, G. Mast, H. Richter, W. Zimmermann. See Beicken, p. 303.

Kafka is surely making a statement on the dichotomy between the performer and the performance. The letter to Felice showed him capable of putting himself as writer specifically into the role of circus equestrian, and his perceptions in that regard show him articulating an insight similar to Rilke's, whose elegy on the nature of saltimbanques reveals an art which camouflages the artiste's fate from the eyes of the unobservant spectator. (See Chapter III, 3) What in the first half of this piece is described in exaggerated terms of exploitation and suffering is shown in the second setting to be a hollow routine. Once again the initial subjunctive situation — by virtue of the overall reversal — describes the actuality of the "real" performer/artiste on a shaky and insecure mount, driven by an unrelenting taskmaster in a literal and figurative rut and rescued by a sympathetic friend from the gallery of grotesquely clapping hands. The indicative mood of the complementary section, however, relates the *Scheinwelt* of a much-practiced performance and an inwardly moved and passively sympathetic spectator. Even with the emphasis shifted onto the performer there is again considerable tension established in the spectator's reaction. One is thus forced by the inversions to question whether the subjunctively expressed reality should more appropriately call forth the weeping of the emotionally moved observer and the indicatively expressed sham, the decisive action of an indignant viewer — or vice-versa as written. In any case, the piece provides the chance to perceive the double-sided nature of the art of the equestrian-performer-artist and encourages us to see here a relationship between the writer and the written, between Kafka as insecure performer in the social *manège,* and Kafka, performer par excellence, routinely denying the vitality and spontaneity of art by virtue of actions ordered, practiced, and polished. At some point it becomes inevitable that the analyst-reader fuse the performer and the spectator into a dichotomous whole — in which case the ingenious Kafka would seem to be offering for consideration (by himself and his readers) the multiple alignments possible with two performers and two spectators. The possibilities seem endless, and one cannot help but be impressed by the virtuosity of Kafka's stylistic camouflage.[10]

Yet another emphasis is possible and inherently related to the previous one: the role of the third person functioning in the piece, referred to as "Chef" in the first sentence and "Direktor" in the second. The character calls forth all the authority figures with whom Kafka was destined to do battle during his lifetime, should they take individual shape as office supervisor, father, God, or someone else. Such figures hide behind the merciless driver of the driven and exploited in the first half as easily as behind the mentor of the second part who is only anxious to preserve the external sham and all the trappings of the performance. The statement cited earlier, however, in which Kafka puts himself into the person of Director Schumann, suggests a slightly different cast of characters – in this instance another dichotomous unit comprising director and performer. Doubtless no single one of Kafka's authority figures drove him so mercilessly as he did himself – so that he could literally cry for some kind of release – and no one could have been so conscious of the requisites of successful and acceptable performance as he himself. He was his own best or worst "director" and "boss": he could envision his own products – "vier oder fünf Geschichten" – standing in disciplined (read "in fear of the whip" or "artistically trained") attention before himself as the man in charge, or he could put himself into that role with the object of his training described as either "irgendeine hinfällige, lungensüchtige Kunstreiterin" or "eine schöne Dame, weiß und rot," depending on whether he, as man in charge, entered the relationship as "peitschenschwingender erbarmungsloser Chef" or "hingebungsvoller Direktor". He could write to Max Brod in 1922 that his writing – his functioning as artist – was a sweet and wonderful reward and in the next breath acknowledge it as service to the devil.

Such a movable emphasis constitutes a problem for the reader but is nevertheless the clearest articulation of Kafka's

[10] A term used by Kobs.

subjective world of infinite possibilities. In Emrich's analysis, his was a struggle "um eine lebensmögliche Existenz in einer Welt, in der aber nicht gelebt werden kann, da in ihr keine absolut sichere, 'wahre' Ordnung vorfindlich ist. Nur Scheinordnungen, die sich aber stets als Unordnungen erweisen, sind möglich."[11] In that sense then, *Auf der Galerie* is a succinct formulation of the Kafkaesque predicament and a straightforward example of the circus employed on a metalevel. The cited instances in which Kafka brings the circus element into play suggest that he was acutely conscious of the circus as an embodiment of that severe separation between audience and performer, between appearance and reality, which he acknowledged but nevertheless sought continually to deny. The "Mandat" fragment ever so subtly expresses his outsiderness while articulating his desire to view the inner circle. By virtue of the recognized demarcation between regular members of society and those of the "show biz" circus/art world, there is little chance of resolution or integration, and the spectator's sadness becomes the sole substance of the lament. Nothing is changed: inaction is only suggestively made relative to possible action, suffering alternates with painless routine on the pivotal question of art. Configurations, relationships (performer/spectator, equestrienne/director) are superimposed within the writer's subjectivity but do not belong to the reality.[12]

[11] Wilhelm Emrich, *Franz Kafka,* Frankfurt/Main, 1961, p. 36.

[12] That Kafka was aware that this world and its members somehow capsulize his own relationship as artist with the real world finds parallel expression in his interest and enthusiasm for the Jewish theatrical troupes which visited Prague and with whose actors and actresses he felt a deep and personal bond. In a 1911 diary entry he articulates his own identification with them as performers as well as his response to them as spectator: "Das Mitleid, das wir mit diesen Schauspielern haben, die so gut sind und nichts verdienen und auch sonst bei weitem nicht genug Dank und Ruhm bekommen, ist eigentlich nur das Mitleid über das traurige Schicksal vieler edler Bestrebungen und vor allem der unseren. Darum ist es auch so unverhältnismäßig stark, weil es sich äußerlich an fremde Leute hält und in Wirklichkeit zu uns gehört.

As outsider on so many counts, Kafka thus keenly sensed a kinship with the arena and could envision himself in it as artist-performer in contradictory modes. Within the most well-known circus act — the bareback equestrienne — he glimpsed a symbolic statement of that basic segregation between the inside and the outside of the circle. He identified with a longing to bridge the gap and to clarify the role and function of both the performer and the spectator. As a writer he was not relieved of the dilemma by virtue of *Auf der Galerie,* but he had given artistic shape to his quandary and had drawn the circus effectively into the writer's domain as a primary and expressive symbol.

2. *Thomas Mann*

The brevity and completeness of Kafka's two-sentence dilemma is countered and somewhat overwhelmed by Mann's epic but unfinished depiction of his picaresque hero Felix Krull. Already when Mann began the work in 1910 he proposed that *Krull* would be something just a little out of the ordinary, writing to his brother Heinrich: "Ich sammle, notiere und studiere für die Bekenntnisse des Hochstaplers, die wohl mein Sonderbarstes werden.“ The work soon turned into an unwieldy mass that frequently caused Mann to despair of ever keeping it in bounds, much less ever finishing it. Some forty years would intervene before the work appeared in its entirety, by which time the figure of Krull had accumulated

Trotzdem ist es aber mit den Schauspielern immerhin so eng verbunden, daß ich es nicht einmal jetzt von ihnen lösen kann. Weil ich es erkennen, bindet es sich zum Trotz noch mehr an sie." *(Tagebücher: 1910–1923*, New York, 1948 and 1949, p. 112). Kafka's sympathies rest here on several factors, not in the least, of course, on the racial bond. But the stigma of the actor which Kafka mentions, the tribulations of the vocation, and the relationship between the actor and the audience place the theatrical sphere in close proximity to the circus and its less-than-"legitimate" performers. See Evelyn Torton Beck's study, *Kafka and the Yiddish Theater: Its Impact on his Work,* Madison, Wisconsin, 1971.

added dimensions and the work itself had acquired a significance for Mann's oeuvre which the original impetus did not fully encompass. As it stands, it appears to be the single work of Thomas Mann in the lighter vein, a factor that has undoubtedly added to its popularity and the readiness with which it was accepted by the reading public both in Germany and abroad. Its external innocence belies a serious and heavier undercurrent, however, and it turns out to be a perfect and logical endpoint to Mann's life work and not, as un unstudied reading would indicate, the work which breaks the Thomas Mann mold.

A glance at Thomas Mann's own statements on the work reveals some of the inflections in the author's relationship to the novel during the lengthy gestation period. In June of 1910 he proposed to the critic Samuel Lublinski that he thought he could corral the two very disparate forces he sensed he was working with. He speaks of "Frivolität" and "Moralismus", of an "erquickliches Blendwerk" produced with "künstlerischer Strenge und Gewissenhaftigkeit", and for his own part, exclaims: "Ja, was ist die Kunst! Was ist der Künstler! Diese Mischung aus Lucifer und Clown." [13] Ten years after the letter to Lublinski he asserts that the "Confessions" could be his best work if he is careful not to spoil it, and by January of 1930 he is clearly still much intrigued by the work's potential. Writing with hindsight that was still a quarter of a century in advance of the final version, he reveals what held him captive: "Es handelt sich natürlich um eine neue Wendung des Kunst- und Künstlermotivs, um die Psychologie der unwirklich-illusionären Existenzform. Was mich aber stilistisch bezaubert, war die noch nicht geübte autobiographisches Direktheit, die mein grobes Muster mir nahelegte, und ein phantastischer geistiger Reiz ging aus von der parodistischen Idee, ein Element geliebter Überlieferung, das Goethisch-Selbst-

[13] Thomas Mann to Samuel Lublinski, June 13, 1910, in *Thomas Mann: Teil I: 1889–1917,* Hans Wysling, ed., in cooperation with Marianne Fischer. Frankfurt/Main, 1975, p. 299. (Vol. 14/1 of *Dichter über ihre Dichtungen,* Rudolf Hirsch and Werner Vordtriede, eds.)

bildnerisch-Autobiographische, Aristokratisch-Bekennerisch, ins Kriminelle zu übertragen."[14] The latter statement is packed with implications, specifically, the acknowledged attraction of the autobiographical element and the desire to extend the complex into the realm of the illicit. This was certainly not a new note for Thomas Mann on either score, although here he senses the opportunity to combine both elements and put them into a larger, more valid framework. Mann's subsequent occupation with the work nonetheless seems to have bordered almost on the point of boredom. He wrote to Hermann Kesten in 1951 that he was again at work on the novel "bloß aus Zeitvertreib ... weil es mir Spaß macht, über all das inzwischen Getane hinweg an ein vor 40 Jahren Liegengebliebenes anzuknüpfen."[15] He acknowledges in the same letter that his Joseph in the meantime had in many ways superseded his Felix, though by the end of the year he could write to Jonas Lesser that while Joseph was preexistent in Felix, Krull was shaping up as a "Joseph redivivus."[16] His final spurt of work on the novel elicited his fascination with "die Idee der wechselseitigen Illusionierung von Welt und Betrüger" — again not a new idea in light of his previous work — though here too it has expanded itself into new dimensions. Whatever the apparent emphasis at any given point it is clear from such comments that Mann always kept his occupation with the confidence trickster within the framework of his entire oeuvre and perceived it not as an exception but as a complement. Ultimately, it was not without considerable pride that he could agree with critics and theorists who, after its publication, accorded the work mythic proportions and a place in a literary tradition that went far beyond the privately autobiographlcal. Their insight confirmed Mann's own sensibilities in regard to the figure he was

[14] Thomas Mann, "Lebensabriß," in *Gesammelte Werke in zwölf Bänden,* Frankfurt/Main, 1960, XI, 122.

[15] Letter to Herman Kesten, January 2, 1951, quoted in Wysling, *Thomas Mann,* p. 323.

[16] Letter to Jonas Lesser, November 6, 1951, quoted in Wysling, *Thomas Mann,* p. 329.

working with and the function it had for both himself and his work.[17]

All of Mann's irony and parodying with his Krull as picaresque hero does not change the fact that this is yet another treatment of the artist type functioning within and outside the boundaries of society. In his oft-quoted interview "Rückkehr" Mann again speaks of the "Grundidee" of the novel as the "travestierende Übertragung des Künstlertums ins Betrügerisch-Kriminelle," and although the statement can be considered valid, it makes the work sound deceptively uncomplicated. If that indeed was the projected shape of the work as first conceived, once Mann took it up again with serious intent after his work on the Joseph tetralogy the added dimension of the autobiographical and mythological gave it increased depth through the polyvalency of its complex meanings. The autobiographical aspect placed him within a long and significant tradition and allowed him to question the validity of the poetic, role-playing existence itself. That relationship permitted him, so to speak, to turn back in analysis of his own life and work, while the mythical expanse invoking the parabolic associations with Hermes and resting on the Kuck-

[17] The following portion of his October 17, 1954 letter to Max Rychner is worth quoting: "Hermetische Stilisierung lag ursprünglich gar nicht in meinen bewußten Absichten; es war eigentlich nur wieder eine Verkleidung und Parodie des Künstlertums, die ich (im) Sinn hatte, und erst bei der späten Fortsetzung war es dann mehr die Nähe des 'Joseph', als der 'Tod in Venedig', die solche mythologischen Assoziationen hineinbrachte. Ihr Hinweis auf Kerényi ist treffend genug und wird gerade jetzt noch treffender: Es ist eine merkwürdige Koinzidenz, daß eben im Rheinverlag ein Buch erscheint: "Der göttliche Schelm", von R. Radin, Kerényi und C. J. Jung in Zusammenarbeit. Es handelt sich um einen indianischen Mythenzyklus, eine archaische Vorstufe aller Schelmenromane, und in seiner mythologisierenden Einleitung weist Kerényi auf die Entwicklung bis zu Rabelais, Spanien, Simplicissimus, Eulenspiegel, Reineke Fuchs – und Felix Krull geradezu hin. Man weiß nicht, was man tut, erfährt es aber gerade, besonders wenn man soviel Wert darauflegt, wie ich, sich in einer festen, möglichst weit zurückreichenden Tradition stehen zu wissen." (Wysling, *Thomas Mann,* p. 368.)

uck privot endowed the work with epic proportions and an open-endedness that made it worth the author's while and worthy of its literary heritage. Helmut Jendreiek suggests that the work's dominant idea echoes Nietzsche's 188th aphorism in the latter's *Menschliches, Allzumenschliches* (II, 1880), to wit: ",Wir verstehen uns darauf, viele Lügen zu sagen' — so sangen einstmals die Musen, als sie sich vor Hesiod offenbarten. — Es führt zu wesentlichen Entdeckungen, wenn man den Künstler einmal als Betrüger faßt."[18] The Nietzschean echo is indeed audible, but surely not all that can be heard. In its entirety, the work is a complex tapestry of uniquely Mannian themes which surfaced with the writer's decision to give his Krull the trappings of a trickster/artist/god.

That finesse which permits Krull to slide along life's way has frequently led readers to find him such a likeable character that Mann's idea of parody and travesty recedes out of the picture. Roman Karst, for example, reads the work as a final synthesis on Mann's part of the dualities that had been the fulcrum of his earlier works. Despite a token acknowledgement that parody is involved, his reading denies the essential equivocalness which allows those two forces Mann spoke of earlier to interact with each other and to shape the meaning of the work.[19]

A substantial part of the work's inherent duality derives to be sure from the picaresque tradition which, if we can believe him, Mann found himself a part of almost unconsciously. Oscar Seidlin's analysis of the work from this perspective[20] was gratefully received by Mann and seems to have been a revelation to him. Such a narrative stance almost dictates that the basic premise of the work involve the reciprocity of *Sein* and *Schein:* that tradition rests on the proof that the world and its values are transitory and illusory and opposed to the King-

[18] Helmut Jendreiek, *Thomas Mann*: *Der demokratische Roman,* Düsseldorf, 1977, p. 515.

[19] Roman Karst, *Thomas Mann oder der deutsche Zwiespalt,* Vienna, Munich, Zurich, 1970, p. 323.

[20] Oscar Seidlin, "Picaresque elements in Thomas Mann's Work," *Modern Language Quarterly,* XII (1951), 183–200.

dom of God which is eternal and genuine. True to form, Krull is indeed forced to do battle with the world — unlike some of his literary progenitors he does not arrive with a silver spoon in his mouth — and his success at playing the game is not only an attest of his own adaptability but also a reflection of the society whose blessings he so avidly seeks. The same multiple *Scheine* that provide him with the ticket to success mirror the sham on which the upper classes stand as they rule the world. Krull can "fake it" so well indeed because the reigning reality is such a counterfeit. The effect is not only a fairly subtle exposé of bourgeois society in the best picaresque tradition, but more importantly, one which simultaneously allows Mann to call into question the whole specter of the *Bildungs-* and *Entwicklungsroman* — nothing less than a bold stroke in light of the German essence of that convention — as well as the role of the authors and writers who produced them.[21] Given the nature of the so-called hero's education and development, the process itself is made to seem questionable; and given the almost consistently close relationship between such works and their authors whose premise has traditionally been to imply far-reaching, symbolic, and sometimes purely aestheticized significance to their literary offspring's experiences, education and development, Mann casts shadows on his own role as memoir-writer-with-a-purpose. The game he was playing with this work was unquestionably far from an innocent one.

Underneath Krull's escapades is nothing other than the challenge of beating the system. That fact, despite the hero's winning charm and philosophizing ratiocination, is the negative force of the work. Mann allows his Krull to create for himself a balloon of ever-increasing size, each episode adding more air until — at some point beyond the unfinished novel's sequence — we are given to understand that it bursts. Each new inflationary encounter is self-contained, and Mann could

[21] See the discussion on Mann in Jürgen Jacobs, *Wilhelm Meister und seine Brüder:* Untersuchungen zum deutschen Bildungsroman, Munich, 1972, pp. 226–244.

have kept going for as long as his patience and fortitude lasted — he promised as much, in fact, by indicating in the work's title that it was only "Part I."[22] The Krull kind of act thrives on repetition and new challenges and cannot exist outside the framework of the performance itself. The incidences in which Felix gets to practice his skills are not only self-contained as links in the chain that constitutes the work; they actually contain the self of Felix Krull. He exists only for the sake of the game, and the game is shown to be one of deception and ultimate selfishness. In the center of all the rationalization and intrigue, of why and how he performs his magic tricks, sits squarely the ego of Krull the performer who longs to bring it off again. Here Mann is at the opposite extreme of his earlier Tonio Kröger, the artist who swore his intention to fashion something useful out of heart and head. Felix is not the final fulfillment of that oath, but rather its travesty. If Kröger's stance was naive, Krull's is farfetched to the point of megalomania. Krull can call on the gods and become one himself — as he does when he equates himself to Hermes and begins to look upon his role in relationship to others as one of a servant. His "service" to others is a two-edged barb: while instilling Felix with a justification all too noticeably lacking, it provides Mann with a focal point on Krull's distorted character. Krull's entire "act," so to speak, comes to be recognizably overblown and out of proportion, and by the time he meets up with Professor Kuckuck he is primed for the supercharge that that figure gives to his already outsized ego. Discussions (or rather listenings) of Kuckuck's theories add fuel to his fires and incite him to Faustian thoughts. The work stops before the fall on the "pinnacle" to which Mann has brought his hero of heroes. Kuckuck is the mentor whose philosophy allows Krull to see his deception as an affirmation of the prevailing laws of nature and himself as the personifica-

[22] Thomas Mann wrote to Paul Burckhart on April 4, 1955: "Aber wäre es denn ein Unglück, wenn die Krull-Memoire weit offen stehen bleiben? Vielleicht sind sie zum 'unendliche Sehnsucht erregenden' Fragment geboren. Qui vivra, verra." Quoted in Wysling, *Thomas Mann*, p. 378f.

tion of some cosmic-absolute validity. In essence, as Jendreiek explains, "die durch Kuckuck vorgetragene Theorie von der totalen Identität des Seins resümiert die von Schopenhauer abgeleitete epische Theorie der Ironie als der erzählerischen Fundamentalkategorie Thomas Manns und wird von dem Memoirenschreiber Krull 'faustisch' benutzt, um Betrug und Hochstapelei als Präsentation der absoluten Gesetze des Seins sehen zu lassen und sich selbst als Erscheinung von kosmisch-absoluter Gültigkeit zu legitimieren. Über die Kuckuck-Mythologie wird der Betrug zur Wahrheit, Schein zu Sein, der Hochstapler Krull zur Offenbarung des Absoluten parodistisch pervertiert."[23] Mann inflates Felix's balloon in full cognizance of the laws of physics governing such phenomena and is all to aware that what fills the inflated object and what remains after it bursts is so much hot air. It is really only upon recognition that he is talking as much about himself and his own art as about Felix and his finesses that the significance of Mann's irony and parody becomes apparent. The work is more than an innocent account about a charming rogue.

Structurally, and as was his usual fashion, Mann is careful to support the narrative super-story on concrete foundational pediments. Although the sweep of Mann's work is indeed Faustian and pretentiously suggestive of a grand scale, three very concrete braces buttress the epic whole. They are with obvious intention spaced evenly throughout the work, and each in its own way serves to state and reiterate what is to be considered the gist of the overall account. The three — the early episode with the actor Müller-Rosé, the evening at the Stoudebecker circus performance in the exact middle (in the 1954 Fischer paperback edition it begins on page 147 of a total 295 pages), and finally, at the end, the bullfight in Lisbon in the company of the Kuckuck family — are unmistakable variations on the "Sein/Schein" theme and can be viewed as three classic instances of games that bourgeois play.

[23] Jendreiek, *Thomas Mann*, p. 544.

The three episodes — in essence the critical mass in which Mann's theme is clearly stated — are virtually of equal value for the total work, but from our vantage point the pivotal circus performance is the most intriguing and ultimately the one least fraught with polyvalent overtones. The Muller-Rosé incident goes a long way to put Mann's feelings about the theater and the artist as an actor in perspective, but it is an experience of Krull's early youth and as such is colored and affected by a juvenile awe and naiveté that takes some of the edge off the discovery that there is a vast discrepancy between *Sein* and *Schein*. The final bullfight episode is similarly diluted by Krull's enamoured state, his intoxication with the Kuckuck mother and daughter pair. The mix between the religious nature of the ceremony-game-struggle and the erotic nature of Krull's passion is a combination with purpose and a tour de force on the part of Mann, but nonetheless a complex whose component parts are difficult to separate. In contrast, the circus performance rests squarely in the middle, is unmuddled by any extraneous or complicating element and provides, as it were, a pristine view of the previously-mentioned game that Krull and legitimate society are playing.

The Circus Stoudebecker is described as an "Angriff auf die Sinne, die Nerven, die Wollust in der Tat" and plays before a mixed public, "dieses einzigartigen Publikums, das sich aus gierigem Schaupöbel und einer Pferde-Lebewelt von roher Eleganz erregend und beklemmend zusammensetzt." Felix is enthralled with Andromache, "la fille de l'air," and in contemplation of her as "star" and main attraction, is moved to question whether she or the other acrobats, clowns, trapeze and high-wire artistes are to be considered actual, ordinary human beings. He answers his own question with the declaration: "Nach meinem Dafürhalten ist es bloße Sentimentalität, zu sagen, sie seien 'auch Menschen', mit den Herzlichkeiten von solchen, womöglich mit Weib und Kind. Ich erweise ihnen Ehre, ich verteidige sie gegen humane Abgeschmacktheit, indem ich sage: nein, sie sind es nicht, sie sind ausgefallene, das Zwerchfell zum Schüttern bringende Unholde der Lächerlichkeit, glitzernde, dem Leben nicht angehörige

Mönche der Ungereimtheit, kobolzende Zwitter aus Mensch und närrischer Kunst."[24] He decides that it is only for the man in the street that these performers must appear to be human: for those more perceptive such as himself, they belong to another realm. It does not take Felix long to get himself aligned with the performers and distinguished from the rest of the audience:

> Es war Hingebung, aber sie hatte — wie soll ich es sagen — etwas Aufsässiges, ich streifte den Rücken dabei, meine Seele — wie soll ich es nur sagen! — übte einen Gegendruck aus gegen die sie bestürmenden Eindrücke, es war — ich sage es nicht richtig, aber ungefähr richtig — bei aller Bewunderung etwas von Bosheit in ihrem eindringlichen Betrachten der Tricks, Künste, Wirkungen. Die Menge rings um mich her gor in Lust und Belustigung, — ich aber, gewissermaßen, schloß mich aus von ihrem Gären und Gieren, kühl wie einer, der sich vom "Bau", vom Fach fühlt. Nicht vom circensischen Fach, vom Salto mortale-Fach, natürlich, konnte ich mich fühlen, aber vom Fache im allgemeineren, vom Fach der Wirkung, der Menschenbeglückung und -bezauberung. Darüm rückte ich innerlich ab von den vielen, die nur das selbstvergessen genießende Opfer des Reizes waren, fern von dem Gedanken, sich mit ihm zu messen. Sie genossen nur, und Genuß ist ein leidender Zustand, in welchem niemand sich genügt, der sich zum Tätigen, zum Selber-Ausüben geboren fühlt.

Now Mann is surely up to more here than just a description of an evening at the circus. While Krull is being quite literal when he qualifies his belonging among the circus artistes — "nicht vom circensischen Fach, vom Salto mortale-Fach, natürlich" — the caveat is highly suggestive of precisely the kind of trapeze act that Krull is engaged in, and it puts the matter of his identification with the performer in the ring in sharp focus. There is hardly any mistaking the parallel associations here: they are distinctly more assumable than either the Müller-Rosé connection by virtue of the youth/age factor or the bullfight analogies by virtue of the North/South cultural differences. The awareness that the entire play before his

[24] Thomas Mann, *Bekenntnisse des Hochstaplers Felix Krull,* Frankfurt/Main, 1954, p. 149.

eyes is constituted of "Tricks, Künste, Wirkungen" for an audience that yearns to be bedazzled and served by such a performance, plus the conscious acceptance of the fact that he is *not* one of the onlookers but rather like in kind to the performers, is an unmistakable and forceful statement of Mann's intentions. He formulates Krull's kinship with the circus, moreover, specifically in terms of those performers on the trapeze — the ones engaged over and over again in the *salto mortale,* the high-wire act that rests on a constant relationship with death.

Mann is thus almost blatantly using the circus context, and the trapeze act in particular, as symbol. In every respect it effectively reflects the artistic dilemma he never tired of treating in his works. That he should choose the circus as vehicle for this purpose stems quite simply from the fact that it served him so well: nowhere could he find a better exponent of the artist's "Außenseiter" status than the circus performer who plays within the circle of the admiring audience, yet who is no more a part of that group than Mann's earlier gypsy in a green wagon. Krull enjoys a similar status, and no matter how brilliant his performance, can never belong to the society which gullibly allows him to play his game. Those who come to town periodically, who lead no settled existence, carry an aura of the illegitimate that borders on the illegality of the criminal — a quality both threatening and intriguing. Krull's adventuresomeness one step in front of the law gives him an élan vital with powerful powers of attraction. Almost invariably the circus artistes' performance is a daring one, and even if not on the high-wire, nevertheless a game of balance between skill and the forces of gravity, between illusion and reality. In their feats they articulate the inhuman in the face of the all-too-human, they are somehow, as Mann says, not to be considered "of this world." Neither is Krull. His provocativeness and his successes are truly "unbelievable," and he, like they, seems to operate according to special capacities not imparted to ordinary mortals. That the circus artistes take on the dimensions that Mann (Krull) prescribes, become such "unreal" figures, is a critical statement of the process whereby such performers — at least within the performance — lose their identity to become both more and less than their real selves. They are never really what they are in performance, just as Krull *is* not the Marquis de Venosta nor Hermes, nor any of the other roles he steals in order to dupe himself and the world as well. Both the circus artistes and Krull perform within a context of demand from the eager spectators who search for relief from reality in the form of play and entertainment, who want to let themselves be transfixed by the magic games of the arena magicians. Both the performers and Krull are able to satisfy their own drives to defy the reality of gravity and can as well legitimize their performance as a service to the social world. The circus has always been the epitome of an adult world on a child's terms, has more often than not been interpreted as a preserved realm of childlike fantasy in an all-too-burdened and responsible world of grown-up gravity. By extension then, the artistry on display in the ring becomes child's play, the artist in performance the game-participant/role-player par excellence. That the game as performed be a *salto mortale* gives the whole affair a negative charge yet propels the performer onward to further feats of daring. The end is as near as the aerialist's potential slip-up. In the circus, that reality rarely happens, but is always admitted as potential — it is, in truth, the factor that gives the act its edge. In *Felix Krull* it has already happened when the "Confessions" begin. Although the knowledge of that fall keeps the old Krull in a state of sleeplessness, the reality of the con game is subtly lost sight of within the sham of the format in the skillful hands of the manipulating author. The *Schein* all but overshadows the *Sein,* we almost forget the truth of the ground in our enchantment with the magic of the air. Andromache prevails — over us as she did over Felix. It is in every way perfectly logical that Krull at the circus is at the center of Mann's work: that represents the essence of Krull's — and Mann's — entire act. The deployment of the motif for such purposes is an exemplary instance of the literary transformation of material basically non-literary in nature. Mann was utterly adept at the process and his work is a grand construction built on piles of such material. One can be duly impressed here by the metamorphosis of a reality from the popular sphere into a symbolic configuration wrought by the most conscious literary manipulation.

Mann's own performance with Krull in that respect is no less impressive than the successes of his hero. His feat as writer can be seen as a high-wire balance act that took him across the accomplishments of his *Schriftstellertum* before the assembly of a world waiting for yet another feat by a seventy-nine-year-old author. He got to the other side once again without breaking his neck, and the applause brought him as much satisfaction as it had always done. "Der Zauberer" had done it again, and the audience reveled in its joy and excitement on watching this hero/confidence trickster who was a real artist. Hardly anyone noticed that the writer/performer/artist was a real confidence trickster.

Felix Krull the work posits provocative questions on the nature of the artist and suggests a number of revealing replies on the nature of Thomas Mann the writer . The central circus symbolism facilitates rather nicely the extensions suggested by Kuckuck's philosophy of *Dasein als Fest* to capsulize the nature of the game Mann was playing and having his Felix play. It had always been a two-pronged affair, a duality that in combination carried both the threat of neutralization and the promise of synthesis. Yet how those opposites attract was testimony of the challenge, and the only resolution was in the performance. There is surely a progression from Tonio Kröger to Felix Krull inasmuch as the latter, by virtue of his name, signifies a smiling German: the rules of the game had finally been recognized and Mann could now play to his heart's content. Andromache and her crew had taught him what he needed to know.

3. *Rainer Maria Rilke*

Rainer Maris Rilke's *Duineser Elegien* prevail as the profound poetry of an anguished soul adrift in the cosmic questions of the early twentieth century. Their elegaic substance is swathed in labyrinthine lines that seem to project them above the level of ordinary experience into the realm of transcendent encounter. Written over a span of some ten years and at various places — in Spain, in Paris, in Munich, and in Switzerland — the cycle of ten poems takes its name from the castle Duino near Trieste where Rilke had gone in October of 1911 to visit his friend the Princess Marie von Thurn und Taxis-Hohenlohe, and where he stayed alone after her departure until April of 1912. After publishing his *Neue Gedichte* in 1907 and 1908 and his novel *Malte Laurids Brigge* in 1910, Rilke was aware that he had still to fashion what could be justified as a major work, as if the earlier publications were somehow less than on the mark. A 1914 poem entitled "Wendung" expresses what the poet felt had yet to be accomplished:[75]

> Werk des Gesichts ist getan,
> tue nun Herz-Werk
> an den Bildern in dir, jenen gefangenen; denn du
> überwältigtest sie: aber nun kennst du sie nicht.

The essence of those internally-snagged images had not yet been expressed successfully, and Rilke spent the entire ensuing decade struggling to articulate what one of his many interpreters calls "some ultimate vision of human life and destiny."[26] Those pictures of which he had spoken, that "heartwork," did not come easily: while some of the poems gushed forth out of galvanizing insight, the work as a whole took shape only in slow and tormented contests with mood, surroundings, and language. The *Elegies* constitute the distilled testimony of a poet literally and figuratively ensconced in the tower, convinced that his wrestling match with the angel articulates an experience worthy of mankind's consideration.

Like much that Rilke wrote, these lyrical outpourings have been met with a kind of awe-filled reverence ever since he

[25] See introduction by J. B. Leishman in *Rainer Maria Rilke, Duino Elegies,* translation and commentary by J. B. Leishman and Stephen Spender, New York, 1963, p. 9.

[26] Leishman, *Elegies,* p. 9.

brought them to a close in 1922 and have remained for the most part too much an ultimate vision from unattainable heights for anyone but a Rilke devotee. Even in the hands of such disciples, Rilke has ended up in limbo somewhere between profundity and decadence, praised on the one hand as an unsurpassed poetic craftsman and on the other, accused of being everything from an aesthete withdrawn into the garden paradise of *Jugendstil* to a fascist with predilections that made him a harbinger of the Nazi terror. Doubtless between such extremes lies a more reliable assessment of the man and his work, though nowhere within the spectrum does he cease to be entirely unique. For all his dependence on others during his lifetime, he was very much his own poetic property and for the most part steered a course clear of movements and literary brotherhoods. To a significant degree he even steered clear of Germany, spending much of his time abroad, ultimately settling in Switzerland and ensuring a reputation not confined except by language to national boundaries. Rilke's indepedence is synonymous with his aloneness, and nothing is likely to dispel the notion that he and his poetry are an elitist aesthetic phenomenon.

At an early point in his career Rilke nonetheless did interact with the *Jugendstil* complex that was dominant for a while at the turn of the century. He was a friend of Heinrich Vogeler and part of the Worpswede colony. True, the principles stemming from that group's reflection of art nouveau ideas were not too out of line with the kind of aristocratic stance that Rilke was capable of assuming almost naturally. Reacting against what showed itself as a socially, economically, politically, and culturally bankrupt society, those who came to demonstrate the properties of *Jugendstil* did so in the dichotomous fashion of withdrawing into resignation, decadence, and intellectualism. while touting ideas and representations of energy, vitalism, and a rebirth of life forces.[27] Thus for all their rejection of manifest reality, the artists associated with

[27] See Karl E. Webb, *Rilke and Jugendstil,* Chapel Hill, 1978, p. 46.

the movement did envision a practical application of their theoretical principles. In this sense *Jugendstil* took a progressive step out into the realm of the everyday world, and the spillover into applied arts such a silversmithing, book illustration, furniture and room design reveals a genuine bond between art and reality that is otherwise conspicuously lacking. Rilke was capable of this kind of vision as well. We find him, for example, advocating the linear principle of *Jugendstil* with references to "the masses": "Die Wiedergewinnung der 'Linie' hat es auch mit sich gebracht, daß die graphischen Künste in vollstem Umfange gepflegt werden, und ihre Ausnützung für die Illustration und Ausschmückung der Bücher und zur Ausführung von Plakatanschlägen hat der Kunst einen neuen, breiten Weg zum Verständnis der Menge gewiesen."[28] We know of his sympathies with the peasant life of Worpswede and Russia, his strong identification with human simplicity (possibly at times with a simplistic view of human purity). We find him in Paris with Rodin, exercising considerable artistic acumen in explicating the sculptor's work for a public he hopes to convince. Later in his career, we can point to what Joachim W. Storck refers to as emancipatory aspects of Rilke's life and work,[29] among them Rilke's basic and ubiquitous premise that change is desirable, his enthusiastic support for new, quite revolutionary, pedagogical ideas (Ellen Key's *Das Jahrhundert des Kindes;* the theories of the Odenwald circle around Paul Geheeb), and a fairly far-sighted theory of a new sexuality that was a serious and insightful critique of the befuddled sexual ethics constricting the society of his day. While these attributes do not transform Rilke into what could be called a poet of the people, they do serve to negate some of the conceptions of him as conservative aesthete, plucking the harp strings of his private poetry. It is entirely possible to view Rilke as an intellectual with genuine and legitimate con-

[28] Rainer Maria Rilke, *Sämtliche Werke,* Frankfurt/Main, 1965, V, 323,

[29] Joachim W. Storck, "Emanzipatorische Aspekte im Werk und Leben Rilkes," in *Rilke Heute,* Ingeborg H. Solbrig and Joachim W. Storck, eds., Frankfurt/Main, 1975, pp. 247–286.

cerns based in the reality of his day. In view of the evidence, this seems to me the more reasonable approach and one, moreover, that makes Rilke a legitimate object of attention for this study. Such a mix of intellectual artistry and realistic interests brings into focus once again the long-standing separation between the spheres of art and life and sets Rilke up as a potential agent through whom the two come to bear upon each other in a rather exemplary way.

The case in point, illustrating how Rilke brings to reality a perspective that is highly intellectually charged while at the same time consciously grounding his poetry in an aspect of common reality, is the fifth of his *Duineser Elegien.* Inasmuch as this elegy's subject matter itself articulates the dialectic between art and reality, it both expresses and represents that dichotomy which Rilke was unable to let cut him in two. And by virtue of its keystone position within the cycle, it suggests that such a split, if it figures centrally in the matter of art, lies at the bottom of man's relationship to life itself.

The genesis of the poem is interesting. Not composed until 1922 (February 14) at the Chateau de Muzot, the fifth elegy was the last one to take shape. It was placed in its central position as number five in a conscious effort on the part of the poet to structure the entire cycle. The elegy came to Rilke in one gush, as it were, and signalled to him the completion of the entire work. In a letter to Lou Andreas-Salomé dated February 19, 1922, Rilke writes excitedly: "Ich hatte vor, Dir heute die anderen drei Elegien abzuschreiben, da es schon wieder Sonntag geworden ist! Aber nun ist, denk Dir, in einem strahlenden Nachtsturm, noch eine Elegie dazugekommen, die der 'Saltimbanques.' Das ist aufs wunderbarste ergänzend, nun erst scheint mir der Elegienkreis wirklich geschlossen. Sie kommt nicht als Elfte hinzu, sondern wird (als Fünfte) eingefügt, vor der 'Helden-Elegie.' Das bisher dort stehende Stück schien mir ohnehin durch die andere Art seines Aufbaus, an jenem Platz nicht berechtigt, obwohl als Gedicht schön."[30] After proposing what he will do with the

30 Rainer Maria Rilke, *Briefe,* Wiesbaden, 1950, p. 749–50.

original fifth elegy, he summarizes: "Und so sind also auch die 'Saltimbanques' da, die mich eigentlich schon seit der allerersten Pariser Zeit so unbedingt angingen und mir immer seither aufgegeben waren."

When Rilke completed this last elegy he claimed a feeling of satisfaction and felt his "real work" to be finished. The elegies may be considered in many ways the product of that earlier-mentioned "ultimate vision of human life," and the poet's struggle to squeeze them into being appropriate to their status as such. According to Leishman, Rilke declared in 1919 that as an intellectual in the postwar world his task would be "to prepare in men's hearts the way for those gentle, mysterious, trembling transformations, from which alone the understandings and harmonies of a serener future will proceed."[31] Even as early as 1912 Rilke appears to have understood his task as such, and it was that weighty a purpose that must have enabled him to bear the process of the *Elegies* for so long. His problem in their creation stemmed from his fervent search to find coordinates in reality which would express and stand for what he perceived in those electric moments of poetic insight into the transcendent world of universal truths.[32] It is in the realm of this almost private expression, of profound, poetic formulation — externalization — that the reader also experiences the problem of understanding. In Rilke's landscape it is a matter of our approaching and approximating the poet's own perception of things, some of which are distinctly not anchored in the familiar, but rather which shift about, coming into and going out of focus as the poet weaves his tapestries of impressions. Posterity's difficulties with the *Elegies* seem to have been almost as great as Rilke's in composing them. Yet it is through the recognition that the ambiguity inherent to them is precisely the result of the poet's having been brought to the verge of inarticulateness that we can appreciate the breakthrough—however excrutiating the trauma had been —

[31] Leishman, *Elegies,* p. 14.

[32] Leishman (p. 15) speaks of "symbolic ... 'external' equivalents for experiences that were becoming ever more 'inward' and incommunicable. ..."

as a gift of what may rightfully be termed some of the German language's mightiest lyrics.

According to the letter to Lou Andreas-Salomé quoted earlier, the original impetus was an earlier episode dating from Rilke's stay in Paris — not as actual, direct experience pushing him to the composition, but rather an event in his past on which he drew and which seems to have been stored for potential use. A letter of July 14, 1907,[33] relates the situation that had left an indelible mark on the poet's mind:

> Ich war eben im Luxembourg: davor, nach dem Pantheon zu, hat Père Rollin mit den Seinen sich ausgebreitet, derselbe Teppich liegt da, dieselben abgelegten Mäntel, dicke Wintermäntel, sind über einen Stuhl gehäuft, auf dem gerade noch soviel Platz bleibt, daß der kleine Sohn, der Enkel des Alten, mit seinem ernsten großen Gesicht ein klein wenig hinsetzen kann (eben soviel als nötig ist, daß es ein Sitzen wird) zwischen der Arbeit. Das ist alles, wie vor einem Jahr. Aber Père Rollin, der die schweren Gewichte schwenkte, 'arbeitet' nicht mehr und sagt kein Wort, Er ist aufs Trommeln gesetzt. Rührend geduldig steht er da, mit seiner Kraft, die nicht mehr recht zu brauchen ist, obwohl sie für das Trommeln noch ein bißchen zu groß ist. Er trommelt viel zu oft, dann pfeift ihm sein Schwiegersohn, und er hört auf, erschrocken, und entschuldigt sich mit einer Bewegung seiner schweren Schultern und tritt umständlich auf das andere Bein. Aber im nächsten Augenblick muß er wieder aufgepfiffen werden, der Alte: er trommelt schon wieder. Er weiß es kaum. Er könnte immerzu trommeln; sie sollen nur nicht meinen, daß er müde würde. Aber es ist nicht sein Schwiegersohn, der jetzt die Hauptsache macht, zwar er arbeitet gut, da ist nichts zu sagen, und gerne, so wie er sein muß, Aber die alles in der Hand hat, und *wie,* das ist seine Tochter, natürlich, das macht das Blut, Die Gewichte sind verkauft worden, die sind nicht mehr Mode und die Kinder gehen mit der Zeit. Aber sie haben sich prachtvolle Sachen ausgedacht: der Alte hat seine Freude. Und wie sie spricht, seine Tochter, so schlagfertig und handfest, fast wie er selbst, der alte Père Rollin, dem keiner nachkam, im Witz nicht und nicht in der Arbeit. Unter den Zuschauern waren welche, die ihn kannten: Hé, Père Rollin! Aber er nicht nur nebenbei; das Trommeln ist eine große Sache und er nimmt es ernst.

[33] Letter quoted in Jacob Steiner, *Rilkes Duineser Elegien,* Bern and Munich, 1962, p. 102.

These very real acrobats who at the time presented their shows over and over again to the Parisian crowds gathered to celebrate various occasions (as here, the 14th of July) had intrigued Rilke for some time. His sympathies in this instance seem particularly directed to the old man who had been forced to retire to the sidelines to play the drums and whose questionable existence gives Rilke reason to consider the rather tenuous life of the entire troupe and its kind of people.[34] That memory of 1907 lay dormant until a number of years later when a second impetus for the elegy made itself felt. The elegy bears a dedication to Frau Hertha Koenig, and it was she who brought Rilke into a fruitful union with the 1905 painting by Picasso *Les Saltimbanques*. She had purchased the picture from the Caspari Gallery in December of 1914, and Rilke was excited enough to telegraph her his congratulations. He had known the picture before that point, but subsequently (June 1915) asked Frau Koenig if he might not stay in her home together with the "great" Picasso so that, as he put it, he might find the inspiration which for months had failed to come to him. He then lived in her home in Munich for some five months (June-October 1915) "mit dem schönsten Picasso.“ It was however, not until 1922 that the two stimuli came together in that moment when Rilke "found" the final elegy and completed his cry to the angels.

[34] In the 1907 letter Rilke mentions that the performance was just like it had been a year previous, except for the changes he now notes in Père Rollin. According to Roland Penrose (*Picasso, his Life and Work*, New York, 1962), Picasso's circus orientation was largely connected with Cirque Medrano artistes in Montmartre, but this certainly does not exclude the Rollin troupe, no matter where Rilke saw it in performance. According to Penrose's description of *Les Saltimbanques,* "the elderly jester with a great paunch swelling his red tights who seems to be the father of the troupe or its 'understander,' has an extensive background of antecedents. Usually dressed in red and seated on a block, he has as a companion a slender youth. He is first cousin to the sybaritic Herod of the etching *Salome,* and wears the same mock crown as the bronze head of a jester modelled about the same time. He also reappears as the gargantuan king of a book-plate drawn for Apollinaire." (p. 110)

The question arises, of course, as to the degree to which both (or either) of these external stimuli were incorporated, either purely or transformed, into the elegy. It seems on the one hand rather remarkable how closely the letter account of 1907 fits the Picasso picture of 1905, and one can theorize whether Rilke knew the painting before viewing (and interpreting) the Père Rollin performance, or whether the same troupe of performers might not be the common subject of Picasso's work and Rilke's sympathies? Regardless of how similar these are to each other, however, it seems all but obvious that neither is the exact subject of the elegy. Although within the poem Rilke distinguishes the characters, addresses them, and would seem to be reading into the painting his own interpretations very much as in the account of Rollin, at some point in the associative process the elegy moves beyond the surface of both the picture and the performance to a depth of subjective analysis and lyrical empathy that cannot be tied to any original material. Such material acts only as catalytic agent which after a long dormancy gives issue to poetic originality. The experiences of the performance and the picture become themselves an experience, and the elegy assumes the independent essence with which we must deal and relate to the cycle as a whole.

It is possibly of questionable value to attempt to reduce the essence of this Fifth Elegy to any one specific concern on the part of the poet. Yet if some of its ideas may be considered more weighty than others, the one that seems to be of prime importance to Rilke centers around the idea of genuineness/validity/truth as these qualities apply to Being — that uniquely transcendent state which seems so difficult to express and which Rilke spends so much of his time in the elegies trying to articulate. In the very first line of the First Elegy Rilke establishes a separation between his (man's) own realm

[35] Letter to Frau Hertha Koenig, dated June 1915. Rainer Maria Rilke, *Briefe aus den Jahren 1914 bis 1921,* Leipzig, 1937, p. 47. Also letter of June 28, 1915, to Thankmar Freiherrn von Münchhausen, p. 50.

and that of the "angels," and it is that division and dichotomy that occupies Rilke throughout all ten elegies.[36] In man's attempts to realize the state of the angels he must be attentive to all and everything around him, yet seemingly he is foiled constantly in this effort by false but attractive claims on him. These falsities all revolve in some manner of thinking around an apparent completion, satisfaction, answer, solution, perfection, end, cessation, ad infinitum — all, that is, which in its completeness is positive but in its finality and consumateness is negative. That is the larger framework.

Specifically, the Fifth begins with an initial inquiry into who *les saltimbanques* are and a questioning of their total surrender to what appears as an unexplained yet preordained force. Rilke qualifies their nature as "sham-fruit" and "superficiality." Leaving that thought momentarily to move to a description of some of the troupe's individuals, Rilke returns to a symptomatic smile that covers up much of a pathos-filled essence underneath. Not to belittle that smile, however, for he realizes its effect on those for whom it is projected, be it because, or in spite, of the fact that it is one of "those not yet to us revealed joys." But then subsequently, in direct focus on one of the individuals, Rilke comes to the pervasive issue of these acrobats as "specimens of equanimity." Then after lamenting that status, he poses the idealized context where such is not the case. That state is precisely in terms opposite to the acrobats' one of deceit — false smile, dulling equanimity, sterile ability, and practiced perfection. The total picture of all this he then expresses in terms of life absurdly in the hands of death, wishing finally for its contrast — the more

[36] Leishman defines the angels of Rilke as "the hypostatisation of the idea of a perfect consciousness — of a being in whom the limitations and contradictions of present human nature had been transcended, a being in whom thought and action, insight and achievement, will and capability, the actual and the ideal, are one." (p. 88) As source of inspiration as well as constant reminder of man's shortcomings they are the very real bane of Rilke's existence, the source and object of his outcry. It is the greater consciousness which the angels are able to achieve that he praises and laments at the same time throughout.

genuine, the still-to-be-realized subjectivity of potentiality where *die Liebenden* perform in a more valid, truthful state of Being not yet realized. Here again are the two separate and contrasting spheres, juxtaposed in such a way that the Fifth Elegy can legitimately be seen as central to the complete cycle.

In this definitive elegy Rilke suggests that the acrobats in their practiced perfection, in a show which is so often repeated as to become rote but which attempts each time to produce a degree of spontaneity, offer a performance which demonstrates their accomplishment in such a manner that it appears each time as a unique completion of some potential. Yet they are characterized by the sham-fruit smile and are nothing of the sort. Their achievement of the ultimate perfection is dead, valueless, bored, invalid. Once their striving for the feat has been accomplished, what is left is hollow, void, "ein leeres Zuviel". And they as troupe are then no more than man himself, condemned to this sort of futility by an unknown force to which they (man) have given themselves over by virtue of their (his) very nature. We are all the clay, material, requisites of Madame Lamort as she makes the sham, cheap, winter hats of fate. And even if the opposite were possible, would the spectators — the participants — recognize it, appreciate it? Pessimistically, Rilke seems rhetorically to ask and answer in the negative: certainly not here in this life or on this mortal earth.

In the opening lines of the Tenth Elegy Rilke proclaims the bliss he will feel when he can fully appreciate the pain he has been suffering. The lines are early, written while Rilke was at Duino, and as such are unsuspecting of the pain and anguish he was indeed to go through. But that suffering and pain is the final aspect of this world that Rilke wishes to articulate. In that suffering is contained the most significant element of affirmation of this world. Beyond the marketplace and outside the City of Pain he savors the Land of Sorrow where pain brings insight and negativity transcends itself in a validity otherwise unknown. Then, at the close of the elegy (and the entire cycle) a formulation of the lesson to be learned is offered once again: we the living, who up to now have always contemplated happiness as something positive, rising, and ascending, now feel and appreciate, almost in a state of shock, the happiness implicit in falling and descending so that the negativity imparted by us unknowingly to sorrow and pain and suffering becomes something positive when we achieve that state of knowledge and consciousness that Rilke has been struggling to express throughout.

That ending on the highest note of praise and affirmation as well as of pain and suffering and death appears as Rilke's final say on the matter of the unity and oneness of life and death, being and becoming, striving and accomplishment. Yet it should not be forgotten that this final insight led him to write the elegy on *Les Saltimbanques,* i. e., that the Fifth is as well an extension of the Tenth. If one knows Walter Benjamin's 1936 essay "Das Kunstwerk im Zeitalter seiner technischen Reproduzierbarkeit," one is tempted to believe, despite the far-fetched nature of any kind of parallel, that the poet and the critic had their respective fingers on virtually the same issue. Benjamin's perception of the changes the work of art undergoes against the backdrop of technical facilities that reduce the authenticity of the original and destroy its "aura" is in essence an elaboration of the same insight that Rilke attempts to distill out of his contemplation of *Les Saltimbanques.* Almost imperceptibly we have been brought to the point in time in which the art of these acrobats has become a performance routine, i. e., a repeatable, standardized, reproduction of a model sequence of actions or feats, a forged "act" displayed before a "rose"[37] of indiscriminate onlookers who come and go and watch, but who never really perceive

[37] One of a number of important symbols for Rilke. According to Frank Wood in his *Rainer Maria Rilke: The Ring of Forms* (New York, 1970), it "occurs at every stage in his career with ever increasing complexity until it comes to rest in the epitaph in the churchyard at Raron as 'the rose of pure contradiction/Desire/To be nobody's slumber/Under so many eyelids.'" (p. 37) In this particular instance, Rilke would seem to be harking back to an image similar to that in "Die Rosenschale" (1907) where he draws on a kind of cosmic symbolism in the open, bowl-like chalice

what it is they are seeing. Rilke's lament revolves around that performance of inauthenticity, and one cannot but acknowledge that Rilke saw these circus acrobats in predominantly negative terms, both their lives, servile to a constricting, all-powerful will, more fugitive than even we ourselves, and their art, ingenuous manifestation of something, their accomplishment no more than the very mortal, transitory substance of cheap entertainment. By 1922 Rilke is attuned, if only in indirect and less analytical fashion than Benjamin, to the status of art in an age exhibiting the scars of progress. Such scars were to be perceived in the changes noticeable (already 1905) in Père Rollin's troupe which itself was shifting its emphasis and playing consciously to the crowds under the direction of the more "modern" directress. Not that such a troupe's performance had not always been directed to the spectator, but not to quite the same degree. The circus performance per se had begun as a self-contained feat, the unique demonstration by an artiste anxious to display extraordinary skills. Doubtless the reaction and confirmation by a public as critic worked from the very beginning to transform the nature of the spectacle into one for the benefit and purpose of the spectators instead of the performer, and by the time Paris was treated to the likes of Père Rollin and his progeny the effects had moved fairly noticeably into the realm of the ingenuine. The gradual deterioration in the act of performance that bothers Rilke is not unrelated to Benjamin's deprecation of the falsity propagated by the technical advances of the film, that aesthetic culprit with its mechanical reproduction of reality in edited sequences. The poet was making an issue of the identical phenomenon that the critic would articulate somewhat later. Significantly enough, it was precisely the development of cinematic technology that served to deflect the public's interest from the circus and related popular entertainment forms toward the innovative and ultimately inexhaustible, though less immediate, mechanization of the film.

shape of the rose petals. The "rose" of onlookers here is only a passing reference, but a metaphor pregnant with connotations within Rilke's framework of images.

One cannot lose sight of the fact, however, that the sequence of Rilke's thought processes has led him from the Land of Sorrow back to the acrobat's performance — back to them as representatives of what he had been talking about in the final elegy. Thus while the Fifth took place in the cycle definitely on the lamentation side of the division first made apparent in the Seventh Elegy's glorification of existence, there was always the very positive aspect of the acrobats' smile which Rilke wanted preserved and which he praised in gentle, loving, positive terms. Thus in spite of all that they are *not,* Rilke could and did envision them as the epitome of a sad and suffering kind of human state: in the terms of the Tenth, he makes them into the toys of a "young sorrow," choosing them to represent, if in no other way than by that sham smile of equanimity still remarkably "as yet to us unrevealed," the transformation out of the negative into the positive, the glorious gift of angelic essence manifest through them to us and to our world. These acrobats of Rilke's own experiential background and Picasso's painting thus undergo perhaps the most radical transformation of any of their colleagues from that world on the fringe. Moving from their worn-out tarp spread on the very ground of some Parisian *Vorstadt,* they find themselves transported to a keystone position among elegies resting squarely on the pinnacle of lyric accomplishment.

4. *Georg Heym*

Shortly before his twenty-fourth birthday in 1911 the young German poet Georg Heym suggested that his poetic work could be viewed as "der beste Beweis eines metaphysischen Landes ... das seine schwarzen Halbinseln weit herein in unsere flüchtigen Tage streckt."[38] While such self-judgment seems a little presumptuous, it is nonetheless a fairly astute

[38] Diary entry, September 15, 1911. Georg Heym, *Dichtungen und Schriften,* III, Karl Ludwig Schneider ed., Hamburg, 1960, p. 164.

assessment by an author who was well aware of his leanings toward the ugly and the negative and who was cognizant of a recently acquired maturity in attacking the established order of a superficially beautiful world. Heym's grounding on those dark peninsulas projected him almost from the start beyond his own era, and more than a few critics have been willing to see him as harbinger of the evils not yet fully visited upon early twentieth century society. Others have proposed that he was a perfect reflection of his time, that his was a typical example of the psychology of upper-middle class youth in Wilhelmian Germany and his case uniquely valuable for an understanding of the "interrelationship of the Wilhelmian spirit, the individual personality, and the creative work."[39]

Whatever camp one wishes to follow, one cannot get around the fact that the thematic foci of Heym's mature work mark him as a poet who intended to go against the established grain as stridently as possible, who meant to swim against the aesthetic and cultural current out of total disdain and not a little spite. There were few aspects of the human condition which Heym did not subject to a process of "deidealization" and "debourgeoisification." In Kurt Pinthus' analysis: "Schreckende Visionen und Träume und das zerrütende Bewußtsein, als tragische Gestalt in einer Zeit zu stehen, die ihn selbst und die mit ihm lebende Menschheit zerrütten mußte, peitschte ihn unablässig, pausenlos auf, seine Phantasien, Ahnungen, verwüsteten Landschaften ... in lauttönenden Strophen Gestalt werden zu lassen."[40] Heym's pessimism and his negativity are well-documented, as well as his deliberate attention to those figures and forms which lay on the borders of society — the demented, the blind, the enslaved, and the dumb — those from the fringes whose lurking shadows had been ignored and denied by a society dedicated

[39] Egbert Krispyn, *Georg Heym: A reluctant rebel,* Gainsville, 1968, p. 42.

[40] Kurt Pinthus, "Georg Heym: Zu seinem zehnten Todestag," in *Georg Heym, Dichtungen und Schriften,* VI, Karl Ludwig Schneider and Gerhard Burckhardt, eds., 1968, p. 149.

to Light, Progress, and a blindfolded Justice.[41] As thematic vortices, these fringe elements pull Heym's poetic work into distinct and almost monotonous patterns and create what can rightly be called an aesthetic of marginality. In his own social and aesthetic idiom it was an effort to wake up an age and an art that was either dying or was already dead.

His long poem "Die Vorstadt" may be taken as an example: it is supposedly the first clear statement of his preoccupation with the dregs of society and dates from September 1910. Here he draws a bleak portrait of abject existence in the burgeoning cities of the early years of the century. Heym's sweeping photographic eye looks through no colored glasses. His glance pauses only long enough to describe the perversions of the urban existence. Although not softened by ameliorating lenses, the description nevertheless seems distorted by a fish-eye perspective: the moon is a skull looking down on an underworld of ugliness where toothless beggars, amputees, idiots, and blind men suffer their daily insults. Crippled children hop about like fleas, and infants cry insatiably after non-existent milk. A lame man dances with tied-together shoes to the music of an organ grinder who is blind, and the local pub wakes to the morning light with the lifeless bodies of sleeping drunkards left over from the revels of the night before. A dwarf in grotesquely inappropriate costume displays his outsider status before an uninterested and unresponsive heaven. It is not a pretty picture and in its Baudelairean intensity is not intended to entertain. These afflicted ones are drawn to our attention by a poet who seeks to force a confrontation with the seamy side of life and whose negative statement of what society has become is juxtaposed in the final lines to the fact that above all this is an unacknowledging firmament marked by meteors cruising mutely in their predetermined paths.

[41] See for example: Gunter Martens, *Vitalismus und Expressionismus,* Stuttgart, 1971; Erwin Loewenson, *Georg Heym oder vom Geist des Schicksals,* Hamburg and Munich, 1962; *Georg Heym: Das lyrische Werk,* Karl Ludwig Schneider, ed., Munich, 1977.

Such negative statements articulate Heym's pessimism throughout his work, with an ever-increasing shift from personal dilemma to universal significance as he moves from juvenile youth to young maturity. The idiom of his mature work becomes a complex relationship between a deanimated humanity and a demonized nature, a depiction of alienation most acutely circumscribed within the metropolitan parameters that were delineating life with increasing intensity. There is a severity in Heym's work which seems almost vindictive and which denies the gentleness that his French models were still capable of. What Rimbaud saw as transformed, Heym views as mutilated.

Now within this kind of negative framework – society's dregs as subject matter, the urban ghetto as locale, and as stated earlier, a deanimated humanity at odds with a demonic nature as theme – are three poems that take their cue from the *Jahrmarkt* and the circus. Such subject matter might appear ill-placed within the framework described inasmuch as those forms of popular entertainment have rarely been conceived as negative symbols. One could argue, of course, that such poems and the topic itself rightly belong within such confines – given the traditional outsider status of circus/fair performers who have always been relegated to the other side of the tracks. Both Thomas Mann and Kafka, for example, were seen to draw attention to the negative associations that could be ascribed to those who belonged either in "green wagons" or on the backs of "dapple-gray horses." Yet despite that kind of status for the artistes themselves, the circus and *Jahrmarkt* traditionally have been viewed more from a utopian than from a realist perspective. Even in instances in which these popular forms were proposed as a threat to bourgeois society (e.g., Carl and Gerhard Hauptmann) the pull was clearly in the direction of freedom and release from the strictures of a repressive social code. Particularly within the German framework the circus had enjoyed for a number of decades a consistently positive reputation, and in the period prior to Heym's 1910–1912 social commentary had reached a zenith in its development. Yet in these poems Heym unmistakably sees it in a different light. The circus and the *Jahrmarkt* serve him on the one hand as a metaphor for that deanimated humanity and dehumanized society with which he wanted to force a confrontation. On the other, his negative treatment of them can be viewed as a poetosociological statement in witness of the fact that as popular entertainment forms they were being eased from an earlier, idealized "dreamworld" status — reflecting an élan vital that was a left-over from la belle époque — into a less glamorous sphere that signalled a dissolution in the quality and character of modern life. If in his pervasively non-idealistic Weltanschauung critics have been able to find an anticipation of our atomic age, in his treatment of these related forms Heym anticipates changes that were only later perceptible in the post-WWI decline of such forms in favor of the film and the general shift from entertainment that was vital performance and living spectacle to more passive forms that were flat and framed and nonparticipatory.

The poems were not published in *Der ewige Tag,* the single volume of poetry which appeared during Heym's brief lifetime, but are among those registered in his *Nachlaß*. The earliest dates from April 1910 and reads:

Wo eben rauschten noch die Karusselle
In weißem Licht zum Lärme der Musik,
Die Wolke Dampfs beglänzt ins Dunkel stieg,
Und hoch sich schwang des Riesenrades Welle,

Wo zwischen Buden sich die Leute schoben,
Wo heisere Rufer schrien, und klang Geläut,
Und wo die Birken, wie von Schnee bestreut,
In weitem Kranze um den Platz sich hoben,

Da ward es stille nun mit einem Male,
Des Mondes rote Sichel schwamm im Schoß
Der tiefen Nacht. Die Birken wuchsen groß,
Steinbildern gleich in altem Marmorsaale.[42]

42 *Georg Heym,* Ausgewählt von Karl Ludwig Schneider and Gunter Martens, Munich, 1971, pp. 54–55.

Here the *Jahrmarkt* context is described within an extremely regular (5 ft. iambic) abba rhyme pattern to form a "still life" that is in contrast to the earlier liveliness referred to in the first two stanzas. The entire description is in the past tense, the cessation of previous action underscored by each past-tense verb until the final stanza transforms the halted movement into engravings in stone. The poet's eye freezes in a single photographic frame, the poem becomes a description of the optical details involved. Two spheres are placed in apposition: the carousel-related details are set within the drawn context against the silence of the surrounding landscape, the birches drawing a containing circle around the noisy life which had moved around the carousel. The aspects enumerated in the first half of the poem exactly to the midpoint — the merry-go-round turning in the brightness of a white (artificial?) light to the noise of the music, the clouds of steam from the calliope rising with a shimmer into the heights, and the fun-seekers noisily moving among the booths and the hoarsened cried of the barkers — are contrasted to the counterforce of the silent birches. The second half paratactically describes the moon as scythe floating in the womb of night, the birches in exaggerated growth surrounding the whole with a static permanency. The sudden cessation indicated in line nine stops the poem with the finality of a period and the summary statement confirms the silence of a now-frozen frame. In more than one respect the poem is a good example of Heym's tendency to articulate his poetic statement in purely visual terms. Yet it is more the subtleties of the subject matter that signal it as noteworthy and draw us to the poem: the blaring noises that shape the *Jahrmarkt* context emerge as part and parcel of Heym's view of a dehumanized mass culture, and the midway confusion appears here as the thrust of that cultural milieu against the *Steinbilder* of a nature that looks on unmoved and unfeelingly. Such a culture, in all its hoarsened noisiness, fails to impress the natural order of things. Nature is the same nature depicted in "Die Vorstadt," that unacknowledging firmament mutely ignoring the tumult of modern life below. The rude and brightly superficial world of the circus/fair has effectively been silenced "nun mit einem Male."

The carousel image recurs the following year in a poem entitled "Fröhlichkeit" (September/October 1911):

Es rauscht und saust von großen Karussellen
Wie Sonnen flammend in den Nachmittagen.
Und tausend Leute sehen mit Behagen,
Wie sich Kamele drehn und Rosse schnelle,

Die weißen Schwäne und die Elefanten,
Und einer hebt vor Freude schon das Bein
Und grunzt im schwarzen Bauche wie ein Schwein,
Und alle Tiere fangen an zu tanzen.

Doch nebenan, im Himmelslicht, dem hellen,
Gehen die Maurer rund, wie Läuse klein,
Hoch ums Gerüst, ein feuriger Verein,
Und schlagen Takt mit ihren Mauerkellen.[43]

The editor of Heym's works, Karl Ludwig Schneider, suggests a possible relationship with Rilke's well-known poem "Das Karussell" (June 1906), though it is questionable whether Heym in 1911 would have been interested in imitating Rilke. He had by then outgrown copying others. The moods in the two poems are dissimilar and the poetic formulation better shaped by Rilke: Rilke's control of form (the rhythmic, repeated refrain) is unmistakable and shows up Heym's rather sloppy metre and anomalous fourth line. Rilke's elegaic treatment unquestionably results in a more refined product. Yet it is not farfetched to suggest that Heym's is the more honest and acute formulation. The difference doubtless lies in what Erich Mühsam proposed as the essential vitality in Heym's poetry: "Er schrieb seine Gedichte, weil er ein Dichter war, nicht weil er die Absicht hatte, Gedichte zu machen."[45] Common to both poems, however, is the implication that the mer-

[43] Georg Heym, *Dichtungen und Schriften,* I, Karl Ludwig Schneider, ed., Munich, 1964, p. 389.

[44] See his afterword to the dtv edition of Heym's poetry, *Georg Heym: Das lyrische Werk,* Munich, 1977, p. 389.

[45] *Dichtungen und Schriften,* VI, 111.

ry-go-round is less than merry, an eternal circling in a hollow and pointless charade, and it is doubtful that Heym needed Rilke to suggest that to him.

The Heym poem devotes the first two stanzas to the carousel's lively turnings, though the proceedings appear somehow passive, the crowd observing rather than participating. The various participants of this wooden menagerie come to life in stanza two and the circular dance is set in motion. But then — the contradiction: The final stanza moves offsides into the bright light of reality to break the mood with a group of masons whose busy movements cause Heym to see them as a "hot" group of little lice keeping time with their trowels. The shift in focus in the three stanzas brings into question the relationship between the world of the carousel and that of the workers and the public. In the first stanza the crowd looks on dispassionately — "mit Behagen" — at the waltz of the animals circling in a separate fantasy world. "Behagen" is a well-chosen term, descriptive of class sensibilities that were beginning to find purpose in the ability to enjoy withous having to be involved. It is not synonymous with *Fröhlichkeit* and casts an ironic shadow on the poem as titled. This observing, nonparticipating crowd is as disconnected from the dance as are the frenetic masons who on their scaffolding high above keep time to the music but never go on the ride. As for them, we cannot fail to note that the animal sequence has gone from bad to worse — from swans, to elephants, to pigs, and finally, to lice — so that by the time the poet focuses on them in stanza III their status has been effectively negativized. The masons' participation in this scene is certainly qualified: their place is in the scaffolding of a society that was just launching a building boom and whose expansiveness and technolozation is aptly symbolized by the construction image. They are clearly means to an end and will be dispensed with when their work is done. Their enjoyment of the ride is only indirect, though their unison rhythm makes them as wooden as the fake performers on the carousel itself. In the mass audience (stanza I) Heym subtly suggests the effects of an increasingly modernized and technologized society: dulled senses and the inability to participate beyond the satisfaction of comfortable passivity. In the carousel itself (stanza II) the balm of a fantasy world has been cancelled, an inanimate animality reduced to machinated figures turning in circles of regular and regulated thythms. And ultimately (stanza III), with hardly a missed beat, the masons are transformed into automatons in a separate dance who appear to move in concert but whose participation is only by means of their tools. In the first poem Heym brought the carousel to a standstill and suggested that it was the symbol of an invalid world to begin with. In the second one he starts it up and intimates that as the mechanized turnings of a wooden existence it produces either a kind of invalid passivity or an equally delusive synchronization that belies the reality. In both cases the effect of the poem is heightened by a negativity that cancels any anticipated positive symbolic value.

There exists a variant version of this poem in a short memorial piece on Heym written by Erich Mühsam. It is the version Mühsam reports receiving in a letter from Heym's friend Robert Jentzsch, who wrote to Mühsam on the 3d of February 1912, telling of Heym's death on January 16. This particular poem (and possibly others) was apparently enclosed as representative of Heym's later work not previously published. Jentzsch proposes: "Bei der — hoffentlich bald erfolgenden — Herausgabe des Nachlasses wird sich zeigen, wie er so die starre Grausigkeit, die an seinen älteren Versen Fremde erschreckte und auch wohl abstieß, in klingende Farbigkeit auflöste." It is impossible to determine whether the version sent by Jentzsch pre- or post dates the version published in the still incomplete edition of Heym's works. Nonetheless, the few changes made are revealing. In the first stanza of the Jentzsch version, Heym speaks of "manchen Karussellen" instead of "großen Karussellen", of "viele Leute" instead of "tausend Leute". Neither change is overwhelming, but both reveal the poet's concern with the matter of size and quantity. The changes in stanze II have primarily to do with the nature

[46] Ibid., p. 110–11.

of the animals of the carousel: the difference between "starre" and "weiße" swans, between a "schwarzer" belly and a "hohler" belly reinforces the idea stated earlier that Heym perceived the merry-go-round itself as a hollow sham. In stanza III, the changes relate to the workers — in one instance their movements are described, in the other, Heym qualifies them — negatively as we might expect. The last word in the Jentzsch version places the emphasis on them as workers, not on their tools. In all, the changes — whether or not we know their sequence, i. e., *from* what *to* what — make the triple focus of Heym's concerns apparent and confirm the idea that the poem is more than descriptive play. Mühsam read it and would have agreed. He wrote: "Man kann sagen: ein schlechtes Gedicht, ein nachlässiges Gedicht, ein schluderiges Gedicht, — aber nie kann man sagen: ein belangloses Gedicht."[47]

A third poem "Die Seiltänzer" is clearly derived from the circus and is consistent in mood and intent with the two carousel pictures. Four stanzas in impure sonnet form describe the high-wire artistes' performance before a gawking, though essentially unappreciative, audience:

> Sie gehen über den gespannten Seilen
> Und schwanken manchmal fast, als wenn sie fallen.
> Und ihre Hände schweben über allen
> Die flatternd in dem leeren Raum verweilen.
>
> Das Haus ist übervoll von tausend Köpfen,
> Die wachsen aus den Gurgeln steil, und starren
> Wo oben hoch die dünnen Seile knarren.
> Und Stille hört man langsam tröpfeln.
>
> Die Tänzer aber gleiten hin geschwinde
> Wie weiße Vögel, die die Wandrer narren
> Und oben hoch im leeren Baume springen.

[47] Ibid., p. 111. A second variant can be found in *Umbra vitae,* the posthumously published volume of poems from Heym's *Nachlaß* (Leipzig, 1912). This version incorporates some of the changes outlined above and exhibits some deviations in punctuation. To elaborate on these, however, adds little to the discussion.

Wesenlos, seltsam, wie sie sich verrenken
Und ihre großen Drachenschirme schwingen,
Und dünner Beifall klappert auf den Bänken.[48]

The first stanza places the tightrope walkers dangerously high above the audience. The empty space above and between the performers and the spectators in line four is countered in the next line in the description of the house as "übervoll von tausend Köpfen". The careful reader is tempted to relate this crowd to the previous poem. The tightrope walkers perform almost effortlessly in the first terzett and are likened to white birds that come to rest in empty trees. In the second terzett the poet reflects on these beings before closing the performance and the poem with thin applause from the audience. The poem deftly separates the spheres of the performers from that of the stolid spectators, the alternation between the airy, empty heights on the thin tightrope and the crowded, packed terra firma occupied by the thousands down below keeps the eye of the reader moving back and forth. The brief shift in rhythmical pattern from iambic to dactylic in line twelve momentarily enforces the distinctions and places the desired emphasis on the fact that those on the wire are "wesenlos" and "seltsam". The final lines are an anticlimax, and the point of it all seems to escape the spectators, unimpressed as they appear to be. For the reader acquainted with the two previous poems, however, the point is not obscure: whatever fascination it may once have held, the high-wire act of these circus artistes is now performed before an insensitive and ununderstanding audience. The performers almost irritate more than they please or thrill, and the lifeless and strange nature of the performers is indicative of how little relevance they have for those in the galleries. What formerly was considered the daring spectacle that no one could resist has been reduced to an empty exercise that fails to move the crowds to more than listless applause.

One may question whether the young Heym was sensitive to the positive potential of the circus/ *Jahrmarkt* world in the

[48] *Georg Heym,* Ausgewählt von Karl Ludwig Schneider and Gunter Martens, Munich, 1971, p. 108.

scheme of bourgeois society, to its function, as Ernst Bloch was to analyze it, as a kind of "kindliche, uralte medizinische, kriminelle, exotische Rauschwelt," i. e., as a form of entertainment preserving in an almost grotesque way facets of life longed-for in the subconscious of society: "Sein wollen ... das fehlende Leben ... buntes Glück."[49] For Heym. there was virtually nothing in his time to warrant a sense of happiness, certainly not in the traditionally merry (go-round) world of acrobats, clowns, and fairground joviality. His melancholy and a sense of resignation prevail: both aspects of mood are underlined in the three poems by the near monotony of the iambic rhymed pattern which Heym used over and over again and the effects of which were intentional. That such a rhythmic pattern served his purpose more than only superfically is attested by his diary entry of September 27, 1911, in which he states: "Der Jambus ist eine Lüge ... der gezwungene Reim ist eine Gotteslasterung."[50] Heym was a poet consciously using an outdated form which he recognized as false and meaningless to articulate with a facade of metrical regularity and harmonic pattern a condition he saw rather as warped and dissonant.

It is not enough, however, to read these poems purely as the lyric expression of the vacuity of an increasingly industrialized, urban, technological age with the circus/*Jahrmarkt* as Heym's metaphor in service to his disappointment and his anger. It is indeed the case that within the larger framework of Heym's aesthetic of marginality there occurs a confrontation between the basic contradictions of a dishonest time, between the accepted and the unaccepted, the haves and the have-nots, the legitimate and the illegitimate. The spheres in reality are nonetheless all too separate and touch each other only in the poet's work. Insofar as these poems bring an essentially marginal sphere, i. e., the world of popular culture, into the central arena of the legitimate lyric they are consistent with Heym's attempts to force the confrontation which he

[49] Ernst Bloch, *Erbschaft dieser Zeit,* Frankfurt/Main, 1962, p. 174ff.

[50] *Dichtungen und Schriften,* III, 166.

sensed was all too often avoided by the bourgeois society of which he was a member. In this way he finds his niche honestly, as it were, in that line of poets stretching back to Francois Villon: his list of acknowledged favorites, those with "a heart torn apart" — Kleist, Grabbe, Hölderlin, Büchner, Rimbaud, and Marlowe — demonstrates the tradition with which he wanted to be associated and the direction he consciously followed. Of greater importance, however, are the statements the poet makes about his society by virtue of that circus/ *Jahrmarkt* metaphor and what he was able to say with regard to the evolution of those popular cultural forms themselves. Heym, I would assert, has genuinely grasped the fact that facets of a technological age had irrevocably affected these forms, and that within a changing framework the mutation, say, of the circus from horse show to fashionable spectacle to technological experiment to big-business enterprise was symptomatic of much that was wrong with his time. While 1912 may be a little early to signal the deterioration of the modern circus, it was not long after that point that it began perceptibly to move toward its nadir. Already by the 1920s it was to be superseded by the film, from which point its magic became a thing of the past. The nature of performance and spectacle had moved and changed in consort with the times, and technological progress and sophistication inevitably changed their function and effect on audiences. In these three poems Heym effectively and rather profoundly puts the world of the circus and *Jahrmarkt* in paratactic alignment with his own world and adeptly preserves the integrity of a dual kind of statement. What he has to say about the former impinges on and supports the judgement he pronounces on the larger social context. For both realms those darkened peninsulas of which he spoke loomed so large that they effectively canceled any hope of a brighter tomorrow. More than circus fans have come to agree with him and to find his intuitions borne out by more contemporary developments. His was a keen poetic perception that could look to carousel and clown, artiste and arena, to discover telltale signs of the impending decline.

FOUR:

Form and Structure

1. *Frank Wedekind*

While other writers have picked and chosen aspects of the circus to use as suited their purpose, few quite so obviously demonstrated their enthusiasm for the circus and its people or made such a point of their association, connection, and interest in the circus world as the dramatist Frank Wedekind (1864–1918). Within the entire gamut of German writers influenced by the circus, Wedekind represents its most mesmerized spectator and its most avid disciple. For Wedekind the circus was more than subject matter, motif, or symbol to be manipulated. His discipleship was rather a case of total idealization whereby his personal and aesthetic principles, his ideas on life and the theater, and, not the least, the form of his dramatic practice were affected and molded.

When and where the young Wedekind's interest in the circus arose is not known. The fist mention surfaces in 1885 when he was in Munich and then again in 1887 then he was in Zurich and a frequent visitor to the circus there. His initial enthusiasm while still in Munich is attested in an unpublished ballad of 1885 entitled "Ännchen Tartini" in which he sings the praises of a high-wire artiste by that name. Then two years later, after having moved to Switzerland, he wrote a series of essays on the circus, the first of which appeared June 29 and 30, 1887, in the *Neue Zürcher Zeitung* under the title *Zirkusgedanken,* followed the next year by two more essays published in the same paper (Nr. 215, 2b and Nr. 218, b, 1888), entitled *Im Zirkus* and *Das hängende Drahtseil.*[1] In addition, his in-

[1] These two 1888 articles were not available to me. I have relied on the account given by Artur Kutscher in his *Frank Wedekind, Sein Leben und seine Werke,* Munich, 1922, I, 146ff.

terest at this time was sufficient to cause him to write, possibly that same year (1888), a poem which be called "Fräulein Ella Belling," either out of captivation with her as a person (she was the daughter of the famous circus clown Tom Belling) or with qualities which she personified. A later dance poem entitled "Ella Belling/Sonne, Mond und Sterne" indicates Wedekind's continued interest in this particular performer.

Based on these early works, Wedekind's ideas on the circus at this stage were limited and rather superficial: he seems to have been most enthusiastic about the physical aspects and charms of the performers. The young author's attitude was not altogether sensually oriented, however. Already in that first *Zürcher Zeitung* essay *(Zirkusgedanken)* we detect his concern with certain aesthetic principles involved in the circus. Here it becomes clear that even at this early stage Wedekind sensed that the circus contained an intellectually stimulating element, that the circus was in essence a visual allegory of a practical wisdom to which his contemporaries might well pay some attention. These first impressions endured throughout Wedekind's career and were later to prove influential in forming many of his subsequent ideas on the theater.

There is no word on Wedekind and the circus during the three years from 1888 to 1891. In December of 1891, however, we find him in Paris, and it is during the ensuing period up until 1895 — spent mostly in Paris and briefly in London — that the playwright's involvement with the circus is most noticeable. The atmostphere in Paris at the time was exciting. These were "the banquet years," to use Roger Shattuck's terms, and Paris was playing the hostess. Together with the opera, the theater, the café, the music hall, the *café chantant,* the circus had become an organic part of Parisian life: "Three permanent circuses and a new Hippodrome fringed Montmartre along the boulevards. The clown, the horse, and the acrobat here earned their place in modern art: The Degas ballet dancer became the Toulouse Lautrec cabaret entertainer, and then became the Picasso Harlequin. The team of clowns, Footit and Chocolat, developed the first comic stooge act (known as *clown et august*). Groc and Antonet, the American Emmet Kelly, and the Fontellini Brothers all achieved fame in Paris before the turn of the century."[2] Within such a stimulating context Wedekind began to work productively, and the pieces stemming from this period reveal the extent to which the playwright was able to incorporate his enthusiasm for the circus into his works.

It was primarily through the Parisian circus that Wedekind became aware of the pantomime as a dramatic form. We noted earlier that the pantomime had become very much a vogue in the circus, had become, in fact, one of the chief reasons for the circus' widespread success.[3] Records of the Parisian circuses during this period attest to the elaborateness of these pantomimic performances. Most of the circus buildings were designed to facilitate large productions on a central arena-type stage. The Cirque d'Hiver and the Cirque Nouveau both had rings which could be converted into pools, and aquatic pieces proved consistently attractive to the populace. To complement this elaborate and complex stage and building design, vast amounts of money were spent on props and large numbers of performers. Grandiose spectacles were the order of the day. Typical of such exhibitions was the Hippodrome's immense production "Neron" in which there were some five hundred and fifty participants – mimes, singers, animal trainers, horsemen, dancers – all performing to the music of Eduard Lalo.[4] Large crowds, realistic sets, dancing, music, and lavish display around a relatively threadbare plot had become the circus pantomime's formula for popular success by the end of the nineteenth century.

Wedekind was sufficiently convinced of the pantomime's potential and hopeful that his career could benefit from its popularity that he tried his hand at writing four of them: *Der Schmerzenstanz, Der Mückenprinz, Die Kaiserin von Neufund-*

[2] Roger Shattuck, *The Banquet Years,* Garden City, New York, 1961, p. 9.

[3] Especially at the Cirque Nouveau. See Paul Adrian, *Histoire Illustrée des Cirques,* Bourg-la-Rein, 1957, p. 62.

[4] Adrian, *Histoire Illustrée,* p. 32.

land, and *Bethel.*[5] In many respects Wedekind's interest in the pantomime may be considered the most direct result of his circus experience in the French capital. Nonetheless, he was able also to finish a farce, *Der Liebestrank,* as well as *Die Büchse der Pandora* out of which he later formed the two "Lulu" tragedies *Erdgeist* and *Die Büchse der Pandora.* He also completed work on his scenes of brothel life *Das Sonnenspektrum* and wrote texts and music for many of the *Bänkellieder* which somewhat later helped make him a cause célèbre in the artistic circuit of early twentieth-century Munich.

There is little direct information concerning Wedekind's stay in Paris other than that contained in two notebook diaries which concentrate on more personal and private experiences. These diaries do record, however, that after his arrival in December of 1891 he settled down to a routine in which his chief interests were the theater, the circus, the music hall, and amorous adventure. Among the places Wedekind frequented were the famous Hippodrome, the grandiose edifice suitable to all sorts of large-scale productions, the Eden Theater, a small but popular boulevard theater, and the well-known Folies Bergère and Moulin Rouge. He spent a significant amount of his time in the three large circuses, the Cirque d'Hiver, the Cirque d'Été, and the Cirque Nouveau. His preference is clearly for those entertainment forms catering to the masses, rather than to the elite. That interest was not a passing fancy: planning a return visit to Paris in 1898, Wedekind wrote that on the first evening he would doubtless go to the Folies Ber-

[5] *Der Schmerzenstanz, Der Mückenprinz,* and *Die Kaiserin von Neufundland* were all first published in 1897 in *Die Fürstin Russalka. Der Schmerzenstanz,* however, is dated 1892 in Wedekind's *Gesammelte Werke,* and *Der Mückenprinz* was completed in 1895. Joachim Friedenthal (*Das Wedekindbuch,* Munich, 1914) claims that *Bethel* was completed during the Winter of '93–'94, and proposes that *Die Kaiserin von Neufundland* likewise originated during the period 1892–97. *Die Kaiserin von Neufundland* was written specifically for the Circus Renz and was supposed to be set to music by Wedekind's friend Richard Weinhöppel. See letters of April 1, 1897, and July 15, 1897, in Frank Wedekind, *Gesammelte Briefe,* I, Fritz Strich, ed., Munich, 1924, pp. 280 and 283.

gère; as late as 1913 he wrote from Rome that it was a lovely city but not as interesting as Paris since there was no boulevard theater, circus, or varieté to be found there.[6]

Wedekind was impressed not only by the performances but also by the unique construction of the circus buildings. A diagrammatic sketch[7] he drew to accompany the theater building in the novel *Mine Haha* shows an edifice which bears a striking resemblance to the Cirque Nouveau. The sketch shows a circular building with seats arranged in amphitheater form around the central stage. Performers enter the building from below by means of an underground tunnel. The stage is disc-shaped, may be raised or lowered, and is lighted by a large chandelier hanging from the center of the ceiling. A stage of this type — pure theater-in-the-round — is particularly suited for pantomimic performances, allowing an equal view of the action from all sides and giving a dimension to the purely visual aspect which would otherwise be lost in a proscenium perspective. It is for just such performances that Wedekind intended this rather specialized structure. The building itself figures importantly in his pantomime *Der Mückenprinz,* the performance of which plays a significant role in the novel *Mine Haha.*

Both before and during his stay in Paris Wedekind enjoyed the friendship of many circus personalities. Particularly valuable and influential was his acquaintance with W. W. Rudinoff (pseud. Willi Morgenstern). Born in 1866, Rudinoff had developed by his late twenties into a dynamic personality and man of many talents, equally proficient as a singer, artist, actor, or clown. He had studied the art of the pantomime and as early as 1884 had been engaged as a pantomimist with a traveling circus in Munich. His subsequent career was increasingly successful, and he became one of the leading attractions at the Parisian Cirque d'Hiver and the London Alhambra.

[6] Letter of June 24, 1913. *Gesammelte Briefe,* II, p. 283.
[7] Accompanying an article by Kutscher, "Wedekind und der Zirkus," *Faust, eine Monatsschrift für Kunst, Literatur und Musik,* III, No. 7, p. 5.
[8] Kutscher, *Frank Wedekind,* I, p. 192.

Rudinoff was apparently an extremely dedicated artist, one who approached his profession with intimate devotion. For him, as the following passage from his travel diary reveals, art took on the nature of religion, and practice of it was in service and praise of something supreme: "Bevor du, Künstler, an die Arbeit gehst, sollst du deine Seele sammeln und dein Herz der Weisheit zuwenden, dein Körper sei fein wie dein Verstand. Deine Stimmung vor der Natur und vor seiner Idee sei dergestalt, als seiest du auf dem Wege zur Mitternachtsmesse, um die Geburt eines Heilands zu feiern. So beginne dein Werk, und deine Arbeit wird Gottesdienst sein."[9]

Wedekind had become acquainted with Rudinoff during the latter's visit to Munich in 1884 and met him again in Paris at the Cirque d'Hiver where Rudinoff was engaged.[10] Wedekind had valued the friendship from the very beginning and as late as 1912 referred to Rudinoff as "prince" in his role as artist and friend, praising him as "one of the very best."[11] Through Rudinoff Wedekind became acquainted with other circus personalities and the life they led. He enthusiastically writes of meeting Rudinoff at the Cirque d'Hiver and of the evenings spent with the circus personnel.[12] Among the personalities Rudinoff introduced to Wedekind was the weight lifter and strong-man Holthoff who possibly served as model for the Empress Filissa's successful suitor in the pantomime *Die Kaiser von Neufundland.* It was likewise through Rudinoff that Wedekind met the well-known Russian clown and trainer of small animals Anatol Durow. In 1892 Durow performed at the Folies Bergère with his trained mice and rats, and there is possibly a connection between him and Professor Pantaleone with his trained fleas in *Der Schmerzenstanz.* Durow's popularity, however, did not rest solely on his skill as

[9] W. Rudinoff, "Ein Selbstbekenntnis," *Zeitschrift für bildende Kunst,* N. F., XVII (1905–1906), p. 46.

[10] According to Kutscher, on December 5, 1892.

[11] Letter to Rudinoff dated Munich, August 21, 1912. *Gesammelte Briefe,* II, p. 271.

[12] See letter dated January 9, 1893, to his friend Karl Henckell, *Gesammelte Briefe,* I, p. 147.

animal trainer. According to one source, his political satire and pointed irony was the basis of the audience's enjoyment: "Seine Monologe, Späße, Reprisen und Szenen mit dressierten Tieren zeichneten sich stets durch Geist und Witz aus, seine Darbietungen waren fast immer satirisch und ein deutlicher Ausdruck seiner Opposition gegen die Regierung." The following excerpt from one of his monologs suggests distinct similarities to the opening scene of Wedekind's *Erdgeist,* or even to some of the scenes in the later *König Nicolo:*

> Seht mich hier in der Arena,
> Faulheit hab ich nie gekannt,
> Und die Geisel der Satire
> Ist das Schwert in meiner Hand.
> Trotz' Verboten und Gendarmen,
> Auch das Kittchen schreckt mich nicht;
> Wahrheit schleudre ohn' Erbarmen
> Euch, ihr Herrn, ich ins Gesicht! ...[13]

Both Durow's style of declamation as well as his insubordinate and somewhat subversive stance within the context of an animal (circus/stage) act touched a responsive chord in the rebellious young Wedekind.

There can be no question that these acquaintances constituted a significant bond between Wedekind and the circus world. They gave him the opportunity to observe the inner aspects of circus life and to become familiar with the tenets and principles, aesthetic and moral, by which these people lived. Even some six years after the Paris period Wedekind had not given up his desire to be, or at least appear as, a person well informed on the circus. In the brief account entitled *Autobiographisches,* which dates from 1901 and which was written in response to questions about his background, he reports: "1888 reiste ich ein halbes Jahr lang as Secretär mit dem Zirkus Herzog und ging nach dessen Auflösung mit meinem Freunde, dem bekannten Feuermaler Rudinoff nach Paris und begleitete ihn als sein Mitarbeiter auf einer Tournee nach England und Südfrankreich ... Dann ging ich, da meine Vater

[13] S. Radunski, *Erinnerungen eines alten Clowns,* Berlin, 1956, p. 109.

indes gestorben war, nach Paris zurück ..."[14] He says further that after leaving the Circus Herzog he traveled as a plant with the Circus Franconi, moreover, that he intended to make a tour as a *Gedächtniskünstler* with Rudinoff. The veracity of this report is extremely doubtful, however, for there is no evidence to substantiate Wedekind's claims: his going back to Paris is impossible since he went there for the first time in 1891, and Rudinoff denied that such a tour was ever made.[15] That Wedekind should have promulgated such a sequence as part of his autobiography either in jest or as wishful thinking is indicative nonetheless of the significance the circus experience held for him.

Wedekind's enthusiasm for the circus cannot, of course, be viewed as existing in a vacuum. Going to the circus was obviously not his sole activity nor was it the only factor to leave its signature on his work at the time. One must take into account other aspects of the Parisian context inasmuch as they form a meaningful pattern and a frame for the circus itself as dominant factor. What Wedekind saw in variety theaters, night clubs, and cabarets was probably all rather much the same, performed in a more intimate setting than in the circus. One popular element here that seems to have taken on special importance for him was the figure of Pierrot. This Commedia dell'arte figure had begun to enjoy a renewed popularity even before Wedekind arrived, particularly in dramatic pieces in the nature of operettas *(operettes bouffes)*. In 1890, however, the tradition reached its culmination with the purely mimetic play *L'Enfant Prodigue* by Michel Carré Fils. In the original production of *L'Enfant* as well as in every revival the role of the male Pierrot was played by a woman: "He is shown wearing a suit of knee breeches and skirted coat, with a Pierrot ruffle, in white for the first scene, denoting the youth and innocence of Pierrot; black in the second and third acts, suggesting his disillusionment and despair."[16] While there is no

14 Kutscher, *Frank Wedekind,* I, p. 149.

15 Paul Fechter, *Frank Wedekind: Der Mensch und das Werk,* Jena, 1920, p. 9.

16 Irene Mawer, *The Art of Mime,* Boston, [n. d.], p. 121.

certifiable, direct connection here to any specific Wedekind character, one is teased by the similarity between *L'Enfant* and Wedekind's Lulu, who in the prologue to *Erdgeist* (which Wedekind appended later) first appears out of a circus tent dressed as Pierrot and whose portrait in such a costume is responsible for the success of the artist Schwarz. In addition, her portrait in that costume figures significantly throughout the play. The probable origin of Wedekind's Lulu in the general Parisian context has been convincingly argued by Kutscher.[17] As he points out, by the time Wedekind arrived in Paris in 1891 the character "Lulu" was a common concept, and the name had become synonymous with the power and attraction of physical beauty. There was even, in fact, a pantomime by that name, one written by the popular French author Felicien Champsaur. The first performance of the piece had been given at the Cirque Nouveau in 1888, and the production was accompanied by publication of the scenario in book form. It went through two printings, and Wedekind had a copy of it in his library. While it is possible to propose a general relationship between the Champsaur pantomime and Wedekind's character Lulu, the connection is admittedly somewhat tenuous. What is significant is the fact that the Lulu/Pierrot context is circus-oriented by virtue of the Champsaur pantomime's premiere at the Cirque Nouveau as well as the heroine's specific designation as a female clown. On a somewhat deeper level the Champsaur pantomime also provided a pantomimic context (which, as has been demonstrated, is part and parcel of Wedekind's circus interest) and furnished a rudimentary expression of the heart/mind conflict that was central to Wedekind at this time.

The Grand Guignol was another aspect of Parisian life which Wedekind found fascinating. As early as the eighteenth century "Guignol" had been the name of a marionette; but the term by some twist later came to be attached to cabarets

[17] A. Kutscher, "Eine unbekannte französische Quelle zu Frank Wedekinds 'Erdgeist' und 'Büchse der Pandora'," *Das Goldene Tor,* II (1947), p. 497.

featuring performances of "horror" plays. The tradition ultimately became centralized in the Théâtre du Grand Guignol where short plays of violence, murder, rape, and suicide were the specialty. One can detect the genre's influence in aspects of two of Wedekind's pantomimes: the heroine's self strangulation in *Die Kaiserin von Neufundland* and the hero's wanton and sadistic murders in *Der Mückenprinz*. In this regard it is worth noting that the original version of the Lulu drama was subtitled "eine Monstre-Tragödie." Wedekind seemed particularly attracted to the figure of Jack the Ripper, the London murderer, and in 1892 proposed writing a "horror tragedy" with the "belly slasher" as his subject.[18] The figure was subsequently incorporated into the "monster-tragedy" *Die Büchse der Pandora*. During the 1890s the Guignol's appeal was given added prestige by Alfred Jarry, who by 1896 was a master of the surrealistic grotesque and whose *Ubu Roi*, performed that same year, took Paris by storm. Like Wedekind, Jarry had arrived in Paris in 1891 and from the first moment become the epitome of unconventionality. By 1893–94 he was a well-known figure and had published in *Mercure de France*, *L'Echo de Paris*, and *L'Art Littéraire*. It is unlikely, however, that Wedekind knew Jarry personally; there is no mention of a meeting between the two, and neither claimed to have been even slightly aware of the other. This is not surprising. Jarry and Wedekind can be seen as representing two opposite poles of life in Paris, the one the friend of Mallarmé and seated at the head of the "banquet" tables, the other, friend of tightrope walkers and horseback riders of the sawdust ring. Although it was doubtless unintentional and unconscious, it was a separation which Wedekind would have cultivated. He managed at any rate to take from the Guignol that which suited his own purposes.

The rhyme and reason for Wedekind's receptiveness to some of these elements is also of importance and is best understood in terms of what the playwright was turning *from*. In much the same way that he disdained any association with

[18] Kutscher, *Frank Wedekind*, I, p. 361.

those at the banquet tables he seems to have remained indifferent to the sophisticated life in Paris, to the Parisian literary circles and their credos. And beyond the Parisian sphere, he most definitely wished to disassociate himself from the current literary fashion on the stage, particularly the German stage. He was far from indifferent, however, to what was going on in those quarters. It was precisely in his strong, almost vehement reaction to the Naturalistic trend of the day that Wedekind gravitated to the demimonde represented by the small boulevard theaters, the cabarets, the music halls, and the circus — they were all one in his veto of Naturalism. On the surface at least, almost all the features of that literary movement were uncongenial to him: its concern with man determined by his social environment, the use of art in the service of society, the use of popular intellectual ideas from science, technology, and politics, the search for determinants. All of this, as far as Wedekind was concerned, was too superficial, too intellectual, and overlooked the real governing forces of life. In the drama especially, he objected to the Naturalist's reformist attitude which left the existence of the bourgeoisie and its values untouched. Instead of being genuine works of art, the products of the Naturalist playwright seemed a tendentious effort to arouse sympathy for a passive hero, a good bourgeois whose admirable qualities either could not be sustained within a hostile environment or else were perverted by the forces of society. Wedekind probably would have agreed with Fritz Strich's characterization of Naturalist dramaturgy as too lacking in courage to fashion either the passions, the pathos, or the emotional glow of its heroes. Only passively groveling characters, not actively resolved, purposeful characters lay within the realm of its possibilities.[19]

Wedekind's distaste for Naturalism and the Naturalists — encouraged not a little by personal envy of their success, particularly that of Gerhart Hauptmann whom he had known as

[19] Fritz Strich, *Dichtung und Zivilisation,* Munich, 1928, p. 191.

a young man in Zurich —[20] was given direct expression in his early play *Kinder und Narren: Die junge Welt* in 1891. He articulates a less rancorous but equally adamant condemnation of Naturalism, or more precisely the literary trend toward intellectualism, in *Die Büchse der Pandora* when he has Alwa Schön credit his association with Lulu and her world of pimps, prostitutes, and gangsters for having brought him into contact with real life and thus provided him proper material for art: "Das ist der Fluch, der auf unserer jungen Literatur lastet, daß wir viel zu literarisch sind. Wir kennen keine anderen Fragen und Probleme als solche, die unter Schriftstellern und Gelehrten auftauchen. Unser Gesichtskreis reicht über die Grenzen unserer Zunftinteressen nicht hinaus. Um wieder auf die Fährte einer großen gewaltigen Kunst zu gelangen, müssten wir uns möglichst viel unter Menschen bewegen, die nie in ihrem Leben ein Buch gelesen haben, denen die einfachsten animalischen Instinkte bei ihren Handlungen maßgebend sind."[21]

Wedekind was thus obviously an advocate for a more natural attitude toward life. He favored individuality instead of group identity, vitality instead of lassitude; above all, he advocated that Eros be separated from Love. The torpor of the Naturalists, the vain strivings of the intellectuals unable to find life because of the book page obstructing their view, and the bourgeois suppressed in his proper but constricting morality were all scorned by the rebellious young playwright.

It was the conjunction of this largely negative reaction toward the theatrical fad of the day together with his enthu-

[20] And whose play *Vor Sonnenaufgang* had been produced in Berlin in 1889. Wedekind, moreover, was bitter about Hauptmann's having used some Wedekind family gossip as dramatic material in the latter's *Das Friednesfest* (1890) — a plagiarism to which Wedekind responded by fairly blatantly caricaturing Hauptmann in *Die junge Welt*.

[21] Frank Wedekind, *Gesammelte Werke*, Artur Kutscher and Joachim Friedenthal, eds., Munich, 1924, III, 125–26. Hereafter referred to as *GW* with appropriate volume and page numbers cited in parentheses in the text.

siasm for the circus that nurtured Wedekind's positivistic stance on life and art during the 80s and early 90s. The circus revealed to him society's paralysis, a paralysis that signified the era's incapacity for life. He sensed that a genuine zest for life had been lost: "Was aber versiegt, was dahinfällt von Mal zu Mal und von uns scheidet, unwiederbringlich fürs ganze Leben, das ist die goldene, sonnige Jugendfröhlichkeit, der harmlose Genuß, lachendes Spiel und süßernstes Träumen...." (*GW,* IX, 295) What concerned him was that contemporary man had lost his capacity for happiness, the ability to consider and live life as a game. In his view, his contemporaries seemed singularly inept in overcoming the hurdles which life presented. In *Zirkusgedanken* he had proposed a solution derived from the central, life-affirming principles of the circus: "Das maßgebende Prinzip der Manege ist die Elastizität, die plastisch-allegorische Darstellung einer Lebensweisheit, deren gerade wir Kinder des neunzehnten Jahrhunderts ... am meisten bedürfen." (*GW,* IX, 297) These principles of elasticity and equilibrium had significance outside the sawdust ring as well, for Wedekind could see that that circus equilibrium had its equivalent in the balance necessary to maintain oneself on the tightrope of life. It was an instinctive, basic affirmation of life and an expression of delight in its continuation: action in the arena never appears passive and cumbrous, but rather is consistently animated and bouyant. Wedekind could perceive that no one ever got "licked" or defeated in the circus, and that realization became an integral part of his philosophy to the extent that it determined his dramaturgy. What he ultimately managed to do was to force a circus vitality onto the legitimate stage and in no small way affect the course of theatrical art that was to follow. If the *Elastizität* he detected in the ring was felt by him to be the kind of philosophical stance necessary to get along in the contemporary world, that same *Elastizität,* put into dramatic practice, gave the theater a new and rejuvenating breath and opened it up to new modes of thought and action that surged into the forces of Expressionism. There was every reason for the fact that Wedekind found little favor among the dramatic powers that were, and more than ample cause for him to feel it necessary to act in his own plays. His dramatic style, tempo, and dialog — the composite force of his dramas — was such that few could understand them, much less accept them. The classical dramatic idiom — both tragedy and comedy — was simply not ready for him. The Naturalists had required of the theater audiences a mood of serious and lethargic dramatic contemplation. Wedekind was prepared to singe them with a tragicomic acerbity that was embarrassing whether one laughed or whether one cried. His was not what Brecht would later refer to as "culinary" theater, and there were few to appreciate or acknowledge as Brecht did that Wedekind deserved to be placed, together with Tolstoy and Strindberg, among the greatest educators of the new Europe.[22]

For Wedekind, the circus also furnished an alternative to the prudishness of a hypermoral age and its restrictions, especially with regard to the human body. As he saw it, the predominant moral attitudes were inimical to any appreciation or enjoyment of the human form. His complaints are laced with scorn: "Was jedoch das lebendige Leben anbelangt, so befinden wir uns wie gesagt in der Epoche der bis unters Kinn hinauf krampfhaft zugeknöpften Taillen, der trostlosen Fracks und röhrenförmigen Beinkleider, alles ungemein praktischen Erfindungen zur Nivellierung der höheren Gesellschaft, die an Humanität, an christlichem Wohlwollen gegenüber stiefmütterlich Bedachten nichts zu wünschen übrig lassen, die aber schwerlich dazu geeignet sind, der Veredlung der Rasse erfolgreich unter die Arme zu greifen."[23] How different it was in the circus! There one could observe beautifully strong bodies performing graceful, tempered movements, or beautiful bodies exhibited for no other reason than that they were beautiful bodies. Wedekind appreciated the

[22] Bertolt Brecht, "Frank Wedekind," in Bertolt Brecht, *Gesammelte Werke in 20 Bänden,* Frankfurt/Main, 1967, VII, p. 4. See also the discussion of Wedekind's dramaturgy by Paul Böckmann: "Die komödiantischen Grotesken Frank Wedekinds," in *Das deutsche Lustspiel,* II, Hans Steffen, ed., Göttingen, 1969, pp. 79–102.

[23] Cited in Kutscher, *Frank Wedekind,* I, p. 148.

freedom and beauty of the undecorated human form and declared that it was unnatural that that form be hidden. In this world of scanty costumes, moreover, one could not but recognize another, more sensual realm of life in which the body was expressive of the mind and where subjective, inner moods or states were objectively, externally depicted by the physical form. Ultimately, Wedekind derived from the circus world his principle of the close relationship between the body and the mind, in essence, the body as expressive of the mind. He would advocate, in effect, not simply one realm or the other — the spirit or the flesh, the soul or the senses — but propose that fulfillment or happiness of the spirit was in proportion to perfection and satisfaction of the body. His ideas in this regard were not significantly different from those advanced much later by Ludwig Klages in his study of the "science of expression." Even allowing for the variance between the two German terms *Geist*= spirit/mind/soul, and *Seele*= soul/mind/spirit, there is little difference between Klages' dictum that "der Leib ist die Erscheinung der Seele, die Seele der Sinn der Leibeserscheinung"[24] and the aesthetic developed by the young playwright/circus fan. The kind of physical, anatomical context he creates in his *Mine Haha, oder die körperliche Erziehung der jungen Mädchen,* for example, is an obvious reflection of the circus ideal to which he subscribed. In view of his enthusiasm for the circus as an institute of learning, the transference of such an ideal to a pedagogical province is a logical extension of his real life experiences in the circus into the corpus of his artistic production.

A similar indication of Wedekind's fascination with the physical body can be seen in his interest in the dance. Like most of the Parisian elements that inspired him, it remained an interest throughout his life. If the tightrope "dancing" of Ella Belling had captivated him in 1888, the numerous popular dances in vogue in Paris convinced him of the grace of the body when governed by dance movements. Like many others

[24] Ludwig Klages, *Grundlegung der Wissenschaft vom Ausdruck,* Leipzig, 1943–49, p. 7.

at the time he became an enthusiast of the cancan and other popular dances, for example, the tarantella; he also showed a pronounced interest in the standard ballet forms such as the pas de deux and the gavotte.[25] Traditional dance forms, as well as numerous programmatic dances of his own invention — *Freudentanz, Schmerzenstanz, Siegestanz* — occur in the pantomimes and are used in moments of high emotional content where in an "unrestricted" context, as it were, the character is allowed to "let go" and "naturally" express feelings in a physically emotive manner, i. e., in dance. The pantomimes themselves are classified in the collected works under the title *Tanzdichtungen*. Folk dancing likewise appealed to Wedekind, and once in an interview he praised such dancing as "das Höchste an Harmonie, was sich von persönlichem Ausdruck, von Temperament, von Geschmeidigkeit, Verve und Adel der Bewegung in einem menschlichen Körper vereinigen kann."[26] Wedekind's continuing interest in the dance is demonstrated in his subsequent efforts in the area of the *Tanzlied,* an artistic form combining the lyric and the dramatic, a mixture of musical rhythm and movement with accompanying verse. Several of the later dramas have such a dance-song as an integral part of their dramatic plan. *Die Zensur,* for example, contains a scene in which Buridan sings and plays the lute while Kadidja dances; in *Franziska* Veit Kunz sings to a

[25] Kutscher claims that Wedekind's interest in the dance stemmed primarily from the inspired definition given to it by Nietzsche. He was nonetheless aware of certain classical models and not unaware of his literary predecessors who had given the dance/mimic tradition in Germany steady, if somewhat sparse, support, e. g., Goethe and Heinrich Heine. The parallel with Heine is particularly noteworthy: Heine was one of Wedekind's admitted literary mentors from the very beginning and had twice tried his hand at the genre — in 1847 with his "Tanzpoem" *Der Doktor Faustus* and in 1853 with his *Göttin Diana*. One is struck by the fact that in both instances the dance element is a factor of a "foreign" aura: Heine wrote both pieces for possible production at London's Covent Garden, and Wedekind, as we have seen, was adapting a form whose origins were distinctly not German.

[26] From an interview concerning Tortejada, a Spanish dancer. Quoted in Kutscher, *Frank Wedekind,* II, p. 122.

lute accompaniment and Karaminka dances; in *Simson* a dance-pantomime routine is performed by Simson and Delila.

In his conviction that fulfillment of the spirit is only possible through fulfillment of the flesh Wedekind criticized society for its sexual inhibitions and outdated moral attitudes and advocated a stronger sexuality and sexual freedoms. Especially in the pantomimes, but also in other works of the Paris period, he places extraordinary emphasis on the catastrophe resulting from the absence of an integrated sexuality. The formula common to all these works which might be expressed as "satisfaction of the senses brings satisfaction to the mind" is covertly the point in *Die Kaiserin von Neufundland* when the court physician Dr. Didi Zeudus warns the soul-sick empress: Marry or die! Similarly, Maria Lezsincka in *Der Schmerzenstanz* sleeps peacefully for the first time in years when she has the flea Nostradamus under the covers and between her legs. Katharina in *Fritz Schwigerling* suffocates in her lonely world for lack of sexual fulfillment. At the beginning of the play, she fumes: "Ich habe Zaire zuschanden geritten, ich werde nicht ruhiger. Ich habe Beethovensche Sonaten geklimpert, ich werde nicht ruhiger. Ich habe Wölfe gebändigt, ich werde nicht ruhiger. — Das Leben hegt noch geheime Schätze, was es auch sei, von denen man sich hier nichts träumen läßt." (*GW,* II, 194) Wedekind seems to propose that only those who satisfy the senses can achieve any sense of inner well-being. The catastrophic results that arise when the sexual sphere is denied is a significant point in the *Mine Haha* novel despite all its positive emphasis on physical training.

While in each of these cases the emphasis is predominantly on those misfortunes which the sexually misinformed or uninformed character brings down upon him/herself, Wedekind *does* consistently offer an antithesis in one way or another by a figure whose connection or association to the circus world is visible. In *Die Kaiserin von Neufundland* Didi Zeudus, so knowledgeable about the problems of the Empress, is a clown figure; in *Der Schmerzenstanz* Nostradamus the flea belongs to Professor Paulo Pantaleone and serves more or less as his agent; Katharina's salvation lies in Fritz Schwigerling — clown, animal trainer, gypsy, etc.; and in *Mine Haha* the solution to the sexual perversion in the pantomime is provided by the magician Hachi-Bümbüm.

Perhaps the most radical formulation of Wedekind's ideas with regard to the necessity of sexual freedom is the utopian piece *Das Sonnenspektrum*. The work is subtitled "eine Idylle aus dem modernen Leben" and is set in the environs of a park-like brothel. The one act centers around Elise who arrives "still a virgin" and begs the Madame to employ her because she finds herself no longer able to deny her body its desires. Wedekind may not have meant this depiction of carefree and happy girls engaged in prostitution as a serious description of reality, but it was clearly a plaidoyer for granting Eros its due independently of Love and was intended to shock the complacent bourgeois by idealizing the woman whose body ruled her actions and whose morality was independent of the accepted social standards. In addition to his exposure to women whom he could have thought to be the paragon of this ideal (in the circus and cabaret where the physical aspect was allowed to dominate), Wedekind had a practical basis for his theory: prostitutes were to a large extent his preferred company, and his notebooks and diaries give evidence that many of his days and nights were spent in their company. It is likely, in fact, that he did research on the subject: in his library was the six volume disquisition by Pierre Dufour, *Histoire de la prostitution chez tout les peuples de monde depuis l'antiquité la plus reculée jusqu' à nos jours,* Paris, 1851–53.[27]

Wedekind's awareness of the importance of the elemental instincts in human life and how they relate to life and art is closely associated with his ideas on the relationship between animal and human nature. His enthusiasm for the achievements of circus animals caused him to question how these dumb creatures could be so graceful and to ask how the qual-

[27] Kutscher, *Frank Wedekind,* I, p. 337.

ities so valued in humans were more often found in animals. Wedekind could give no higher praise than to describe the former in terms of the latter; thus Leona in the pantomime *Bethel* is compared to the prize mare with the same name; and Lulu in *Erdgeist* is referred to as "a magnificent animal! – an elegant animal! – a champion!" Wedekind had no difficulty imagining human qualities transferred to animals or animal characteristics transposed onto the human plane. In *Mine Haha,* Hidalla describes her beloved supervisor in terms of a horse: "Ich sah die Augen und fühlte, daß ich ein menschliches Wesen vor mir hatte. Mein nächster Gedanke war Gertrude. Diese Stellung der Füße war Gertrude. Diese stolze Haltung hatte ich nur an Gertrud gesehen. Dieses sprühende Feuer in den Blicken, die Art, den Kopf zu schütteln, alles rief mir Gertrud vor Augen." (*GW,* I, 348) A summary of the animal-human parallel is given by Fritz Schwigerling when he tells Katharina: "Wir taxieren eine Künstlerin nach ihrer Grazie, ihrem Temperament, auch ihrer — Seele. ... Ob sie eine Schauspielerin als Ophelia oder eine Seiltänzerin auf dem hängenden Draht sehen, das Ausschlaggebende ist immer nur der Mensch, die geistige und körperliche Schönheit. Und was wir auf dem Draht, im Trapez, am Reck, in den römischen Ringen vom *Menschen* verlangen, das suchen wir beim *Tier* durch die sorgfältigste, umsichtigste Erziehung zu wecken. Der Geist, die Seele, die in dem schönen Organismus schlummert, muß in vollendeter rhythmisch gebundener Form zutage treten." (GW, II, 219) Wedekind's frequent inclusion of "animals" in the four pantomimes allowed him to show or symbolize visually the acquisition and transference of desired qualities onto the human plane through the judicious mixture of human and animal instincts. He gives the animal a role in which human characteristics govern its actions and relegates to the human actor qualities best identified with the animal.

Wedekind systematically viewed animal-training techniques as applicable to humans:

> Erziehung ist gegründet auf Ausdauer und Konsequenz und wird unterstützt von Tadel und Strafen einerseits, von Lob und

> Belohnung andrerseits. Beide so sparsam, so weise zu verwenden, wie lebensgefährliche Gifte bei der ärztlichen Behandlung eines zarten Körpers, ist eine der größten Aufgaben des guten Bereiters. Wie die Erziehung des Jünglings sowohl auf Kräftigung wie auf harmonische Ausbildung seines Geistes ausgeht, so bezweckt diejenige des jungen Pferdes die Entwicklung sämtlicher Körperkräfte und damit ein effektvolles, gleichmässiges Hervortreten der einzelnen Formen, eine Veredelung der Erscheinung. Indem die Gliedmassen entbunden, die Gelenke frei gemacht, alle Halbheiten, Unregelmäßigkeiten bekämpft werden, beginnt ein dauernder Rhythmus, ein gewisses erhabenes Pathos das Tier zu durchdringen. Es erscheint von Stolz auf seine Leistung erfüllt, die es selbst zu beurteilen gelernt, und hegt einen künstlerischen Ehrgeiz, der ihm unter den Bewegungen des Reiters in hellen Funken aus den Augen sprüht. In dieser Vervollkommnung, frei von den Schranken des Gesetzes, bäumt sich der junge arabische Schimmelhengst im Zentrum der Arena mächtig vor unsern Augen empor und bietet dem Ästhetiker einen Hochgenuß, wie er ihm großartiger nur in der Magie himmelanstrebender Berge, wie er ihm feiner, durchgeistigter nur in den Linien des menschlichen Körpers entgegentritt.[28]

In advocating the technique of animal training Wedekind was criticizing contemporary educational practices at the same time he was affirming and advocating an alternative. To him the matter of educating animals was not the grammar-school-like process of forcing fabricated information into the minds of students, information oftentimes totally inapplicable to practical life. Wedekind directly criticized such an educational system in *Die junge Welt* (1891) and extended his criticism in *Frühlings Erwachen* into farcical scenes showing how pedantic and meaningless the system could become.

Wedekind seems to have been particularly interested in the training potential of the whip — one of the technical aids used by the *Dresseur* in the circus ring. Employed primarily by the trainer to communicate his wishes by the subtlest touch, it is used only in cases of disobedience or inattention as means of punishment. We find Wedekind incorporating this idea in *Mine Haha,* for example, in a scene in which Ger-

[28] From one of the 1888 circus essays. Cited in Kutscher, *Frank Wedekind,* I, pp. 146–47.

trude instructs the young children in walking: "Dabei hatte sie ihre Rute fortwährend auf unseren Fußspitzen, unter unseren Knien oder unter den Waden, wenn eins den Fuß zu rasch sinken lassen wollte." (*GW,* I, 325) In *Fritz Schwigerling* he emphatically condemns the misuse of the whip. The prince attempts to force Schwigerling into using it on his two sons: "Meine Kinder sind von der Wiege auf an die Knute gewöhnt. Wenn die drei Stunden aufhören, Striemen zu spüren, dann tanzen sie ihnen auf der Nase herum. ... Wenn sie ihnen Savoir-vivre beibringen wollen, dann müssen sie etwas in der Hand haben." Schwigerling replies simply: "Das ist meine Art Dressur nicht. ... Im Zirkus hat man andere Begriffe von Erziehung. Das Tier muß seinen Stolz dareinsetzen, hinüberzukommen, mit Anmut, mit Sicherheit über jedes erdenkliche Hindernis!" (*GW,* II, 191) The ultimate goal of the trainer is to develop in his animals qualities normally associated with human spiritual development — freedom, joy, grace, and the like — and Schwigerling is convinced that his methods accomplish this: "Ich löse die Glieder, damit der Geist sie durchbebt, damit Freiheit und Freude durch jeder Ader zittert, bis die Faszination in hellen Funken aus beiden Augen sprüht — Das Tier muß seine Muskeln schwellen, seine Brust sich heben fühlen, wenn es der Welt gegenübertritt." (GW, II, 192)

In addition to both the emphasis upon the sensual/physical as a door or gateway to the spiritual and the parallelism between the animal and the human, Wedekind was doubtless aware of another aspect peculiar to the circus world, that is, the ease with which it is able to unite disparate social elements. It is true that the personnel of the circus form a world unto themselves and are apt to be regarded as less than equal by those in the audience. Nevertheless, Wedekind must have appreciated the irresistible attraction of that world for the respectable citizen as well as its ability to set aside all differences in status and station among the masses in the audience. The action in the arena inevitably transforms spectators into galleries of naive and enraptured children listening and looking at a world they once all shared. Not only are they united, relieved, as it were, of their separateness due to social factors, but they are allowed to return to a state uncomplicated by all the rules of life. The circus, in other words, facilitated a return to a childhood state, and that, for Wedekind, was of utmost significance. Life could assume the nature of a game.[29]

It is in this connection that Wedekind must have considered the clown a figure that uniquely expressed some of the ideals he held at the time. The clown, or a variation of him, appears in all four of his pantomimes: in *Der Schmerzenstanz* he appears as Professor Paulo Pantaleone; in *Der Mückenprinz,* Leonor has characteristics of that comic figure — particularly in the love scenes; numerous clown routines appear in *Die Kaiserin von Neufundland,* most obviously in the actions of the four suitors; in *Bethel,* Kneebs, Sanftleben, Schmetterling, and Hufeland are all dependent on clownish actions for their comic effect. Wedekind also gives a significant role in *Bethel* to the true clown "der dumme August" — the circus figure who since the days of Tom Belling had delighted audiences with his naive clumsiness and playful shenanigans.

Most of these clown figures encourage the development of a comic situation and are used merely to provoke laughter. Yet with these figures Wedekind actually accomplished two more serious purposes beyond the theatrical one of entertainment. On the one hand these figures can be seen as representatives of the attitude Wedekind proposed in the early *Zirkusgedanken* essay: the ability to overcome obstacles which the circus of life puts in one's path — a comic attitude as opposed to the tragic defeat at the hands of life. In *Bethel,* for example, both horse and Leona are able to defeat the intrigues against them, and Leona in particular realizes the fulfillment of her nature with the aid of "der dumme August." In *Der Schmerzenstanz* the heroine's mental and physical indisposition is healed with the aid of Pantaleone. The same thing is true of the figure of Fritz Schwigerling, who in spite of his appearance within a dramatic context is in reality a clown

[29] Recall that in the early 1888 essay *Im Zirkus* Wedekind had ascribed some of the charm of the circus to "das Kindliche."

thriving on tight situations and narrow escapes, always in control of himself and the circumstances. Just how strongly this function of the clown would have appealed to Wedekind becomes clear when one considers the figure in Bergsonian terms: tension and elasticity are the two complementary forces which life brings into play; if lacking to any considerable extent in the body, sickness, informity, and accidents result; if lacking in the mind, there is mental deficiency and insanity; if lacking in character, there is inability to adapt to social life; therefore, what life and society require of one is alertness, adaptability, and a sense of savoir faire. Such an attitude incorporates the concept of elasticity that functioned so centrally in Wedekind's philosophy, and the clown as the epitome of this positive force, constantly superior to defeat, is a figure that would have obviously appealed to him.

Wedekind was able to turn another facet of the clown figure to his advantage as well. Through the channel of the clown he could criticize those aspects of society opposed to what he envisioned as a positive life force. Understanding that society (the audience) is suspicious of every evidence of inelasticity of character, of mind, or of body and reacts to it by laughing, most clown figures display some form of rigidity in attitude or movement, or in most cases, a combination of both. Taking that principle of rigidity as the comic and laughter as its corrective, Wedekind had no difficulty finding social institutions characterized by rigidity. Once found, he relentlessly pushed them into the limelight. Held up thus to scorn, society (the audience) could be brought to laugh at itself. Although the clown's role is largely a matter of self-irony, his exaggerated spasticity makes it possible for the spectator to unconsciously grasp the slighter spasticity of his own routine (life), and lets him see the foolishness of his own situation. Helmuth Matiasek called them "Komiker der Unzulänglichkeit" working to make the public recognize itself in the most distorted forms of humanity;[30] Thomas Mann called them "Mönche der Ungereimtheit" — implying that they are

30 Helmut Matiasek, "Zeitlose Satire des Ewig-Menschlichen: Der Clown," *Maske und Kothurn,* IX (Heft 2), 1963, p. 192.

agents as well as confessors of our own nonsense. Wedekind used the figure as a double-edged sword, embodying his criticism of society in the rigidity of the figure itself, while at the same time making the audience see it as such and criticize it by laughing at it — and, of course, at itself.

In the light of these observations it is almost obvious that this very purposeful and compound use of the clown figure by Wedekind corresponds to, and arises out of, an aesthetic doctrine of tragicomedy. As soon as the clown's general purpose or function is understood to move beyond the sphere of laughter, naiveté, and indefatigability, as soon as he functions to remind us of the catastrophies, the obstacles, the barriers life sets up for humankind, he assumes a partially tragic, negative configuration. Seen from this perspective, the clown embodies a world that is not so much nonsensical as it is out-of-joint with the parts still intact. His is a disorientation over which one can both laugh and cry. In this way, then, this figure endemic to the circus becomes the externalization of Wedekind's tragicomic philosophy and attitude. This is not to argue that this aesthetic conception of life originated in the author's circus experience: Wedekind had hinted at such a philosophy already in some works prior to his stay in Paris so that the circus experiences are more appropriately viewed as reinforcement. The reinforcement was sufficiently dynamic, however, to carry a similar aesthetic stance over into the playwright's later plays, so much so that it would be difficult to imagine their development without taking the circus and related experiences into account.

In specific regard to the Paris period, a tragicomic orientation shows up significantly in two of the pantomimes, *Die Kaiserin von Neufundland* and *Der Mückenprinz*: in both we are struck by the counterpoint between a tragic theme and its expression in comic form. In *Die Kaiserin von Neufundland* the heroine's happiness depends on her being sexually fulfilled, and when her desires prove insatiable she strangles herself with some of her own hair. The "action" is consistently built around the element of exaggeration and is therefore comic. Yet the story is intended to be tragic, for it is precisely the heroine's inner exaggeration that causes the catastrophe. Once introduced to the realm of sensual pleasure, she exhibits a great imbalance and excess and so moves over to the tragic side of life. Here the very qualities that for Wedekind were positive — sex and physical prowess — are depicted in comic fashion by means of a distortion, and through this comic externality of excess and exaggeration emerges the playwright's questioning of a sexuality that has become excessive and therefore tragic. In the second pantomime *Der Mückenprinz* the tragic elements are inherent in the sexual excesses of the hero Leonor; the entire shocking (1890!) stage action, however, is comic in its performance before a stage audience obviously enjoying itself and makes the entire sequence almost lewdly antic. The same simultaneity of the comic and tragic poles can also be seen in *Frühlings Erwachen* where the fate of young people in conflict with the paralyzed morality of an older generation is destined, except for a few cases, to a tragic end. Yet humor pervades the play: Moritz' concern about his academic future and his sexual experiences is comic because of the exaggerated degree of his anxiety; the school board members' comic actions, their curious names, and their absurd preoccupations provide the audience with a hearty laugh; Wendla's naiveté is humorous at the same time it is tragic. In these latter instances it is not so much a matter of the broad tragedy of theme/comedy of form combination as in the pantomimes, but rather cases in which Wedekind used individual comic aspects to heighten the overall tragedy and where the latter imbues the former with a very special edge. A further example can be seen in the prologue to *Erdgeist:* despite the fact that it was composed some years after the play itself, the circus setting imparts an initial air of gaiety, fun, and entertainment which, however, does not mask, but rather sharpens, the effect; the barker's boast that "das wahre Tier, das wilde schöne Tier, Das — meine Damen — sehn Sie nur bei mir" (*GW,* III, 8), proclaimed as Lulu steps forth in her Pierrot costume, gains penetrating significance after the spectator becomes acquainted with the nature of the animal. Lulu's "Pierrot" debut is itself a statement that grows in meaning as one watches the progress of the "show." In *Marquis von Keith* we find a humorous line of action imposed on the hero's rather tragic existence. Keith's final pronouncement that life is a sliding board is almost symbolic of a comic grin that betrays a fundamental desperation. Even in later plays such as *Nicolo* and *Karl Hetmann,* Wedekind continued to mix the tragic with the comic, cauterizing the poignant with the flippant, shapening the point of his "audience-jabber" so that it made its puncture less painfully, though none the less effectively.

Wedekind's demonstrable debt to the circus world was an early impetus that kept its charge throughout the playwright's life. The effects of the Paris period and the circus experience are probably more pervasive and more completely organic to his creative products than in the case of any other German literary figure. The circus as an element of the popular cultural world was for Wedekind more than emblem, more than useful symbol, more than metaphor. It was in the playwright's formative period that which he actually lived, and in all probability the most receptive, tolerant sphere in which he moved or tried to move during his entire lifetime. Whether or not he himself was cognizant of the fact, it was really where he belonged. Small wonder, then, that it could shape his work to the extent it did, giving him the ability to smile — or sneer — in the face of an essentially hostile world, a world that over and over again insisted on seeing in him the clown instead of the tragic hero.

2. *Bertolt Brecht*

In his essay "Bertolt Brecht und die Tradition" Hans Mayer parallels Brecht's youth in Augsburg with Thomas Mann's in Lübeck. Mayer acknowledges that Brecht never would have presumed to refer to his native city as "geistige Lebensform" as Mann had done, but contends that without Augsburg Brecht nevertheless "ist nicht zu denken." It was not a case of the native city providing the writer with a framework for the traditional conflicts of family and youth à la Hasenclever, Bronnen or Kafka, however. For Brecht, Augsburg revealed conflicts of a wider scope despite the apparent personal tranquility of his early years. "Schon die ersten Konflikte, die dieser Schriftsteller gestalten möchte, sind unmittelbar gesellschaftlich. Sie behandeln das Verhalten des Einzelnen zur Umwelt, Aussenseitertum oder Konformismus."[31] But the provinciality of Augsburg also served as Brecht's haven against trends that did not correspond with the role he saw for himself. It allowed him non-participation in the tendencies of Expressionism, and kept him from following too closely in the shadows of Wedekind's moralistic preachings. Mayer's formulation "Rückzug auf die Augsburger Provinz als Gegenposition zur expressionistischen Menschheitsdämmerung" signals Brecht's individualistic rejection of much that constituted the contemporary literary vogue despite the fact that his own programme was only in its formative stages.

Much later in his life (1954) Brecht would acknowledge that the Augsburg connection had provided him with an initial and critical link to a particular folk tradition: "Die Einflüsse der Augsburger Vorstadt müssen wohl auch erwähnt werden. Ich besuchte häufig den alljährlichen Herbstplärrer, einen Schaubudenjahrmarkt auf dem 'klein Exerzierplatz' mit der Musik vieler Karusselle und Panoramen, die krude Bilder zeigten wie 'Die Erschießung des Anarchisten Ferrer zu Madrid' oder 'Nero betrachtet den Brand Roms' oder 'Die Bayerischen Löwen erstürmen die Düppeler Schanzen' oder 'Flucht Karls des Kühnen nach der Schlacht bei Murten'."[32] This popular world of the *Bänkelsänger* and *Schaubudenjahrmarkt* exerted a significant influence on Brecht in his lyric production and it is of utmost importance to his conception

[31] in Hans Mayer, *Brecht in der Geschichte,* Frankfurt/Main, 1971, p. 29.

[32] Bertolt Brecht, "Bei Durchsicht meiner ersten Stücke," *Gesammelte Werke in 20 Bänden,* Frankfurt/Main, 1967, XVII, 950. Subsequent references in this edition will be cited as *GW* with appropriate volume and page numbers.

of the theater as well. As a chronicle type of presentation with placards and pamphlets illustrating the high point of the narrated action — an oral comic strip, as it were — the *Bänkelsang* assumed critical mass for Brecht as a fairground presentation at once theatrical, pictorial, and musical. As a creative stimulus, it came to bear on his stage works so that, as Sammy McLean writes, "his scenery [illustrates and comments] on the subject matter being presented on stage in the manner of the picture sheets of the *Bänkelsänger,* his scene titles as narration and and commentary [serve] to make the individual scenes [pictures] within a play, his songs and musical presentation [provide] both internal commentaries on the story lines of plays and external narrative frames for complete plays and [function] thus in relation to the context of plays as did the *Bänkellieder* in relation to the prose tales of the *Bänkelsänger* pamphlets, and his actors as direct mediators ... present and interpret the story lines of plays to the audience through songs, through prologues, interludes, and epilogues spoken in verse and through direct addresses to the public in prose."[33]

Albrecht Schöne had suggested already in 1958 that Brecht's guiding principle of *Verfremdung* was derived from the fairground panoramas and that the nature of the *Bänkelsang* gave his plays their unique structure: "Das Stück verliert die all seine Teile zusammengreifende Gespanntheit auf den Höhepunkt, die Katastrophe, den Schluß und zerlegt sich in eine parataktische Reihe eigengewichtiger Szenen, Bilder, Stationen, die etwas Revue-Haftes, Panorama-Artiges haben ..."[34] Brecht, of course, was not the first or only playwright to find his dramaturgical métier in this kind of structure, i.e., in a form of dramatic action which Volker Klotz would later analyze as "offen." Klotz, who also explicated the *Bänkelsang* background to Brecht's poetry in his study *Bertolt Brecht: Versuch über das Werk,*[35] developed his ideas on the

33 Sammy K. McLean, *The "Bänkelsang" and the Work of Bertolt Brecht,* The Hague, 1972, p. 312.

34 Albrecht Schöne, "Bertolt Brecht: Theatertheorie und dramatische Dichtung," *Euphorion,* LII, 3 (1958), p. 275.

35 Darmstadt, 1957.

dichotomies of formal structure in an article "Lied im Drama"[36] and subsequently in his important study *Geschlossene und Offene Form im Drama.*[37] The distinction he formulates comes down to the basic fact that the movement of the action in open drama tends much more to a circular arrangement than to a linear process moving from a beginning toward a conclusion. Klotz' broadly based analysis definitively established the distinction as fundamental to the history and development of the drama. In view of the substantive nature of these contrasting formal structures, the early influence of the fairground on Brecht's own principles of structure is pushed onto a critical level, and the significance of this element is expanded far beyond the measure of a simple stimulus. At issue is basic aesthetic policy.

The Augsburg fairground/*Bänkelsang* influence acquired significance for Brecht's dramatic practice in conjunction with a number of other stimuli, one of which was the playwright's friendship with Karl Valentin. Brecht greatly admired the Munich comedian and drew from him in much the same way that Wedekind had drawn from Willi Morgenstern.[38] Hans Mayer grounds the Brecht-Valentin bond in a mutual *Außenseitertum.* That outsider stance was the crux of many of Valentin's skewed dialectical dialogs with his partner Liesl Karlstadt, and it matched an attitude that had already become basic to Brecht: "Bei Valentin wird daraus immer wieder die Unmöglichkeit der Hauptgestalt, sich der Umwelt verständlich zu machen: bei innigstem Bemühen, verstanden zu werden ... Der einzelne, den der vertraute Alltag keineswegs vertraut anmutet; was er den Partnern mitteilt, ohne daß sie ihn begreifen könnten. Der Konflikt zwischen vertrauter und entfremdeter Umwelt durchzieht alle Szenen des großen Münchner Schauspielers und Szenenschreibers. Brecht hat mit ihm von Anfang an nicht bloß das spannungsreiche Ver-

[36] *Akzente,* VII, 4 (August 1960), pp. 309–320.

[37] Volker Klotz, *Geschlossene und Offene Form im Drama,* Munich, 1972.

[38] See Sol Gittleman's article, "Frank Wedekind and Bertolt Brecht," *Modern Drama,* X (1967/68), pp. 401–409.

hältnis des Außenseiters zur Umwelt gemein, sondern auch die Neigung zum Denken in Widersprüchen, die Weigerung, das Alltägliche und Vertraute als fraglos zu akzeptieren.“[39] The skewed exchanges between Valentin and Karlstadt become an exposé of the rigidity and paralysis of language, the reduction of life to a series of clichés. The logic of dialog careens into the realm of the absurd, and the reduction brings the listener up with a start. Turning onto itself, Valentin's circular repartee takes the form of a dialectical argument at the core of which lay an element of criticism. The comedy was not without its dialectic edge, a combination Brecht would employ and develop throughout his work. Valentin's technique of a cultivated distance between himself as performer and the stage action — his ability to divorce his characters from his own stage presence — was likewise adapted as a basic attitude by Brecht and was a germinal idea that evolved into an entire program for the Brechtian actor.[40]

Valentin was not Brecht's sole model in this regard. Of equal importance was his admiration for Charlie Chaplin. His esteem for the British actor grew out of his enthusiasm for the American silent movie comedy, particularly for comedians like Buster Keaton and Laurel and Hardy. Brecht was an avid filmgoer and a genuine fan of the new art form.[41] Almost from the very beginning he was a Chaplin admirer, by the time he got to Berlin in 1924, a veritable devotee. Of all those legendary figures who polished slapstick comedy to its 1920s film brilliance, Chaplin left the deepest impression. While

[39] Mayer, *Brecht in der Geschichte,* p. 37.

[40] See further Bernhard Thole's Marburg dissertation, *Die "Gesänge" in den Stücken Bertolt Brechts,* Göppingen, 1973.

[41] The extent of his involvement has been investigated by Wolfgang Gersch in his study *Film bei Brecht,* Munich, 1975. One is reminded of a similar situation with Georg Kaiser (see pp. 188–190): Brecht was certainly the more successful in terms of actual involvement in the medium, though his success in film was often in the shape of an argument, to wit, the *Dreigroßchenoper* film that brought forth both a legal suit as well as much theoretical analysis on what is now called a "Brechtian" film aesthetic. The overall scenario of Brecht's involvement requires considerable qualifying commentary.

some of the others apparently served as specific models, for example, the Laurel and Hardy routine in the *Badener Lehrstück* clown scene (1929), Chaplin's influence was more pervasive. In any larger frame of reference Charlie and Company are prime reference points for a kind of dramaturgical routine that functions centrally in Brecht's work. These classic clowns epitomize the naive hero to whom Brecht gives the lead and around whom he builds so much of his dialectical dramatic structures. In many ways they are the mimic counterparts to Valentin's verbal exercises and reproduce both the dry presentational character of the sketch as well as the naiveté at the core of the comic routine. In a mention of Chaplin's 1914 *The Face on the Barroom Floor* Brecht talks about the stoic countenance of Chaplin in his conservative expression of *Gestus:* "Chaplins Gesicht ist immer unbewegt, wie gewachst, eine einzige mimische Zuckung zerreißt es, ganz einfach, stark, mühevoll."[42]

This kind of unemotional portrayal through controlled facial gesture was related by Brecht to another aspect of film that attracted him, namely the documentary nature of some of the early films. News strips, for example, he found intriguing for their ability to portray objects functionally, i.e., with clarity and considerable background but without complicating elements. This rather obvious interest in cinematic forms that permitted the degree of objective rationality Brecht found lacking in the "culinary" traditionalism in most of the theater of his day was given further support by the experimentation going on in Berlin through the efforts of both Reinhardt and Piscator. Erwin Piscator took charge of the Berlin Volksbühne in 1924 and "began to apply the principles of fluidity, simultaneity and cinematic cutting to the topical, historical, factual material that was now beginning to invade the arts."[43] Stage action against a backdrop of film clips, narrative commentary (both spoken and sung) mixed with dramatic action, became common. Brecht had already prescribed the use of placards in

[42] Brecht, "Schriften zum Theater," I, *GW,* XV, 61.
[43] See John Willett, *The Theatre of Bertolt Brecht,* Norfolk, Conn., 1959, p. 110.

Trommeln in der Nacht, and in his own 1924 production of *Eduard II* used silent-film screen titles. Concomitantly, the staging of Pirandello by Reinhardt in 1924 and 1925 brought Brecht face to face with a new vision of the actor and the breakdown of traditional dramatic unities which lay at the center of the Italian playwright's conception of the stage.

Now in all this it is fairly easy to see that the various elements that appealed to Brecht fall into a synchronous and almost circular pattern. The pull of the early fairground *Schaubude* and the illustrated *Bänkelsang* finds support and confirmation in the early film — whose subtitles explain the action or, vice versa, whose fast-moving frames illustrate the narrative of the subtitles. From the *Bänkelsang* to the film is but a very short step with the *Bänkelsänger* easily replaced by the film projector. Illustrative placards, projections onto the stage backdrop, narrative, epic commentaries and songs are the logical extension and bring about a new conception of the actor's role. The latter again harks back to the *Bänkelsänger* "relating" the chronicle of some figure removed from his time and place and self. The early film, whose silence itself distanced the actor on screen from a narrated action and made him dependent on a *Gestus* was but a variation on the fairground technique of demonstrative illustration. Enter Pirandello with the actor released from the constraints of traditional drama, facilitating an almost surreal, farcical mix between the actor and the audience (Brecht had already approved of that in Iwan Goll's farces which he labelled "surreal"). Farces take us to clowning and clowning back to the films of Chaplin and the others. In the requisite stylization and exaggeration of mime lay the kernel of comedy, and slapstick grew to fill the void that would have been filled by words. Here was support and confirmation for the dryness and rudeness *(Derbheit)* characteristic of folk comedy and farce, the acerbity of Valentin's lines matched by the sobreity of Chaplin's non-expressive face.

The precipitate of this grand mixture of variations of narrative frame and clown routine is Brecht's 1924–26 play *Mann ist Mann.* Through an analysis of that play as a clown number we see the direct effects of popular elements, transmuted with various other stimuli, coming to bear on Brecht's first comedy — on a play that gave definitive shape to his conception of "epic" theater and therefore to the whole of his dramatic production. The *Bänkelsang*/Valentin/Chaplin/documentary impeti come together creatively as factors of a pronounced anti-bourgeois effort to create an effective theatrical aesthetic based on decidedly unliterary, markedly visual, and radically objective elements.

Externally, the play is a demonstration. From the very beginning it is perfectly clear to the audience that it is to witness the transformation of Galy Gay into another character. The play-line, or *Fabel,* has of course to be introduced and set up, but any tension arising from the unknown is quickly dispelled. By the time the core of the action is at hand, the demonstrative/illustrative configuration is blatantly exposed. The action on stage becomes action in a fairground booth.[44] Various elements contribute to that atmosphere: songs help set the framework and mood; there is a *Zwischenspruch* to comment on the action and channel the audience's perceptions; an announcing voice narratively sets the stage for the important ninth scene, the *Montageakt,* which itself is divided into five "numbers," three of which are announced in circus-barker fashion; actors fall in and out of roles. In sum, no attempt is made to delude the audience into thinking that the stage action is anything other than just that — stage action illustrative of a point. The purposefully naive and unsophisticated level of the play reinforces the audience's awareness that it is all explicitly a demonstration. There is a shocking lack of finesse in this "poorly-made" play. Should anyone be so obtuse as to miss the central idea of the transformation of a character — what Brecht calls *Ummontierung,* i.e., breakdown and reassembly — there are three sub-transformations paralleling the main one: the soldier Jip is transformed into a Chinese pagoda-god, Widow Begbick's canteen is disassembled and packed up, and Bloody Five becomes a civilian and

[44] See Schöne, "Bertolt Brecht," p. 309.

then a soldier again. The last transformation constitutes, of course, the real parallel in the dialectic that Brecht wishes to demonstrate. These several epic features thus signal the successful integration of theory-barely-developed into concrete dramatic praxis, and the nature of the *Montageakt* makes Brecht's inspiration in the fairground and his indebtedness to the *Bänkelsang* with its narrative/chronicle format fairly explicit. Yet the play involves more than that.

Brecht's conspicuous interest in new forms, his exploitation of "trivial" forms, specifically the detective and adventure novel (to wit, his essay *Über die Popularität des Kriminalromans)* and his enthusiasm for the relevance of sport and technology (his essay *Mehr guten Sport)* form the background for his conscious desire to produce a play of non-literary substance. In an almost obvious parallel to Georg Kaiser's putting on the stage what he proposed as colportage (*Kolportage,* 1924) *Mann ist Mann* represents the younger playwright's rather audacious attempt in the same year to go against the grain of convention by presenting the theater audience with a play in the shape of a clown number. The five "numbers" of Scene 9 would seem to offer fairly undeniable proof that such an intention lies at the center of the play, and the theatrical spectacle "Das Elefantenkalb" which is given as an appendix to *Mann ist Mann* and subtitled "Ein Zwischenspiel für das Foyer" (in Esslin's translation "an interlude for performance in the foyer during the interval") clearly points in this direction. Having seen what Georg Kaiser was up to, Brecht seems to have wanted to go him one better in exploiting a nonliterary form for the serious purposes of the theater. That he should dare to incorporate a fairground/circus routine into his theatrical praxis was nonetheless a quite logical choice, given his background and his concurrent interests.

Just what are the implications of Brecht formulating his play as a clown number? The essence of the "number" as a brief sketch or routine is apparently assumed by Brecht to be readily understood by the audience. He makes no attempt to explain it to them. After Jesse's lengthy exposition at the end of the introductory passage in Scene 9 Uria simply calls out:

"Nummer eins: Das Elefantengeschäft. Die Mg-Abteilung überreicht dem Mann, der nicht genannt sein will, einen Elefanten." Three successive sketches are similarly announced. The end of number four leaves Galy Gay lying in feigned death, and the interlude with Fairchild is not announced as a numbered sketch. It falls into the main action and functions here as an interruption in the sequence. The fifth number restores the sequence and is announced as such. These sketches constitute a fair bulk of the play's action and together with "Das Elefantenkalb" (which is clearly in the nature of a sketch) give the work the overall contour of a series of "numbers." This was formally the essence of "epic," an easy, almost natural slip into that open-ended, serial format that was to dominate Brecht's dramaturgy and which facilitated the addition of most of the properties of the epic mode that he made a permanent part of the modern theater. Moreover, if Brecht saw theatrical potential in the demonstrative/illustrative nature of the clown *number,* he also appreciated the possibilities inherent in the routine itself by virtue of it being a *clown* act. In virtually every clown number (e. g., Chaplin, Valentin, or any circus clown) one is confronted by a peculiar kind of comedy, a dialectic which is unique. Basically it is the fact that the exterior never matches the interior. Inasmuch as the clown operates consistently within a framework of exaggeration, we in the audience are kept aware of the discrepancy between the clothes and the man, the painted features and the facial reality, the mimic action and the actual movements. The clown is consistent *acting.* Behind such an obvious mask there must obviously be a performing agent. The clown, moreover, is the essence of contradiction: all his actions bring about contrary results. He cries when he is happy and laughs when things get rough; he is the "dumbest" who survives by thinking he is the smartest; he thinks himself the "smartest" and falls all over himself in his stupidity. His nonsense always makes sense and his logic is the opposite of rationality. His modus operandi within this contradictory framework is one of adaptation in the face of odds that always threaten to get the better of him. He can be agile or spastic, cunning or naive, fast or slow, go backwards or forwards, lie down, sit up, turn around — in short, whatever the situation demands. He is threatened by disaster but never is its obvious victim, he never falls down without getting up. Nothing does him in — or so it seems. Always he is programmed to teach us, the spectators, a lesson about ourselves. His routine allows us a quick glance into life's routine, and places us momentarily into the actor's role. Our laughing at him is ultimately at ourselves.

None of this apparently escaped Brecht's attention. Four facets of the clown routine in particular must have seemed to him made-to-order: in the clown's obvious projection of a mask he was an embodiment of the distance between the actor and the action which Brecht deemed essential to a non-culinary theater; in his contradictory actions the clown was the essence of an ambiguity that always left the door open for a new insight, and in the very least discouraged a pat analysis, the likes of which allowed the theater audience to check their minds along with their coats; in the adapability that puts the clown in apparent control of the situation Brecht saw his developing ideas on the mutability of man given dramatic expression; and finally, the clown number embodied a kind of actor-audience relationship which complemented his inclination toward the theater stage as a didactic institution. There was thus reason enough to utilize this popular form for the theater that Brecht was planning for the present and the future.

On the surface, the facets of the clown routine that involve that figure's relationship to himself and to the audience, i.e., the alienation (actor-mask) and the didacticism (action-audience) appear uncomplicated and would seem to fall easily into place with other patterns that culminate in the totality of Brecht's theater. The other two points, however, are more complex and deserve closer attention. We ultimately get involved both in the substance of what uniquely lies at the center of this play as clown routine as well as in what causes it to be sometimes less than satisfactorily interpreted.

Brecht called *Mann ist Mann* a comedy and it was the first

of his plays to be so designated.[45] The specification is not without significance, and Eric Bentley, for one, gives it considerable status: "With *A Man's a Man* emerges the Brecht the world knows. The transition is rather an abrupt one ... Formally speaking, it could be taken as a switch from tragedy to comedy. Brecht's final attitude would be vehemently anti-tragic. The newfangled notion of Epic Theater can be construed as a synonym for traditional comedy."[46] That formulation, however, while accurate in calling attention to the fact that the play signalled a change in Brecht's stance, is a gross oversimplification. What Brecht was up to within the framework of the comedy is not so easily dealt with. The matter, to be sure, has not gone undiscussed: Brecht's own statement that "der V-effekt ist ein altes kunstmittel, bekannt aus der komödie, gewissen zweigen der volkskunst und der praxis des asiatischen theaters"[47] has alone provided sufficient fuel to the fire to generate a goodly number of analyses. Of significance here is Helge Hultberg's argument that Brecht's theories diverge considerably from traditional conceptions of comedy, that the matter is not as simple as the equation "comedy equals alienation" might appear. In his *Forschungsbericht,* Jan Knopf sides with her as follows: "Die Komödie ist traditionell auf den guten Schluß abonniert, der alle gezeigten Widersprüche nur als scheinbare, ex eventu als nicht wirkliche erweist. Auch von grundsätzlicher Distanzierung, in dem Sinn, daß das in der Komödie Dargestellte auf Reales zeigt und die Bühnenwirklichkeit als solche sprengt und aufhebt, kann in der traditionelle Komödie nicht die Rede sein ... Die traditionelle Komödie hat das tragische Il-

[45] *Baal* was simply termed "a play"; *Trommeln in der Nacht,* "a drama"; *Im Dickicht der Städte,* "a contest"; *Leben Eduards des Zweiten von England,* a "history."

[46] Eric Bentley, "On Brecht's *In the Swamp, A Man's a Man,* and *Saint Joan of the Stockyards," in Brecht: A Collection of Critical Essays,* Peter Demetz, ed., Engelwood Cliffs, N. J., 1962, p. 53.

[47] Note dated August 2, 1940. Cited in Jan Knopf, *Bertolt Brecht: Ein kritischer Forschungsbericht,* Frankfurt/Main, 1974, p. 32. See also Bertolt Brecht, *Arbeitsjournal 1938–1942,* I, with notes by Werner Hecht, Frankfurt/Main, 1973, p. 137.

lusionstheater zu keiner Zeit in Frage gestellt; sie war bloß sein Pendant und hat es als solches nur bestätigt."[48] The traditional mode of comedy thus seems to contradict the view Brecht had of comedy as a source for the V-effect. Knopf proposes that the two are related only if the point of fusion rests on what he calls *Einheit des Uneinheitlichen* — the unity of the ununiteable. He explains:

> Immer ist es die Widersprüchlichkeit und zugleich die Schlüpfrigkeit, d.h. das grundsätzlich nicht Festzuhaltende, das Unstabile und Prozessuale der Begriffe, worin sich der Humor nach Brecht äußert. Damit aber wird Dialektik zu einer grundsätzlich humoristischen Welthaltung, weil sie sowohl mit dem Ernst des Feststellbaren und Fixierbaren — 'der' Wahrheit, 'dem' Menschen etc. — bricht, als auch auf alle Metaphysik verzichtet.... Komik und Verfremdung sind nur, insofern sie die Widersprüchlichkeit des Bekannten durch Verfremdung aufdecken und als reale Widersprüchlichkeit der Sachen selbst im schlüpfrigen Begriff einer sich selbst widerstreitenden 'synthetischen Einheit' ... fassen, 'wesensverwandt', nämllch als Logik der ungleichen Gleichheit, die auf Identität und Widerspruchsfreiheit verzichtet.[49]

Comedy and alienation, slippery contradictions and a dialectic that turns on itself — these requisites enumerated in Knopf's analysis all find validation in precisely the clown routine rather than in traditional theatrical comedy. It was the clown's comedy and not dramatic comedy that allowed Brecht to cite *Komödie, Volkskunst,* and *asiatisches Theater* in one breath. *Mann ist Mann* was a prime example of all three in interaction.

The play, however, has rarely, if ever, been allowed to exist as a clown routine, i.e., as a piece whose form is demonstrably slapstick in the repartee between the "smart" and the "foolish," whose construction as a series of numbers demonstrates the clown's adaptability, and whose essence is enigmatically contradictory. Like the fate of most of Brecht's plays, this one has not escaped the critics' and interpreters' penchant for tying things in neat packages. Despite Brecht's char-

[48] Jan Knopf, *Forschungsbericht,* p. 37.
[49] Ibid., p. 35.

acteristic ability to change his mind, his interest in always leaving the door open, and his willingness to view any and everything from all and other angles, his public is most often intent on getting a firm grasp on the "morals" of his plays, putting his dialectic to rest so that the "definitive" Brecht can be savoured and enjoyed. In the case of *Mann ist Mann,* these efforts revolve around the "point" of Galy Gay's transformation: is it to be interpreted as something positive or something to be feared? Those anxious to see it affirmatively are those who see the beginnings of Brecht's Marxist stance proposing the necessary elevation of the individual from self-centered singularity to purpose-filled collectivity. Those arguing negatively see the danger of the individual being exploited for society's less than idealistic goals such as war and destruction. Some, for example Ronald Gray, allow the equivocal nature of the play the significance it justly deserves: "The play reveals a deep ... anxiety which can be met only by a feverishly exaggerated depiction of it, and the working of a desire either to escape from the flux or to canalize it in a particular direction. Brecht is still indeterminate, wanting the vivid intensity of varied life, but perceiving how, in present society, it can be immensely dangerous."[50]

A fair reading of the play virtually prevents one from jumping onto one side of the fence or the other: one cannot, for example, discount the structural relationship between Galy Gay and Bloody Five — opposites in that as Bloody Five turns civilian, Galy Gay turns soldier, as Bloody Five struggles with himself to maintain the role he likes to play, going to the extreme length of castration to accomplish it, Galy Gay gives up his self with virtually no effort at all. The castration of both is the persistent symbolism, however, and the complex inverse relationship is countered by the simple parallel. All the negative qualities of the military personality are reiterated, but they frequently are made to characterize something preferable to the zero character of Galy Gay. Widow Begbick's *Zwischenspruch* is the epitome of equivocalness: the lines "Hier

[50] Ronald Gray, *Brecht the Dramatist,* Cambridge, England, 1976, p. 33.

wird heute abend ein Mensch wie ein Auto ummontiert / ohne daß er irgend etwas dabei verliert" are in counterpoint to the admonition which follows: "Herr Bertolt Brecht hofft, Sie ... werden schon merken bei dem Packer Galy Gay, daß das Leben auf Erden gefährlich sei." The final scene (1926 edition) in which Galy Gay as soldier par excellence destroys the mountain fortress also contains the *Ferne Stimme* which interjects: "Die Bergfestung Sir El Dchour steht in Flammen, welche 7000 Flüchlinge aus der Provinz beherbergt hat. Bauern, Handwerker und Kaufleute, zum großen Teil fleißige und freundliche Menschen!" Galy Gay's response "Aber was soll das mir? Das eine Geschrei und das andere Geschrei!" cannot be taken without some reservation. The clown number has turned serious but no less enigmatic.

Brecht's own pronouncements on his play do nothing to clear the air. Collectively they indicate the "flow of things" of which Widow Begbick spoke and the shifting sands on which the play's structure rests. In a 1926 interview, for example, when asked whether the play showed the development of "der ideale Mensch" Brecht replied simply: "No, not particularly." In the 1927 *Vorrede zu Mann ist Mann* things look a little different. Brecht proposes: "Sie werden sich auch sagen, daß es eher bedauernswert sei, wenn einem Menschen so mitgespielt und er einfach gezwungen wird, sein kostbares Ich aufzugeben, sozusagen das einzige, was er bestitz, aber das ist es nicht. Es ist eine lustige Sache. Denn dieser Galy Gay nimmt eben keinen Schaden, sondern er gewinnt."[51] In the 1936 essay *Zur Frage der Konkretisierung* the play is interpreted as a veiled warning of impending Nazi "transformation," and as late as 1954 in his *Bei Durchsicht meiner ersten Stücke* Brecht acknowledges this change in perspective represented by the 1926 and 1931 performance versions (the earlier one contained scenes 10 and 11, the later one ended after the "Montageakt" (Scene 9)): "Ich hatte 1931 das Stück nach dem großen Montageakt enden lassen, da ich keine Möglichkeit sah, dem Wachstum des Helden im Kollektiv einen nega-

[51] Brecht, "Schriften zum Theater," III, *GW*, XVII, 978.
[52] Ibid., p. 987.

tiven Charakter zu verleihen, so hatte ich lieber auf die Beschreibung des Wachstums verzichtet. Bei einer gut verfremdenden Darstellung ist aber dieses Wachstum ins Verbrecherische durchaus zeigbar. Ich versuchte, sie durch ein paar Einfügungen in die letzte Szene zu erleichtern.“[53] The probability of a definitive position on the part of the playwright seems patently unlikely.

Perhaps, however, Brecht's 1935 essay *Über die Verwendung von Musik für ein Episches Theater* in which he places the emphasis on the social fabric allows us to find a key to the play in its equivocal form. Here the didactic element gets heavy coverage:

> Das Interesse des epischen Theaters ist also ein eminent praktisches. Das menschliche Verhalten wird als veränderlich gezeigt, der Mensch als abhängig von gewissen ökonomisch-politischen Verhältnissen und zugleich als fähig, sie zu verändern. Um ein Beispiel zu geben: Eine Szene, in der drei Männer von einem vierten Mann zu einem bestimmten illegalen Zweck gemietet werden ('Mann ist Mann'), muß vom epischen Theater so geschildert werden, daß man sich das dabei zum Ausdruck kommende Verhalten der vier Männer auch anders vorstellen kann, das heißt, daß man entweder sich politisch-ökonomische Verhältnisse vorstellen kann, unter denen diese Männer anders sprechen würden, oder eine Haltung dieser Männer den gegebenen Verhältnissen gegenüber, die sie ebenfalls anders sprechen ließe.[51]

Here the emphasis falls on enabling the audience to envision a *change,* either changed conditions or changed attitudes to the same conditions, but in either dase, different actions than are acutally depicted. The *Ummontierung* of Galy Gay is thus set into a greatly expanded context and the whole procedure is felt by Brecht to be something really innovative: "Der Zuschauer erhält die Gelegenheit zur Kritik menschlichen Verhaltens vom gesellschaftlichen Standpunkt aus ... Der Zuschauer soll also in der Lage sein, Vergleiche anzustellen, was die menschlichen Verhaltungsweisen anbetrifft. Dies bedeutet, vom Standpunkt der Ästhetik aus, daß der Gestus der

[53] Ibid., p. 951.
[54] Brecht, "Schriften zum Theater,“ I, *GW,* XV, 474f.

Schauspieler besonders wichtig wird."[55] This *Gestus* lay precisely in the previously mentioned ambivalent qualities of Galy Gay as simultaneously *abhängig* and *fähig,* in other words, precisely in the dialectical nature of his adaptability and in the essence of his persona as clown. The ambiguities of the clown number, the equivocalness of Galy Gay and the questions raised by virtue of his "transformation" expand into the dialectic of the whole play and the questions posed by a thinking audience. The question raised at the end of "Das Elefantenkalb" — the apparent absurdity of which is really the epitome of the dialectical — is still open: "... ob das hier die Wahrheit war ... ob es ein gutes Theater war oder ein schlechtes ..." The comedy and the contradictions, the dilemma and the dialectic were always the properties of the clown. It was Brecht, however, who was ultimately responsible for giving him a place on the stage of the Epic Theater.

3. *Georg Kaiser*

It is a fact that at one point during his career the German dramatist Georg Kaiser set a kind of record for having the most plays produced in a single theatrical season. So feverishly did he turn out play after play from the turn of the century until his death in 1945 that there was a rumor that he was in reality a collective of writers duping the public.[56] His name was of sufficient renown that Bernhard Diebold wrote a mon-

[56] Six Kaiser plays enjoyed premieres during 1917, with openings in Hamburg, Berlin, Frankfurt/Main, and Munich. In a 1918 essay *Vision und Figur* Kaiser articulated his own, almost frenetic, dramatic activity: "Vielgestaltig sind die Figuren, die Träger der Vision sind — von den heißen Fingern des Dichters beladen mit großer Fracht seiner Mitteilung. Sie würde zehn und hundert erdrücken — so müssen Scharen hinausgehen und Teile des ganzen tragen, soviel ihre Schultern tragen. ... Immer bunter flirrt die Gestaltung der Vision — es wird schwer eine Übersicht aus der Vielheit der Teile das Ganze zu erkennen." Georg Kaiser, *Werke,* Walther Huder, ed., Frankfurt/Main, 1971, IV, 548.

ograph on him as early as 1924.[57] Yet for all but Kaiser afficionados he is now no more than an obscure German playwright — if his name is known at all. Marked fairly early as a leading dramatist of German Expressionism, Kaiser got locked into that category despite the work that he produced after that movement had waned, and today he remains all but banished to that historical realm of theatrical and literary history. The recently published edition of his *Werke* is filled with plays that would have to be termed unknown except to a group of disciples and experts, and the 1978 Alberta Symposium[58] celebrating the centenary of his birth was an event of decidedly limited interest — except, again, to specialists in the field.

Despite numerous anthologists' tendency to perpetuate Kaiser's pre-1920 fame and Expressionist tag, Kaiser's own testimony would support the premise that the twenty-five years between 1920 and 1945 were ones of considerable vitality and productive of plays worthy of more than a specialist's attention. The playwright's comments right up to his death indicate that Kaiser never had any intention of withdrawing from the fray — not in his dramas at least. Even if his post-Expressionist period seems to defy organization, it does not follow that the dramatist had been overtaken by insecurity, nor that the products of such a period are the hackwork of a mind in limbo — two fairly common claims that have contributed to an unfair and distorted view of this complex and enigmatic figure in the history of modern German theater.

Three of Kaiser's post-1920 plays slipped quickly into oblivion. In few critical studies do the plays *Nebeneinander, Kolportage,* or *Zwei Krawatten* receive more than cursory mention. Frequently they are ignored completely, and on the basis of dramatic content, they have probably been dismissed with some justification. In 1960 Wolfgang Paulsen did suggest, albeit in a footnote, that *Nebeneinander* qualified as

[57] *Der Denkspieler Georg Kaiser,* Frankfurt/Main.

[58] Georg Kaiser Symposium, sponsored by the Department of Germanic Languages, The University of Alberta-Edmonton, October 11-14, 1978.

"eines der interessantesten Stücke der zwanziger Jahre, auf das näher einzugehen sich verlohnen würde,"[59] and at least two contemporary literary analysts have deemed two of them worthy of examination and explication.[60] The three plays demand our attention here for what they tell us about Kaiser's relationship to popular entertainment forms of his day and how the latter – similar to what we have seen in the case of the circus – affected his conception of dramatic form. Though Kaiser wrote for the stage in a variety of forms, and the comedy to which these three relate was by his own admission one of his strongest dramatic impulses, *Nebeneinander* (1923) is the only play he labelled a *Volksstück, Kolportage* (1924), while subtitled *Komödie,* is clearly the best single representative of the generic designation itself, and *Zwei Krawatten* (1929) is the only piece classified as a *Revuestück.*

Kaiser had demonstrated an early interest in innovative dramatic form in *Europa* (1914/1915), a play he called "Tanz und Spiel in fünf Aufzügen". The piece attests to his awareness of the public's enchantment with "natural" dance, a vogue that had taken dance out from under the shadow of traditional balletic forms, given it freedom of movement, and clothed it in diaphanous gowns. Kaiser's sensibilities in this regard may be seen as an early example of his tendency to break new ground in the theater, to go against traditional forms.[61] But while the impetus in *Europa* was grounded in a

[59] Wolfgang Paulsen, *Georg Kaiser: Die Perspektiven seines Werkes,* Tübingen, 1960, pp. 64 and 119 (note 52).

[60] See Peter U. Hohendahl's treatment of *Nebeneinander* in his discussion of the fool figure in *Das Bild der bürgerlichen Welt im expressionistischen Drama,* Heidelberg, 1967, pp. 269–293, and Reinhold Grimm's analyses of *Kolportage* and *Nebeneinander* in his *Nach dem Naturalismus,* Kronberg, 1978.

[61] A number of statements by Kaiser, though later in origin, bear this out. For example, "Der lebendige Autor muß wissen, daß er der Widersacher der Sitten und Formeln seiner Mitzeit ist – sonst griffe er fehl im Mittel seiner Äußerung, die Kunst heißt." ("Dichter und Regisseur," *Werke,* IV, 553); "Drama ist Bedrohung des Zuständlichen. ... Jedes Dichtwerk verrichtet eine vernichtende Niederlage der Geborgenen." ("Methusalem oder der ewige Bürger," *Werke,* IV, 575).

"popular" and culturally "new" form, and while in many ways he did transform the dramatic stage action into a dance revue, this humorous piece was nevertheless conceived in terms of the traditional five acts, and it is clear that an "old" mythology shapes the development of the plot. In the three later pieces, Kaiser takes bolder steps, revealing in all of them a similar popular orientation and a consistently more conscious effort toward theatrical innovation. Each one can be viewed as an experiment in form.

Kaiser the man is still very much an enigma, and the essence of his work emanates out of paradox. There are few questions one can ask and expect a definitive reply. I nevertheless want to suggest that in these three plays Kaiser is at work in typical paradoxical fashion, and that instead of relegating these plays to the fringes of his total work by virtue of their apparent light tone and slightly frivolous form, it is more appropriate to view them as evidence that Kaiser was consciously and deliberately making use of popular entertainment forms for very specific dramatic purposes.

It is helpful to consider the broader context in which Kaiser found himself when involved with these plays. By 1923 he was a man of forty-five. He had behind him a theatrical record as well as a police record.[62] Judgment had been pronounced on both the plays and the playwright, and there was reason enough to see that in the playwright's eyes the public had not been overly understanding of either the man or the work. Despite the fact that Kaiser claimed with a touch of bravura that he never viewed his own plays in performance, that he wrote only for himself, that it was sheer accident that the theater and its audience found what he had to say of interest, he nevertheless admitted that he enjoyed success and the money it brought in. Despite all the disclaimers, Kaiser knew that he was writing for a public, that whether or not he was giving them what they wanted he was nonetheless giving them something. For the numerous times he expressed his ab-

[62] Kaiser was tried in 1921 for selling furnishings from a villa he was renting at the time. He was sentenced and spent several months in prison.

horrence of the idea of sitting back and resting on the successes of the past, it was probably equally a matter of not being financially able to do so in the first place. He could propose that upon completion the products of his activity — whatever the original impetus — were finished and done with, but the producer knew full well that their reception was relevant to his own private purposes: each success was a means to an end — "Mittel, (seine) Passionen zu befriedigen." The very fact that Kaiser's personal situation was almost always highly precarious put him in an antagonistic position relative to his public, and the trial and sentencing in 1921 must have reinforced this to an indelible degree. Beyond this, moreover, was the ample evidence that the world had not changed its ways, and that the ideals and visions he had articulated had not had any effect at all. In the most secure of writers all this might have called forth a stock-taking, a kind of self-assessment, and Kaiser's *Noli me tangere* of 1920/21, written while he was in prison, can indeed be read as Kaiser contra Kaiser in veiled terms. Self criticism, however, was never Kaiser's forte — he was much more inclined to self delusion than introspective analysis — and he was ever on his public guard. Nonetheless, most of his statements *off* the stage *about* the stage show him at the time viewing his own position as one of constant struggle, of energetic efforts to find the right vehicle for his ideas, the best form for articulating his argument. Within this complex context, then, it is ultimately more logical to accept as entirely plausible the variety of Kaiser's dramatic formulations than to fault him for inconsistency and what in some instances appear to be deviations from an established norm. The three plays treated here illustrate the dimensions of this more positive approach.

A purely external impetus behind Kaiser's work at this point, and one with particular significance for the kind of formal experimentation in which he demonstrates an interest, was the film. The development of the movie industry and the concurrent public interest in the new art form were obvious to anyone involved in the theater at this time, and Kaiser was not completely blind to what was going on in the world outside his villa. His own work with the genre attests to his lasting interest in this regard as well as to his awareness of the film's monetary and aesthetic potential. Kaiser wrote some thirty-three film plans/sketches/synopses, although only one actually became a film script. Eight ot these (of varying length) are contained in volume IV of Kaiser's collected works. The editor Walther Huder points out that while most of the films are but variations on the theme of the antithesis, polarity, or dialectic of appearance and reality, i. e., the favorite theme of Kaiser, it is important to note that the playwright recognized that for the representation of those themes the technical possibilities of the film were greater than those of the stage.[63] Kaiser, of course, was not alone in his appreciation of the new form's relevance to the theater. The entire Expressionist movement existed in competition with the new form in ascendancy, and not a few characteristics of Expressionism — and the early film as well — evolved from the interpenetration of the cinema and the literature of the day. Ultimately, the film/cinema proved more successful for the Expressionists than did the stage, at least as an aspect of mass media. The film functioned so successfully precisely because it could, and did, relate to the masses to a considerable degree more effectively than the established dramatic literature. In his analysis of the film and expressionist literature, Silvio Vietta explains: "In einer Zeit, als die Literatur in symbolisch-neuromantischen Bahnen sich apart vom Leben hielt, das Schöne zu kultivieren und eine 'reine' Kunstsprache zu konservieren suchte, wird hier im außerliterarischen Medium Stummfilm das moderne Lebenstempo selbst zur Darstellung gebracht. Während hohe Literatur um die Jahrhundertwende nur durch ihre Verweigerungsgeste sich auf die Moderne bezieht, spiegelt sie der Film naiv und direkt, ja, die unprätentiöse Naivität des neuen Mediums ist vermutlich die Voraussetzung einer solchen Form von Mimesis gewesen."[64] Success in this field, Kaiser doubtless perceived, would have brought

[63] See *Werke,* IV, 740.

[64] Silvio Vietta, "Film und expressionistische Literatur: Simultaneität des Disparaten und Ablösung der Literatur durch den Film,"

him much needed financial security. This, however, proved as elusive as some of his other dreams. But whatever the reality, the playwright's awareness of the fact that the film enjoyed a significance both for the present and for the future is articulated in the play *Nebeneinander,* where one-third of the play's action revolves around the line: "dem Kino gehört die Welt."[65]

I would propose, then, that the three Kaiser plays in question take their cue from the then-current popularity of the cinematic form and may be viewed as the playwright's attempt to incorporate aspects of this and related popular forms into the legitimate theater. Part of his interest might be ascribed to a desire to "cash in" on the wave of public enthusiasm; in part it was surely the recognition that these forms might well work better than some of the constructions he had previously put before the audience. There is a noticeable progression from *Nebeneinander* to *Zwei Krawatten* in the direction of formal simplicity, as if Kaiser sought to go each time one step further toward the naiveté that marked the early film's approach to its subject matter (dictated, to be sure, by the state of the technology involved) as well as to a populist attitude that was in evidence in other popular forms. All three plays represent a kind of reactionism and anti-traditionalism on the part of Kaiser, not only against and with respect to the traditional theatrical heritage, but also with reference to his own earlier work. The three plays serve a more important function, then, than hackwork or flippant exercises to relieve the playwright's tension after a recent burst of dramatic energy. They are the products of a Kaiser working within a broadened framework, a playwright keenly attuned to the relevance of form, the *Denkspieler,* as Bernhard Diebold had called him, playing in a new key. The light tone of these plays (not quite comic in *Nebeneinander,* progressing to the almost farcical in *Zwei Krawatten)* would seem to work counter to a well-planned and tight construction underneath. But Kaiser had al-

in Silvio Vietta, Hans-Georg Kemper, eds., *Expressionismus,* Munich, 1975, p. 123.

65 Georg Kaiser, *Nebeneinander* (Act II), *Werke,* II, 301.

ready successfully wrought the apparent looseness of the *Stationsdrama* in *Von morgens bis mitternachts* and other plays, and there is every reason to believe that he was intrigued by the dialectic between form and content here as well. In the first play (which has most often been given significance relative to the status of the Kaiserean old "new" man, the pawnbroker[66]), the "nebeneinander" refers to the tri-partite construction of this *Volksstück* — five acts and fifteen scenes evenly divided among three parallel actions — a kind of dramatic sequencing not unlike the paratactic sequencing possible in the film, or for that matter, not too different from the three rings of the American circus tradition. The action in the center portrays that aspect of the play's plot involving the pawnbroker and his harried attempts to prevent what appears

[66] Paulsen views it as a later realization of the idea of personal responsibility within the social and cultural fabric. Kenworthy is willing to see the central figure as a statement of "the isolation of modern man, and the lack of human sympathy in a competitive world." In the fairly recent study by Wilhelm Steffens for the Friedrich series *Dramatiker des Welttheaters,* the central point is related to the idea of *Erneuerung* so that the main character can be viewed as dying "mit dem unsichtbaren Gewinn des wunderbarsten Gefühls: für einen fremden Menschen sich auf den Weg gemacht zu haben." (Wilhelm Steffens, *Georg Kaiser,* Velber, 1969, p. 115). Diebold sees it as more Kaiser sermonizing, the pawnbroker falling into place alongside the Kassierer in *Hölle Weg Erde,* and the Kanzlist in *Kanzlist Krehler,* i. e., as yet another variation on the same theme, all of them Don Quixotes running their heads against the brick walls of an absurd ideal. Although he points to the tragic/comic nature of the struggle — "der Pfandleiher glaubte an das Ineinander der Menschenseelen ... und starb an der Tragikomödie des Nebeneinander" — he sees the ultimate point in the question of guilt, in general a rather heavy-handed interpretation of a *Volksstück.* (See Diebold, *Der Denkspieler,* p. 121) For Eric Fivian it is the senselessness of modern existence that places it in the Kaiser pattern: in his analysis Kaiser's point is that "wir leben nicht mehr füreinander, miteinander, sondern in furchbarer Gefühlskälte nebeneinander." It is this lack of connection, "das kalte, geschäftsmäßige Beiseiteschieben der Empfindungen des Mitmenschen" that occupies Kaiser's attention. (Eric A. Fivian, *Georg Kaiser und seine Stellung im Expressionismus,* Munich, 1946, p. 92f.)

to him as an imminent suicide, with two levels of action on either side, the one involving Luise who, instead of taking her life, takes a husband and lives happily ever after, the other, the successful realization of Neumann's enterprising undertaking in the financially-rewarding world of the film. It is very neatly balanced out in a one-two-three sequence, each act opening with the pawnbroker's tribulations. The three actions run parallel and separate, though obviously connected and fatefully intertwined in the cyclical pattern. The pattern appears simple enough, and Kaiser would seem to be advertising an obvious plot line by labelling the piece a *Volksstück*. More than the traditionally accepted genera of comedy and tragedy, the *Volksstück* designation indirectly implies a simplicity easily comprehensible by the popular body, a level of dramatic intent not too demanding. In the third act, the cue/statement is made: "Nur der Zufall schafft Klarheit" as if to suggest that the seemingly accidental reappearance of the three plot tunes in the cyclical melody should produce a certain clarity. Again in the fourth act, the line "Da ist nichts schleierhaft" proposes an uncomplicated point commensurate with the "folk" grade of the play. Or is this reading Kaiser naively? Should we not be slightly more suspicious of the *Denkspieler?*

Most interpreters, as already indicated, have been inclined to take the play as Kaiser engaged in a more or less serious sermon, and Diebold finds elements as well to mark the play as "regular" Kaiser.[67] Even though Diebold suggests in passing that this is after all not as naive a piece as the subtitle would indicate, he and others seem intent on ignoring the implications of the play's subtitle, that is, the piece as a more direct appeal to the masses, by denying the folk-specific nature

[67] Diebold, *Der Denkspieler,* p. 122f: "außerordentliche Formeln der Gedankenknappheit, der rapiden Assoziationen. ... Kontraste in zwei Gegenwarte, die bereits einen Dialog ersetzen. Bombastische Ausdrücke des simplen Pfandverleihers bezeugen grotesk die 'tiefere Bedeutung'. ... Die Sprache magert ab zum Begriff. ... Dies unnaive 'Volksstück 1923', wie der Untertitel sagt — es wird Schule machen."

of the form that bears the subtitle out: the three-fold plot structure suggestive of the multiple actions of the circus arena, or the serial nature of the film and less sophisticated theatrical forms such as the variety stage and burlesque (including the musical revue), or the "epic" form as Brecht was to develop it, or what has been termed "open" form in contrast to "closed." It is, of course, unlikely that Kaiser would all of a sudden become a "playful" playwright, that he would forego the prerogative of the serious artist to do more than entertain. Yet given the formal structure of this work it is likewise unlikely that it is to be interpreted purely and simply as the fateful demise of a "new" man out to serve his fellowman in a dog-eat-dog world. Overserious intent is mollified by less-than-serious form. The two side actions involve plots which run in counterpoint to the central action and effectively subdue a totally serious "unnaive" interpretation of the pawnbroker's fate. Luise quickly recovers from the desertion by Neumann and in a new setting finds her bourgeois equilibrium in the match with Franz Krüger. Neumann — the Nieman(d) sought so desperately by the pawnbroker — wraps up a deal with brother and sister Borsig to the satisfaction of all concerned and with promise of a bright future that was not so hard to achieve after all. The audience can be expected to applaud the action in both side rings. While champagne flows at the Borsigs, the music plays on — "diesselbe Melodie ad infinitum" — at the wedding celebration of Luise and Franz. The pawnbroker meanwhile has been brought to the end of his tether and is sacrificed to what must appear as totally foolish ideals. No one could be so stupid as to act the way he did — to assume so much responsibility for actions which were independent of him and which only by sheer accident came to his attention — and then commit suicide because he could not find a sympathetic ear in the world outside his private room behind the counter of his pawnshop. Now either the pawnbroker is made to look foolish in the context of the other two actions or else the audience that can be expected to empathize with Luise and Neumann is forced to assume the role of the fool. The latter interpretation restores the piece to the status of a variation on a Kaiser theme in which Kaiser shows once again the difficulties encountered by the "new" man in the philistine world of the twenties. But was Kaiser's vision so myopic that he could propose such idealism before an audience in 1923, a year in which rampant inflation brought more members of the audience into more pawnshops than could ever be depicted on stage? Or is his irony more directed at himself? Although definitiveness still eludes us, there is considerable evidence to indicate the latter as the more reasonable approach to the play.

Hohendahl treats this play at length in his discussion of the fool figure,[68] pointing to the traditional status of the fool as outsider, and in the case of Kaiser, relating the playwright to the dramatic tradition of Wedekind and his prototypes. He proposes that while there are numerous examples of the fool depicted in isolation from society, most authors portray the figure positively. Of more interest, he suggests, are those cases, "in denen mittels der Narrengestalt die Zweifel an dem eigenen Protest ausgedrückt werden. Um sich in der ideologischen Auseinandersetzung behaupten zu können, mußte das Stigma der Narrenhaftigkeit ja als eine positive Eigenschaft umgedeutet werden. Sobald aber das Vertrauen in die eigene Position nachläßt, gewinnt der öffentliche Vorwurf den Anschein der Berechtigung."[69] This he finds to be the case in *Nebeneinander,* an almost classic example in which the depiction of the fool figure ends in *aponie.* Willing to accept the fact that Kaiser forces a negative interpretation onto the pawnbroker by virtue of the other two subplots, i. e., that the playwright wanted to criticize the old man's excessive humanity by carrying his actions to the absurdity of suicide, Hohendahl nonetheless rescues Kaiser and proposes that while the play obviously lends credence to the realistic world of the subplots, the humane ethic of the pawnbroker remains as its polar opposite. "Die blinde Nächstenliebe des Pfandleihers ist zwar in der Welt eine Torheit; aber ist es nicht besser ein

[68] Hohendahl, *Das Bild der bürgerlichen Welt im expressionistischen Drama,* pp. 272–288.
[69] Ibid., p. 292.

Narr zu sein, wenn die Gesellschaft so ist, wie sie dargestellt wird?"[70] In this interpretation the whole dramatic process would end up an equivocal statement of the playwright – castigation of the world for its inhumanity, self-castigation by leaving the central character a victim of his ridiculous righteousness. Now that is a more likely interpretation than those which totally ignore the play's revolving structure, yet it too seems overly intent on keeping the play in a strict Kaiser mold. It draws out of the play a kind of static equilibrium, and transforms the triangular format into a straight line with polar opposites at either end.

The direction in which Kaiser was subsequently to move in both *Kolportage* and *Zwei Krawatten* possibly sheds some light on what he was up to in *Nebeneinander:* the irony is pronounced in the execution of the colportage of his material in the one, and moves into comic sarcasm in the other. Kaiser was apparently interested in new directions not only structurally but also in relation to content. The latter plays are almost anti-Kaiser in their pronounced departure from the tone of previous years and other works, and *Nebeneinander* in this regard falls into place as the first in that series.

What Kaiser has fashioned in *Nebeneinander* is the equivalent of the *Drehbühne* which Brecht was to bring into fashion only a little later. It is also the execution of the technique of the film in which several actions can be made to run parallel and serially. In its cyclical, revolving manner the fate of the pawnbroker turns with the other two. The structure is triadic, and through five acts the triplex turns like a theatrical carousel before a crowd of fairground spectators, the plots spinning their development in a kind of everchanging and entertaining tableau only limitedly united by time and space. But the Neumann-Luise plots oppose the pawnbroker's plight, the two, as it were, in league against the third. And in this instance the last word does *not* go to the pawnbroker, the spotlight does *not* focus finally on the action in the center ring. In this *Volksstück* Kaiser gives Luise and Neumann the distinct edge. He

[70] Ibid., p. 288.

can ill expect that the audience will swallow the pawnbroker's misguided sacrifice, and the penultimate words, descriptive of Neumann, "Das ist der Typ, der durchkommt. Wenn wir alle in Dreck und Speck verrecken, pfeift das noch die Wacht am Rhein mit vollen Backen," push the existence and death of the pawnbroker further into the shadows. The final words, spoken almost as a toast, "Ex Kino lux! Stimmt's?" ring out as the curtain falls. The "folk" agree and applaud, and only the playwright remembers the pawnbroker.

Thus by virtue of its open form the play is neither simply Kaiser lamenting a *nebenher* kind of fate relegated to an old "new" man nor the evenly-drawn sides between a fool and a foolish society. The first of these three "divergent" pieces almost defies a simple interpretation, operating as it does on several levels. From the hints furnished by its formal construction, however, *Nebeneinander* would seem to lean toward an acknowledgment by the playwright that two against one are uneven odds and always will be, no matter how long the carousel keeps turning. That would be Kaiser looking at Kaiser from a slightly critical stance. In a piece designated as *Volksstück,* however, the point seems less sharp and appears to carry a less serious intent. This is in many ways Kaiser's well-practiced paradoxical approach to the theater — full of escape hatches for the playwright. By fashioning his play formally on structures inherent in those forms contemporarily popular with the public, Kaiser could take stock of an old idea that possibly no longer belonged to the future and suggest to the audience that such an idea was legitimately overwhelmed by more current attitudes. If on the other hand he intended to preach the old sermon once again, he almost begs the audience to miss the point, and in their ridicule to perceive that the sarcasm is directed at them and not the pawnbroker. It is a dramatic hall of mirrors that suggests that in *Nebeneinander* Kaiser is profoundly aware of his audience, critically aware of himself, and playing to both elements at the same time.

Kolportage, which followed in 1924, is possibly less problematical. Here Kaiser constructs a well-made play around a totally unrealistic plot line and comes up with such blatant colportage that he cannot resist titling the play with that term. A marriage for money, a change in the will; a greedy father and a well-meaning and determined mother; false heirs and fresh beginnings for someone willing to play the game; the outcome as planned — only better; a multitude of beneficiaries and lessons learned; love triumphant and happy ever after. All this in traditional form — "Komödie in einem Vorspiel und drei Akten nach zwanzig Jahren" — but in such farfetched proportions as to *appear* to ridicule the tradition, the playwright, and the audience.

The piece has suffered much the same fate as its predecessor of the previous year. Diebold takes Kaiser at face value and cannot forgive him for writing such trash: "'Kolportage' scheint nun wirklich ein Meisterwerk an Fehlgeburt zu sein." He finds it lacking in irony because Kaiser proposes within the play that such colportage is life itself. He even fears for the fate of the German theater which might be taken in by Kaiser's poorly conceived joke: "So wenig ist hier echte Ironie und Dichterüberlegenheit gegeben, daß harmlose Provinzdirektoren dieses Drama in vollem Ernst als 'feine Konversation' akzeptieren dürften — im Bewußtsein, ihrem weiteren Publikum wieder einmal ein kerngesundes Stück Literatur auf die Platte zu legen. Und das Publikum reagierte denn auch mit allen seinen theatralischen Atavismen und fand es wunderschön. Denn zwischen Kitsch und Wahrheit schwebet hier zweifelnd jede Brust. Und das Renovance des Dichters bebet bedenklich mit."[71] Brian Kenworthy sees it as the simple satirization of shallow conventional plays so much in vogue and readily consumed by the public. He cites the suggestion by Max Freyhan *(Georg Kaisers Werk,* Berlin, 1926) that Kaiser wrote the play as relaxation, and on the basis of Victor Fürdauer's assertion that Kaiser was "urged to write a play more to the taste of the average theater-goer" *(Georg Kaisers dramatische Gesamtwerk,* Dissertation, Vienna, 1949), refers

[71] Diebold, *Der Denkspieler,* pp. 125, 127.

to the work as "another satire on bourgeois life."[72] Paulsen does not discuss the play at all.

In this play Kaiser would appear to be giving the public what it longed for by virtue of giving them what he accurately calls colportage. As one of the lesser literary forms, colportage has received some attention of late, particularly from the sociological perspective. Gert Ueding's analysis, for example, follows Ernst Bloch's lead in viewing it as a kind of folk placebo: "Kolportage thematisiert derart die jeder Scheinlösung immanente Dialektik, wie sie selber als Tagtraum der Gesellschaft ganz reale gesellschaftliche Bedürfnisse scheinhaft befriedigt: als Glanz in dem das Elend verschwinden soll ... am kruden Widerspruch zwischen Wunsch und Erfüllung hält sie fest: durch sie selber geht der Riß hindurch, den sie glanzvoll verdecken soll und so immer wieder thematisiert: auch deswegen versetzt sie ihre Leser in Spannung."[73] Bloch had seen in colportage a *Ferntraum* functioning similarly to the fairy tale in satisfying an inner longing of a people: "Beiden Eigenschaften des Traums: der kreatürlichen Urspannung wie den Arabesken der Verschleierung, Einkleidung und Verwetterung ist Kolportage der nächste und treuste Ort. Sie wird dieser Art der populäre Widerschein von Urmotiven der Angst, der Rückkehr, des Muts, der Erwartung, Enttäuschung, Rettung und anderer Erschütterungen des Willenslebens *im Spiegel gefährlicher Ferne oder abgrundreichen Glanzes.*"[74] It was for him the paradoxical expression of "manipulierter Bedürfnisse und deren scheinhafter Befriedigung, Quietiv revoltierender Sehnsucht."[75]

These insights notwithstanding, Kaiser has created in this well-named play all the components necessary to colportage — a pieced-together story that condenses twenty years so that we only see the critical moments, dialog which is frequently not a logical development of ideas, statements that are no

[72] Brian J. Kenworthy, *Georg Kaiser,* Oxford, 1957, p. 70.
[73] Gert Ueding, *Glanzvolles Elend: Versuch über Kitsch und Kolportage,* Frankfurt/Main, 1973, p. 194.
[74] Ernst Bloch, *Erbschaft dieser Zeit,* Frankfurt/Main, 1962, p. 178.
[75] Ueding, *Glanzvolles Elend,* p. 185.

more than old clichés and formulated of the most stereotypical dreams. But he presents it with tongue in cheek. What Diebold refers to as Kaiser's misplaced and insufficient irony, i.e., his title-page statement that the play was written in support of child welfare and the contemporary theater, must indeed be taken as a statement of Kaiser's ironic, almost satiric intent. Given our conviction that the formal construction of these three plays is of the utmost importance, however, we are inclined to suspect that Kaiser was offering his work as something more than just satire. By virtue of his earnest experimentation with form and his previous work on *Nebeneinander,* the introduction of colportage into the theater would doubtless have held some degree of fascination for him. Innocent colportage, i.e., the product of an author not consciously adopting the role of colporteur, is the substance of Bloch's and Ueding's analysis. Another matter, however, is the conscious creation of colportage which in and of itself entails an ironic stance on the part of an author, as if playing with some deep-seated shortcomings in the audience itself and forcing them to face this inadequacy in themselves. That would be Kaiser in this piece — but with the addition of yet another twist. The addition of irony to already existing irony is far from innocent. In such a format it creates a dialectic superbly infinite. The interplay between what the playwright proposes within the context of the dramatic action and his own stance with regard to the play (as not too subtly stated on the title-page) can become a game of wits. If the playwright has one of the characters exclaim: "Kolportage, James — aber so ist das Leben" then we are brought to reflect on the relationship between life and its clichés. But if the playwright's stance is from the beginning one of irony and sarcasm so that statements become double-entendres and turn upon themselves, we can hardly afford to take anything at face value, surely not such profundities as offered here, for example, what is referred to as "the recipe for paradise free of charge from Mother Appeblom":"füttert die Kreatur und häschelt sie ein bißchen," or statements such as "Es muß doch in jedem Proletarier ein Stück von einem Grafen und in jedem Grafen ein Stück von einem Proletarier stecken,“ — a pronouncement that appears at the close of the play to be of supreme importance. In instances such as these Kaiser is always one step ahead of the audience by virtue of this *ironic colportage.* It is not a relaxing game, and doubtless one which puts too much of a burden on the audience. Kaiser nonetheless is again working with the exigencies of a new form: while he appears in his title-page stance to be sarcastically throwing garbage to the proverbial swine, in ironizing his irony he ends up being serious — theatrically serious if not realistically serious. The lines which everyone is ready to smile at — and dismiss since, after all, this is colportage — are in fact to be taken in almost dead earnest, Mother Appeblom's recipe and the fact of bourgeois-aristocratic interchangeability included. There is ultimately more than a gratuitous grain of truth in the points the play makes — even if it does so in rather roundabout ways. Paulsen is not giving Kaiser sufficient credit when he reprimands him for doubling his irony. There is every reason to believe that Kaiser knew exactly what he was up to. Not too much earlier than these plays, in a 1920 comment on *Europa* — that early, deceptively light piece that critiqued the new fashion in dance — Kaiser had explained: "Der einzige Vorwurf von Dichtung: der ist die Erneuerung des Menschen — wird in dieser *Umkehrung Europa betont. Das Lustspiel verweist auf die Ernsthaftigkeit des Problems. Seine Tragfähigkeit erprobt sich am Widerspiel. Es ist altes Dramengesetz. ... Einblick ins Unwesentlich ist getan — und Ausblick weitet sich gleich aufs dringende.*“[76] Kaiser would have agreed with Bloch's premise that more lay in colportage than the frivolous and insignificant pabulum of the unsophisticated. It is highly interesting that the playwright who held himself so aloof and apart from the public should have been intrigued by the opportunity to play with a play-form that made him look less Kaiserean and more playful, but which nonetheless afforded him the vehicle for yet another "think-play."

Some five years after *Kolportage* Kaiser was at it once

[76] *Werke,* IV, 556. Italics mine.

again in *Zwei Krawatten* (Revuestück in neun Bildern, 1929). It is probably the lightest of all of Kaiser's plays — not unlike an early Hollywood musical. The plot is simple enough and involves the comedy of a hide-and-seek game in the search for the heir to an enormous fortune. Again, the piece is deceptively innocent fun. Kaiser comes back to the *Stationsdrama* format in the series of nine scenes — this time interspersed with outbursts of song. Here too it is possible to see a form-conscious Kaiser at work, inasmuch as the nine scenes take on the same kind of *Drehbühne* pattern that we observed in *Nebeneinander* — a cyclical 1,2,3-1,2,3-1,2,3 format turning on a lost/found axis: both Jean and Trude are "found" and "lost" in each of the three sets with all the comic hoopla of the time-tested search/escape/discovery routine with disguises (the two ties) thrown in for good measure.

The play does indeed appear to be insignificant in the Kaiser oeuvre[77] — unless one approaches it for its relevance in the playwright's experimentation with form: like the other two plays that preceded it, *Zwei Krawatten* is Kaiser adapting a popular form — here the musical revue — for his own purposes, attempting to work with a lighter vehicle for theatrical effectiveness. Underneath it all is still noticeable the Kaiserean irony and the intent to clothe thought-provoking and critical substance in the guise of innocent fun. The "points" of the play — the role of chance, the rarity of human happiness, the role of money in interpersonal relationships — reveal Kaiser operating here too with his double-barreled irony. If the format was supposed to sweeten the pill, it was not intended to transform the medicine into candy. One cannot relax and be passively entertained when faced with such irony turning on itself in a paradox of form and content.

Against the background of entertaining popular forms, then, Kaiser demonstrates in these three plays a critical acumen that must be read from between the lines. They are really

[77] Kenworthy, for example, makes no more than passing reference to it, mentioning the *Stationsdrama* technique carried beyond comedy to the revue; he calls it "colportage leavened with music and song." See Kenworthy, *Georg Kaiser,* p. 83.

a gentler coaxing of the audience into consideration of less tendentious, but nonetheless serious, Kaiserean truisms. Having observed Kaiser's earlier penchant to preach an idea, we should not be surprised to find him doing so in these works as well. But what we see is the playwright consciously manipulating his material in such a way that he is in control of form in formats that few expected him to take much pains with. Bloch's insightful analysis into the deeper significance of these "forms" supports the thesis that Kaiser was not just frittering away his time when he attempted to work within the popular idiom that was so much a part of the times. In his brief essay on Walter Benjamin's *Einbahnstrasse*, Bloch proposes: "Von der Straße, dem Jahrmarkt, dem Zirkus, der Kolportage dringen andere Formen vor ... und sie besetzen das Feld der Reife. Genau brach der Clown ins sterbende Ballett ... durchbrochene Revue in den alten, schön geschlossenen Bühnenbau ... Kein neuer 'Mimus' ist aus der Revue entstanden, sie diente überwiegend Amüsierpöbel und war amorph wie dieser. Aber mittelbar freilich konnte 'Revue' gebraucht werden, als eine der offensten und wider alle Absicht ehrlichsten Formen der Gegenwart, als Abdruck jenes Hohlraums, worin sich nicht mehr ohne Lüge schließen läßt, worin sich nur noch Teile begegnen und mischen."[78] Kaiser was sufficiently a man of the theater to perceive that such "lesser" forms bridge a gap to the public which more seriously and analytically constructed formats seemed to widen. He was just as much the *Denkspieler* in these plays as in his others. But instead of falling from grace by taking his cue "from the street, the fair, the circus," the playwright par excellence was in fact the more consciously and paradoxically attempting to align his theater with life, keeping his act in step with the times.

[78] Bloch, "Revueform in der Philosophie," in *Erbschaft dieser Zeit*, p. 368–69.

Nachwort

Kaiser's search for dramatic form casts widely for the innovative ploy to make his irony more palatable to a demanding audience as well as to a questioning self with doubts of personal validity: his choices in form are symptomatic of a fusion of ideas relating to both the circus and the cinema, a confusion, if you will, arising from that historical period of transition in which the former found itself being pushed out of popularity by the latter. The analysis of the other authors shows them similarly grounded in an historical and sociological correlate. If we review the individual authors' stances in conjunction with the views of those neo-Marxist critic/philosophers cited in the introductory chapter, we cannot but note a remarkable congruence between that which the authors found in the world of the circus and that which critics such as Bloch, Benjamin, Marcuse, and Adorno postulated as needs, tensions, and/or requisites of modern society. I am not assuming, of course, that theirs is an exclusive theoretical base. Yet is is primarily in the work of these critics that a number of relevant hypotheses are to be found. In contrast to a kind of general neglect of the circus from anything other than a historical or descriptive perspective, these philosopher/critics have concerned themselves with the significance of numerous aspects of popular culture and have placed them in a meaningful relationship within the general contours of western culture. To be sure, their writings on these forms are not easily reducible to definitive philosophical or theoretical statements. I referred to their ideas earlier as "musings" — statements that suggest and open up perspectives otherwise ignored or closed off. In those musings they make it perfectly clear that when they consider the circus and other forms of popular culture, they are conscious of delving into an area of life that lies "without" — outside the traditional spheres of philosophic and aesthetic inquiry and outside the usual domain of traditional culture and social relevance. Their collective efforts to shape an aesthetic theory with particular reference to a social and cultural framework focus in varying degrees on the nature and function of art in society and ineluctably cause them to treat the dichotomy I have analyzed earlier. Their perspective thus serves well to unite the historical, sociological, and aesthetic facets of the literary and dramatic material discussed here.

In assessing the preceding chapters and looking for evidence of an historical correlate, we may conclude that Carl and Gerhart Hauptmann's embellishment of the gypsy ideal proves to be a rather blatant revolt against the strictures and rationality of a turn-of-the-century bourgeois ideal. Carl Zuckmayer's work presents a vision of circus "folk" as the embodiment of those qualities he sensed being trammeled by the advance of a technological and unethical age. Together, these literary cases can be considered an historical prelude and poetic variation on Ernst Bloch's *Wunschbilder* — a desire to escape to an "other" not available from the reality as given. We were witness as well to Wedekind's and Brecht's conscious rebellion in their choice of forms — forms that expressed their disenchantment with the norm and served to raise the hackles of their respective times grown aesthetically and morally stale. Both Wedekind and Brecht are examples of the kind of reactionary, alienated stance that was required as the "culture industry" of which Adorno would speak was beginning to work its effects. In the case of Kafka, we cannot but perceive that the *Sein/Schein* nature of the circus world articulates the predicament of the artist in the peculiarly modern age in which the ambivalence of contradictory forces threatens destruction but serves as inspirational source. Thomas Mann, over the span of time in which he was occupied with *Felix Krull,* clearly came to find the circus context a perfect symbol for a kind of performer in a kind of performance that is both dishonest and intriguing, ingenuine but necessary — for the performer as well as the audience: his is as much a statement about the artist as about the world upon which the artist draws and of which he is a part. Rilke searches among the lowly ranks of a travelling troupe of acrobats to find that quality or aspect of existence that fits into his more comprehensive, almost cosmic, view of life around the first quarter of this century. Already he is able to perceive the toll taken by the advance of time, and relates past glory to present tedium in an elegaic mood that in and of itself signals a loss. Heym harbingers the disenchantment that was becoming more acute and tries to make a statement with broad socio-cultural implications — for the circus itself as well as for the cultural background against which it plays out its more noticeably repetitious and mechanical role. Kafka, Mann, Rilke, and Heym thus all reflect a vision similar to Benjamin's, insofar as their respective worlds are cynosures of the modern evolution toward a questionable democratization in life as well as in art.

Adorno's scepticism about the potential of the avant-garde to successfully withstand the pressures of the "culture industry" and technologized mass society, and Bürger's rhetorical question at the end of his book whether or not, à la Adorno, late capitalist society has become "irrational" to the point of no longer being theoretically comprehensible, both suggest the very questionable status of whatever might be called the avant-garde of the present. To a certain extent, the fate of the circus bears out that kind of negative assessment. Riding on a tide of popularity that carried it far beyond its original design, the circus became a victim of its own desire to accomodate the tastes of an increasingly bourgeois and commercialized audience and a world more and more captivated by technological innovation. When Franz Renz took over from his father in 1892 Circus Renz was only barely related to what it had been at its origin fifty years earlier. Flooded in electric lights, outfitted with decorative palms and mirrors, carpeted except for the stables, it was functioning, we may recall, already as *salon*. What had earlier operated effectively because of its "apartness" was becoming legitimized, commercialized, and technologized, and its negative charge was undergoing the predictable process of neutralization. As the original uniqueness of the circus performance — its immediacy and nonreproducibility in its reliance on the human performer — gave way to elements whose dependence on technics made them the less immediate but the more productive (in the worst sense of the word), the circus was writing its own obituary. Despite Zuckmayer's 1928 affirmative conviction that "circus blood" would be victorious, and later, that the Knie brothers were a model of adaptation to trying times, there is little reason to see in their present enterprise much more than a remnant of former glories. Oskar Schlemmer's 1925 essay *Mensch und Kunstfigur*[1] reveals the degree to which a mechanical ideal had overtaken what had earlier belonged to the realm of horsepower in purer forms and represents an interesting comment on the ubiquitous force of an ideologized technology. By the later twenties it was clear that the circus — not to mention those other popular forms such as the pantomime, the varieté, and the revue that had themselves exerted a force on its forms and content — was being eased out by the newer medium of an increasingly technological age — the film. The development and extreme popularity of that art form is clear evidence of the irresistible power of a non-traditional and blatantly popular form, the cultural and aesthetic significance of which usually catches the legitimate forms of high art off guard and instigates activity in those latter circles only after certain artistic and professional potential has been assessed. In the long run, the process was one in which the film gradually assumed the role the circus had played earlier. It has grown, to be sure, in popularity and complexity to a point never achieved by the circus. Similarly, however, it has developed to a point where it too has been subsumed into the realm of what is now regarded as legitimate art. The coincidence of the one form's retreat and the other's dynamic advance is surely not accidental, but rather attests only to the transference of the public's (the masses') attention to the more inventive and technologically progressive form. The phenomenon whereby a popular form interacts with art to be-

[1] Oskar Schlemmer, et al., *Die Bühne im Bauhaus*, Frankfurt/Main, 1925.

come a popular "art form" with precepts and patterns of its own can thus be seen as a factor of the innovation taking place outside the traditional spheres of artistic endeavor. By the mid-to-late twenties the circus was forced to make room for a new art which successfully drew the eyes of the spectators from the sawdust ring and focused them on the silver screen. The ascent of the film, followed subsequently by the sedative effects of television, continues in fact to make an impact on the remnants of the older form: today's relics of the circus have achieved a definitive sterility that comes by and large from a reliance on technology's props. There is every reason to question whether what could formerly be ascribed to the form under the auspices of "das Wahre am Schein" (Bloch) is even applicable in today's world in which film and television dominate to an awesome degree the contemporary vision of reality. For most spectators the arena now exists only on the television screen, and for some time now, circus management has jumped at the chance — and the implied rewards of status — of having the performance featured on prime-time specials.

It is interesting to observe that even in the face of such developments, interaction between "high" and "popular" continues to occur in sometimes noteworthy ways. One can point to numerous contemporary instances in which the circus element is brought into play with the legitimate world of art, not the least of which is the circus framework in which the events of the entire 1978 Berlin Festival Weeks — one of Europe's most prestigious festivals of art — were set forth. Dietrich Stobbe, the mayor of Berlin, in his official remarks for the opening of the festival, issued the following invitation: "Sehen wir uns also einmal an, wie überraschend viel der Zirkus beigetragen hat und beiträgt zu dem, was wir im Begriff der Kultur zusammenfassen, wie sehr er selbst Kultur ist."[2] In this instance as in others, it is difficult to determine at this point whether the deployment of the circus context is a case of nostalgia, or a kind of last ditch effort to extract the final

[2] *Magazin der Berliner Festwochen 1978*. Berliner Festspiele GmbH, ed., Berlin, 1978, p. 2.

breath from a past exoticism, or a supreme attempt to institutionalize the arena. On the one hand, the perceptible interest during the last decade in aspects of popular culture — not only abroad but in this country as well, and not only by classic-comic-book collectors but also by serious scholars — would seem to indicate that facets of that popular realm do indeed persist in the segregated state necessary for their survival. Despite Marcuse's thesis that the process is one in which society is "flattened out" — and there is evidence aplenty that that is indeed underway — there still appears to be an awareness on the part of artists that, similar to earlier eras, these elements hold some potentially greater significance within the contours of our cultural life. One can even acknowledge that while the nature of the beast has evolved and undergone change, it is still its untamed character that causes the process to be repeated over and over again. On the other, however, Mayor Stobbe's remarks raise the specter of the culture industry's effect: his admonition that for the circus we should take note of "wie sehr er selbst Kultur ist," would seem a sure sign that the beast can now be allowed into the living room (or the museum) with the other members of the resident aesthetic family.

The final note, in any event, belongs to Zirkus Roncalli, a present-day circus miracle of sorts. Through its efforts to bring the circus back to what it once was — a small, intimate, almost poignant, experience in distinctly human proportions — this remarkable German undertaking has found enormous success. It plays outside major cities to crowds that throng to its single ring filled with sawdust. Those who enter the gate get a bit of grease paint and a sprinkle of glitter and thus become performer and participant. This "Reise zum Regenbogen" (subtitled "Ein Zirkusstück sowie ein Stück Zirkus ... Aufführung in zwei Akten auf Sägemehl in zehn Aufzügen zwischen vier Masten"), directed by Bernhard Paul and Emil Steinberger exists as fragilely in our contemporary society as one of the bubbles gently blown by the beloved mime and Pierrot, Pic. Its director Paul addresses the audience in the program as follows:

"Der Zirkus ist das schönste aller visuellen Spiele", schrieb Théophile Gautier 1858. Inzwischen hat sich vieles verändert. So auch die Welt des Zirkus. Viele Unternehmen haben sich der Zeit angepaßt, sich an gängige Trends angebiedert, modernisiert. Dabei ist vieles auf der Strecke geblieben: Die Romantik, die Ästhetik und vor allem der Zauber des Geschehens in der Manege. Wir haben in unserem Programm den Schritt zu anderen außercircensischen Künsten, etwa zum Theater, gewagt. Niemand hat daran geglaubt, daß dieses Experiment glücken könnte. Diesen Zirkus Roncalli ins Leben zu rufen, wäre ohne den großen Aufwand und der Hilfe von Theaterfachleuten, Pantomimen, Künstlern und vor allem von Idealisten nicht möglich gewesen.... Wir wollen ein kleiner Beitrag sein in einer Welt, in der die Phantasie und das Schöpferische ständig zu kurz kommen: den Menschen Freude bereiten und in ihnen jene Gefühle wecken, die in diesen Zeiten verlorengegangen sind. In diesem Sinne: Salto vitale!

Having brought the circus full circle, as it were, back to a unity with those "außercircensischen Künsten," his program quotes, among others, Jean Genet ("Seltsamer Plan: sich zu träumen, diesen Traum greifbar zu machen, um dann wieder zum Traum zu werden, in anderen Menschen"), Walter Benjamin ("Es gibt noch keine geistreiche Konvention, die anleitet, über Dinge des Zirkus zu schwatzen. Sein Publikum ist weit respektvoller als das irgendwelcher Theater oder Konzertsäle. Das hängt damit zusammen, daß im Zirkus die Wirklichkeit das Wort hat, nicht der Schein. Es ist immer noch eher denkbar, daß während Hamlet den Polonius totsticht, ein Herr im Publikum den Nachbar um das Programm bittet, als während der Akrobat von der Kuppel den doppelten Salto mortale macht"), Federico Fellini ("Auch wenn sie sich in der Manege mit Kanonenschüssen bekriegen, am Ende werden der Weiße Clown und der August doch unter Trompetenklang vereint und gehen gemeinsam hinaus. Warum geht uns dieses Finale so nahe? Weil es einen unserer tiefstverwurzelten Mythus verwirklicht: die Versöhnung der Gegensätze, die Möglichkeit für den Menschen, seine Einheit wiederzufinden, ohne die Vielschichtigkeit aufzugeben"), Ernst Bloch ("Der Zirkus stellt heute noch die farbigste Massenschau dar oder das Bild der Sensation; er ist *chinesiche* Fantasie in der aufgeheitersten römischen Arena"), and Karl Kraus ("Im Theater dort, wo viele Worte gemacht werden, ist Zeit, zwischen Tat und Spiel zu unterscheiden. Akrobaten aber und Clowns spielen jenseits der Grenze unserer Möglichkeiten"). What better testimony to the interfaces that have been suggested as possible than this circus program with such quotes as captions for its pictures? While a final theoretical projection based on the Roncalli undertaking would be risky, we can be assured that its future lies to a significant degree in the determination of its directors and performers to resist all the forces that would ruin its delicate charm and ever-so affective moments. Its "Salto vitale!", we hope, will in the best circus tradition carry it far forward into the most uncertain of futures.

Bibliography

Adorno, Theodor W., *Minima Moralia.* Frankfurt/Main, 1975.
Adrian, Paul, *Histoire Illustrée des Cirques Parisiens, d'hier et d'aujourd'hui.* Bourg-la-Reine, 1957.
Appignanesi, Lisa, *The Cabaret.* London, 1975.

Bachtin, Michail, *Literatur und Karneval. Zur Romantheorie und Lachkultur.* Munich, 1969.
Barbu, Zev, "Popular Culture: A Sociological Approach," *Approaches to Popular Culture,* C. W. E. Bigsby, ed. Bowling Green, Ohio, 1976.
Bauer, Arnold, *Carl Zuckmayer.* Berlin, 1970.
Beck, Evelyn Torton, *Kafka and the Yiddish Theater. Its Impact on his Work.* Madison, 1971.
Beicken, Peter U., *Franz Kafka. Eine kritische Einführung in die Forschung.* Frankfurt/Main, 1974.
Benjamin, Walter, *Gesammelte Schriften,* Rolf Tiedemann and Hermann Schweppenhäuser, eds. Frankfurt/Main, 1972.
–, "The Work of Art in the Age of Mechanical Reproduction," *Marxism and Art,* Berel Lang and Forrest Williams, eds. New York, 1972.
Bentley, Eric, "On Brecht's *In the Swamp, A Man's a Man,* and *Saint Joan of the Stockyards,*" *Brecht, A Collection of Critical Essays,* Peter Demetz, ed. Englewood Cliffs, New Jersey, 1962.
Berliner Festspiele, ed., *Magazin der Berliner Festwochen 1978.* Berlin, 1978.
Bierbaum, Otto Julius, *Deutsche Chansons.* Berlin and Leipzig, 1901.
Bigsby, C. W. E., "The Politics of Popular Culture," *Approaches to Popular Culture,* C. W. E. Bigsby, ed. Bowling Green, Ohio, 1976.
Binder, Hartmut, *Motiv und Gestaltung bei Franz Kafka.* Bonn, 1966.
Bloch, Ernst, *Ästhetik des Vorscheins, I.* Gert Ueding, ed. Frankfurt/Main, 1974.
–, *Erbschaft dieser Zeit,* Frankfurt/Main, 1962.
Böckmann, Paul, "Die komödiantischen Grotesken Franz Wedekinds," *Das Deutsche Lustspiel II,* Hans Steffen ed., pp. 79–102. Göttingen, 1969.
Bose, Günter and Erich Brinkmann, *Circus. Geschichte und Ästhetik einer niederen Kunst.* Berlin, 1978.

Brecht, Bertolt, *Arbeitsjournal 1938–1942, I,* with notes by Werner Hecht, Frankfurt/Main, 1973.
–, *Gesammelte Werke in 20 Bänden.* Frankfurt/Main, 1967.
Bürger, Peter, *Theorie der Avantgarde.* Frankfurt/Main, 1974.

Cain, Georges, *Anciens Théâtres de Paris.* Paris, 1906.

Daibler, Hans, *Gerhart Hauptmann oder der letzte Klassiker.* Vienna, 1971.
Diebold, Bernhard, *Der Denkspieler Georg Kaiser.* Frankfurt/Main, 1924.
Domino, Signor, *Wandernde Künstler.* Berlin, 1891.

Emrich, Wilhelm, *Franz Kafka.* Frankfurt/Main, 1961.

Fechter, Paul, *Frank Wedekind. Der Mensch und das Werk.* Jena, 1920.
Fivian, Erich A., *Georg Kaiser und seine Stellung im Expressionismus.* Munich, 1946.
Friedenthal, Joachim, *Das Wedekindbuch.* Munich, 1914.

Gersch, Wolfgang, *Film bei Brecht.* Munich, 1975.
Gittleman, Sol, "Frank Wedekind and Bertolt Brecht," *Modern Drama,* X (1967/68), 401–409.
Gobbers, Emil, *Artisten: Zirkus und Variété in alter und neuer Zeit.* Düsseldorf, 1949.
Goldstein, Walter, *Carl Hauptmann. Eine Werkdeutung.* (Vol. 65 of *Germanistische Abhandlungen,* Walter Steller, ed.). Breslau, 1931.
Gray, Ronald, *Brecht the Dramatist.* Cambridge, 1976.
Grimm, Reinhold, *Nach dem Naturalismus.* Kronberg, 1978.

Häsler, Alfred A., *Knie: die Geschichte einer Circus-Dynastie, mit einem Geleitwort von Carl Zuckmayer.* Bern, 1968.
Hauptmann, Carl, *Einhart der Lächler.* Berlin, 1907.
–, *Die Goldenen Straßen.* Leipzig, [n. d.].
–, *Der Landstreicher und andere Erzählungen.* Stuttgart, 1912.
–, *Leben mit Freunden. Gesammelte Briefe,* Will-Erich Peuckert, ed. Berlin-Grünewald, 1928.
–, *Marianne.* Berlin, 1900.
Hauptmann, Gerhart, *Das Gesammelte Werk.* Berlin, 1943.
–, *Sämtliche Werke.* 11 vols. Hans-Egon Hass, ed. Berlin, 1966–74.
Heuser, Frederick W. J., "The Life of Ida Orloff and her relations to Gerhart Hauptmann," *PMLA,* LXII (September 1957), 737–774.
Heym, Georg, *Dichtungen und Schriften,* I, Karl Ludwig Schneider, ed. Munich, 1964.
–, *Dichtungen und Schriften,* II, Karl Ludwig Schneider, ed. Munich, 1962.

–, *Dichtungen und Schriften,* III, Karl Ludwig Schneider, ed. Hamburg and Munich, 1960.
–, *Das lyrische Werk.* Karl Ludwig Schneider, ed. Munich, 1977.
–, *Umbra Vitae.* Munich, 1924.
Heym, Georg. Selected by Karl Ludwig Schneider and Gunter Martens. Postscript by Karl Ludwig Schneider. Munich, 1971.
Heym, Georg. Dokumente zu seinem Leben und Werk (Vol. VI of collected works, *Dichtungen und Schriften,* Karl Ludwig Schneider, ed.). Karl Ludwig Schneider and Gerhard Burckhardt, eds. Darmstadt, 1968.
Hofmannsthal, Hugo von, *Prosa I.* Frankfurt/Main, 1956.
Hohendahl, Peter U., *Das Bild der bürgerlichen Welt im expressionistischen Drama.* Heidelberg, 1967.
Horkheimer, Max, and Theodor W. Adorno, *Dialektik der Aufklärung. Philosophische Fragmente.* Frankfurt/Main, 1971.

Jacobs, Jürgen, *Wilhelm Meister und seine Brüder: Untersuchungen zum deutschen Bildungsroman.* Munich, 1972.
Jendreiek, Helmut, *Thomas Mann: Der demokratische Roman.* Düsseldorf, 1977.

Kafka, Franz, *Briefe an Felice und andere Korrespondenz aus der Verlobungszeit.* Erich Heller and Jürgen Born, eds. Frankfurt/Main, 1967.
–, *Das Kafka-Buch. Eine innere Biographie in Selbstzeugnissen.* Heinz Politzer, ed. Frankfurt/Main, 1965.
–, *Gesammelte Werke.* Max Brod, ed. New York, 1946–58.
–, *Tagebücher:* 1910–1923. New York, 1948–1949.
Kaiser, Georg, *Werke.* Walther Huder, ed. Frankfurt/Main, 1971.
Karst, Roman, *Thomas Mann oder der deutsche Zwiespalt.* Vienna, 1970.
Kenworthy, Brian J., *Georg Kaiser.* Oxford, 1957.
Kiaulehn, Walther, ed., *Chansons von Frank Wedekind.* Munich, [n. d.].
Klages, Ludwig, *Grundlegung der Wissenschaft vom Ausdruck.* Leipzig, 1943–49.
Klotz, Volker, *Bertolt Brecht: Versuch über das Werk.* Darmstadt, 1957.
–, "Lied im Drama," *Akzente,* VII, 4 (August 1960), 309–320.
–, *Geschlossene und offene Form im Drama.* Munich, 1972.
Knopf, Jan, *Bertolt Brecht. Ein kritischer Forschungsbericht.* Frankfurt/Main, 1974.
Kobs, Jürgen, *Kafka.* Bad Homburg, 1970.
Koegler, Horst, *Balanchine und das moderne Ballett.* Velber, 1964.
Kreuzer, Helmut, *Die Boheme.* Stuttgart, 1968.
Krispyn, Egbert, *Georg Heym: A reluctant rebel.* Gainsville, 1968.

Kusnezow, Jawgeni, *Der Zirkus der Welt*. Berlin, 1970.
Kutscher, Artur, "Eine unbekannte französische Quelle zu Frank Wedekinds 'Erdgeist' und 'Büchse der Pandora'," *Das Goldene Tor,* II (1947), 497-505.
–, *Frank Wedekind. Sein Leben und seine Werke.* 3 vols. Munich, 1922-31.
–, "Wedekind und der Zirkus," *Faust, eine Monatschrift für Kunst, Literatur und Musik,* III, No. 7 (1925), 1-5.
–, *Wedekind, Leben und Werk,* edited by Karl Ude. Munich, 1964.

Leishman, J. B., *Rainer Maria Rilke, Duino Elegies*. Translation and commentary by J. B. Leishman and Stephen Spender. New York, 1963.
Loewenson, Erwin, *Georg Heym*. Hamburg and Munich, 1962.

McLean, Sammy K., *The "Bänkelsang" and the Work of Bertolt Brecht*. The Hague, 1972.
Mann, Thomas, *Bekenntnisse des Hochstaplers Felix Krull.* Frankfurt/Main, 1954.
–, *Gesammelte Werke in zwölf Bänden*. Frankfurt/Main, 1960.
–, *Thomas Mann: Teil I: 1889-1917.* Hans Wysling, ed., in cooperation with Marianne Fischer. Frankfurt/Main, 1975. (Vol. 14/1 of *Dichter über ihre Dichtungen,* Rudolf Hirsch and Werner Vordtriede, eds.).
Marcuse, Herbert, *One-Dimensional Man*. Boston, 1964.
Martens, Gunter, *Vitalismus und Expressionismus*. Stuttgart, 1971.
Matiasek, Helmuth, "Zeitlose Satire des Ewig-Menschlichen: Der Clown," *Maske und Kothurn,* IX, No. 2 (1963), 182-192.
Mawer, Irene, *The Art of Mime*. Boston, [n. d.].
Mayer, Hans, *Brecht in der Geschichte*. Frankfurt/Main, 1971.
Meckauer, Walter, "Carl Hauptmanns dichterische Hinterlassenschaft," *Monatshefte,* 42 (1950), 224-230.
Muschg, Walter, *Gestaltung und Figuren*. Bern and Munich, 1968.

Paulsen, Wolfgang, *Georg Kaiser. Die Perspektiven seines Werkes*. Tübingen, 1960.
Penrose, Roland, *Picasso, his Life and Work*. New York, 1962.
Percival, John, *The World of Diaghilev*. London, 1971.
Petzoldt, Leander, *Bänkelsang. Vom historischen Bänkelsang zum literarischen Chanson*. Stuttgart, 1974.
Poggioli, Renato, *The Theory of the Avant-Garde,* Gerald Fitzgerald, trans. Cambridge, Massachusetts, 1968.

Radunski, S., *Erinnerungen eines alten Clowns*. Translated from the Russian by Ruth Bruckner. Berlin, 1956.
Raynor, Henry, *Music and Society since 1815*. London, 1976.

Razinger, Hubert, *Carl Hauptmann. Gestalt und Werk.* Krummhübel i. R., 1928.
Rilke, Rainer Maria, *Briefe.* Rilke-Archiv, ed. Wiesbaden, 1950.
–, *Briefe aus den Jahren 1914 bis 1921,* Ruth Sieber-Rilke and Carl Sieber, eds. Leipzig, 1937.
–, *Sämtliche Werke.* Rilke-Archiv, ed. Frankfurt/Main, 1965.
Ritter, Naomi, "On the Circus Motif in modern German literature," *German Life and Letters,* XXVII (July 1974), No. 4, 273–285.
Rosenwald, Henry M., ed., *Jahrhundertwende.* New York, 1968.
Rudinoff, W., "Ein Selbstbekenntnis," *Zeitschrift für bildende Kunst,* N. F. XVII (1905/06), 43–46.

Schlemmer, Oskar, et al., *Die Bühne im Bauhaus.* Munich, 1925.
Schöne, Albrecht, "Bertolt Brecht: Theatertheorie und dramatische Dichtung," *Euphorion,* LII, No. 3 (1958), 272–296.
Schumann, Klaus, ed., *Bertolt Brechts Hauspostille.* Beiheft. Frankfurt/Main, 1970.
–, *Der Lyriker Bertolt Brecht, 1913–1933.* Berlin, 1964.
Seidlin, Oscar, "Picaresque elements in Thomas Mann's Work," *Modern Language Quarterly,* XII (1951), 183–200.
Shattuck, Roger, *The Banquet Years.* Garden City, New York, 1961.
Simon, Karl Gunther, *Pantomime: Ursprung, Wesen, Möglichkeiten.* Munich, 1960.
Sokel, Walter H., *The Writer in Extremis.* Stanford, 1959.
Stahl, Ernst, *The Duineser Elegies.* Oxford, 1965.
Steffens, Wilhelm, *Georg Kaiser.* Velber, 1969.
Steiner, Jacob, *Rilkes Duineser Elegien.* Bern and Munich, 1962.
Strich, Fritz, *Dichtung und Zivilisation.* Munich, 1928.
–, *Zur deutschen Literatur seit der Jahrhundertwende.* Stuttgart, 1967.
Storck, Joachim W., "Emanzipatorische Aspekte im Werk und Leben Rilkes," *Rilke Heute.* Ingeborg H. Solbrig and Joachim W. Storck, eds. Frankfurt/Main, 1975, pp. 247–286.

Thole, Bernhard, *Die "Gesänge" in den Stücken Bertolt Brechts.* Dissertation, Göppingen, 1973.
Thon, Christiana, *Französische Plakate des 19. Jahrhunderts* (Bilderhefte der Staatlichen Museen Preußischer Kulturbesitz Berlin, Vol 7/8). Berlin, 1968.
Toole-Stott, Raymond, *Circus and Allied Arts: A World Bibliography.* 3 vols. Derby, England, 1958–62.

Ueding, Gert, *Glanzvolles Elend. Versuch über Kitsch und Kolportage.* Frankfurt/Main, 1973.

Vietta, Silvio and Kemper, Hans-Georg, eds., *Expressionismus.* Munich, 1975.

Völker, Klaus, *Brecht-Chronik: Daten zum Leben und Werk*. Munich, 1971.

Webb, Karl E., *Rainer Maria Rilke and Jugendstil*. Chapel Hill, 1978.

Wedekind, Frank, *Gesammelte Briefe*. Fritz Strich, ed. Munich, 1924.

–, *Gesammelte Werke*. Artur Kutscher and Joachim Friedenthal, eds. Munich, 1919–24.

–, *Ich habe meine Tante geschlachtet. Lautenlieder und 'Simplicissimus' Gedichte*. Manfred Hahn, ed. Munich, 1967.

Wehmeyer, Grete, *Erik Satie*. Regensburg, 1974.

Wood, Frank, *Rainer Maria Rilke. The Ring of Forms*. New York, 1970.

Willett, John, *The Theatre of Bertolt Brecht*. Norfolk, Connecticut, 1959.

Zuckmayer, Carl, *Al's wär's ein Stück von mir*. Vienna, 1966.

–, *Gesammelte Werke*. Frankfurt/Main, 1960.

–, "Von Seiltänzern udn Himmelreichsmännern," *Gartenlaube*, 36 (1930), 747–48.

Index

112,—